10th Anniversary Special Issue “PUBMET2023 Conference on Scholarly Communication in the Context of Open Science”

10th Anniversary Special Issue "PUBMET2023 Conference on Scholarly Communication in the Context of Open Science"

Guest Editors

Iva Grabarić Andonovski
Nikolina Peša Pavlović
Jadranka Stojanovski

MDPI

Basel • Beijing • Wuhan • Barcelona • Belgrade • Novi Sad • Cluj • Manchester

Guest Editors

Iva Grabarić Andonovski
Faculty of Food Technology and Biotechnology
University of Zagreb
Zagreb
Croatia

Nikolina Peša Pavlović
Department of Information Sciences and Technologies
University of Zadar
Zadar
Croatia

Jadranka Stojanovski
Department of Information Sciences
University of Zadar
Zadar
Croatia

Editorial Office
MDPI AG
Grosspeteranlage 5
4052 Basel, Switzerland

This is a reprint of the Special Issue, published open access by the journal *Publications* (ISSN 2304-6775), freely accessible at: https://www.mdpi.com/journal/publications/special_issues/WN3057YCM2.

For citation purposes, cite each article independently as indicated on the article page online and as indicated below:

Lastname, A.A.; Lastname, B.B. Article Title. *Journal Name* **Year**, *Volume Number*, Page Range.

ISBN 978-3-7258-6896-4 (Hbk)
ISBN 978-3-7258-6897-1 (PDF)
https://doi.org/10.3390/books978-3-7258-6897-1

Cover image courtesy of Ivana Končić

Contents

About the Editors

Iva Grabarić Andonovski

Iva Grabarić Andonovski is the Editor of *Food Technology and Biotechnology*, one of the leading diamond open access scholarly journals in Croatia. She is one of the founders and the current President of the Croatian Association for Scholarly Communication (CROASC/ZNAK), Vice-President as well as Chair of Croatian Regional Chapter and Co-Chair of Environment and Sustainability Committee of the European Association of Science Editors (EASE), a member of HRČAK Portal of Croatian scientific and professional journals Advisory Board, and a member of OPERAS Special Interest Group on Best Practices. Her focus is on best practices and sustainability in diamond open access scholarly publishing.

Nikolina Peša Pavlović

Nikolina Peša Pavlović is a postdoctoral researcher in the Department of Information Sciences and Technologies at the University of Zadar, Croatia. She is a member of the Laboratory for Interactive Systems and User Experience at the University of Zadar (UX Lab), where she conducts usability testing and user experience research. Her scientific interests include information behaviour in an online environment, scholarly communication and information literacy: including digital literacy and source credibility assessment, instructional design, human–computer interaction and user experience (UX), with emphasis on usability and user research, online search and evaluation of online services, tools and sources.

Jadranka Stojanovski

Jadranka Stojanovski is a retired associate professor from the Department of Information Sciences at the University of Zadar, where she continues to contribute as a part-time researcher. She holds an MSc in physics and a PhD in information sciences. Her work has focused on the development of open science infrastructures and services, emerging trends in scholarly communication, and support for editorial quality, with particular attention to peer review, research integrity, and research data management. At the international level, she has been involved in a wide range of projects and professional communities, including EASE, OPERAS, OpenAIRE, NI4OS Europe, PEERE, ENRESSH, UNESCO, and CoARA. She represents Croatia in the European Commission Expert Group on National Points of Reference for Scientific Information and serves as an OPERAS delegate to CoARA. She is also a member of the editorial board of the *Journal of Electronic Publishing*. In addition, she is a co-founder and the current Vice-President of the Croatian Association for Scholarly Communication (CROASC/ZNAK), a member of the Peer Review Committee of the European Association of Science Editors (EASE), and Chair of the OPERAS Special Interest Group on Best Practices.

Preface

This Special Issue marks the 10th anniversary of the PUBMET conferences on Scholarly Communication in the Context of Open Science. Over the past decade, PUBMET has developed into a vibrant international community of researchers, practitioners, and enthusiasts dedicated to the global open science movement and the advancement of scholarly communication. This anniversary edition is a significant thematic example of efforts to implement open science and enhance communication within the wider scholarly community. The Special Issue presents selected contributions covering various topics under the main theme of scholarly communication in the context of open science, which is the central theme and motto of the PUBMET conferences. This anniversary reprint includes empirical studies and practice-oriented articles addressing a range of research problems and ideas related to openness, research assessment, infrastructures, FAIR principles, and ethical responsibility in the scholarly communication ecosystem.

It is intended for a broad readership, including scientists from all disciplines, educators, undergraduate, graduate and doctoral students, librarians, publishers, policymakers, stakeholders, and professionals from various communities.

The need for open science in all aspects of academic work has become a central issue for participants in scholarly communication, making this Special Issue a valuable reference for understanding ongoing transformations in open science culture. It also highlights the need for continued discussions about institutional policies, research assessment, and dialogue and involvement across disciplines and professional communities within the scholarly communication ecosystem.

Iva Grabarić Andonovski, Nikolina Peša Pavlović, and Jadranka Stojanovski
Guest Editors

publications

MDPI

Editorial

Editorial: 10th Anniversary Special Issue "PUBMET2023 Conference on Scholarly Communication in the Context of Open Science"

Nikolina Peša Pavlović [1], Jadranka Stojanovski [2] and Iva Grabarić Andonovski [3,*]

1 University of Zadar, Department of Information Science and Technologies, F. Tuđmana 24i, 23000 Zadar, Croatia; npesa@unizd.hr
2 University of Zadar, Mihovila Pavlinovića 1, 23000 Zadar, Croatia; jadranka.stojanovski@irb.hr
3 University of Zagreb, Faculty of Food Technology and Biotechnology, Pierottijeva 6, 10000 Zagreb, Croatia
* Correspondence: igrabaric@pbf.hr

Over the past decade, the Open Science movement has profoundly transformed the way research is conducted, communicated, and assessed. What began as a call for open access to publications has expanded into a comprehensive framework, encompassing research data, infrastructures, peer review, metrics, and engagement with society.

Guided by global and regional initiatives, such as the UNESCO Recommendation on Open Science (UNESCO, 2021), the European Commission's Open Science Policy (European Commission, 2022), Coalition for Advancing Research Assessment (CoARA) Agreement (Coalition for Advancing Research Assessment, 2022), and national Open Science policies, openness is now embedded as a core value of research policy and practices. These developments underscore a shared vision: that transparency, inclusivity, and collaboration are crucial to enhancing the quality and credibility of science and its social impact.

Over the same period, the PUBMET Conference on Scholarly Communication in the Context of Open Science has evolved into a vibrant meeting point for researchers, editors, publishers, librarians, and policymakers. Since its inception in 2014, PUBMET has anticipated and accompanied these changes, offering a space where global trends meet local realities. The 2023 conference, hosted by the University of Zadar, marked its tenth anniversary with a focus on openness, equity, and sustainability in scholarly communication. Discussions spanned a broad range of interrelated topics: diamond open access, open research infrastructures, FAIR data, responsible research assessment, ethics, and the growing role of artificial intelligence in scholarly workflows.

This Special Issue of *Publications* includes selected papers presented at PUBMET2023[1], providing a snapshot of current research and practices in Open Science. These nine contributions highlight the diversity of approaches and the complexity of the challenges faced by the scholarly communication ecosystem, from institutional publishing and data management to citizen science and digital literacy.

The opening paper by Jadranka Stojanovski and Danijel Mofardin explores the diamond open access landscape in Croatia, based on the results of the Developing Institutional Open Access Publishing Models to Advance Scholarly Communications (DIAMAS) project survey (Kramer & Ross, 2024). The study reveals how institutional publishers operate within community-owned, non-commercial models, balancing Open Science principles with limited financial and human resources. Their findings underscore the crucial role of shared infrastructures and public support in sustaining the diamond model.

From a complementary perspective, Jane Mahoney presents the PublishOA.ie (Royal Irish Academy and Trinity College Dublin, 2023) initiative, which examines the feasibility of a shared diamond open access platform across Ireland and Northern Ireland. The project illustrates how collaboration among institutions and funders can overcome fragmentation and strengthen open access publishing at national and regional levels—particularly across differing policy frameworks within and outside the European Union.

A recurring theme across several papers is the management and reuse of research data in alignment with FAIR (Findable, Accessible, Interoperable, Reusable) principles. Radovan Vrana analyses the data practices of Croatian scientists, identifying both progress and obstacles in research data management. Ljiljana Poljak Bilić and Kristina Posavec focus on the FAIRness of humanities data at the European level, emphasising the heterogeneity of data types and the need for domain-sensitive approaches to ensure accessibility and reusability. Luca De Santis, reporting on the GoTriple (OPERAS, 2021) discovery platform for the social sciences and humanities, offers a practical illustration of FAIR-by-design infrastructure development and lessons learned in building interoperable systems that support openness from the outset.

Ethical and disciplinary specificities of data sharing are further addressed by Olga Orlić in a study of ethnological and anthropological research practices. This paper highlights the tension between the ideals of openness and the ethical imperative to protect participants and cultural contexts. By proposing a combined FAIR/CARE framework (balancing reusability with collective benefit, authority, responsibility, and ethics), the author reminds us that Open Science must remain sensitive to the diversity of research traditions.

Several contributions expand the discussion towards education, engagement, and the societal interface of Open Science. Jelena Madunić and Matija Sovulj examine the application of ChatGPT 3.5 in information literacy instruction, exploring both the potential and the limitations of generative AI in educational contexts. Their findings point out the need for human oversight, critical thinking, and pedagogical adaptation when integrating AI tools into academic practice. Dolores Mumelaš and Alisa Martek, in their paper on the benefits of citizen science for libraries, show how libraries can become active partners in participatory research, leveraging citizen involvement to advance both scientific literacy and institutional missions. Mirko Duić adds another dimension by analysing academic attitudes towards Wikipedia, suggesting ways in which researchers can engage more proactively in shaping open and reliable public knowledge.

Taken together, these contributions illustrate how the principles of Open Science are being implemented, negotiated, and reinterpreted across disciplines and contexts. They demonstrate that openness is not a uniform condition, but rather a dynamic and evolving process shaped by infrastructure, policy, culture, and ethics. The integration of FAIR data principles, the advancement of diamond open access, and the emergence of AI as a transformative tool all signal that the future of scholarly communication will depend on continued collaboration, experimentation, and critical reflection.

The 10th anniversary of the PUBMET conference offers an opportunity not only to celebrate a decade of dialogue and community building, but also to look ahead. The studies and reflections presented in this issue reaffirm the importance of inclusive infrastructures, responsible innovation, and capacity building for Open Science. They also remind us that openness is most meaningful when it enables trust between researchers, institutions, and society.

This Special Issue thus serves as both a record and an invitation: a record of how far the scholarly community has come in reimagining research communication, and an invitation to continue this journey towards a more transparent, ethical, and sustainable research culture.

Author Contributions: Conceptualization, N.P.P., J.S. and I.G.A.; writing-original draft preparation, N.P.P.; critical revision of the original draft, J.S. and I.G.A. All authors have read and agreed to the published version of the manuscript.

Conflicts of Interest: The authors declare no conflicts of interest.

Notes

1 PUBMET2023—The 10th Conference on Scholarly Communication in the Context of Open Science, 13–15 September 2023, University of Zadar, Croatia; https://pubmet2023.unizd.hr/ (accessed on 25 September 2025).

References

Coalition for Advancing Research Assessment. (2022). *The agreement on reforming research assessment.* Available online: https://www.coara.org/agreement/the-agreement-full-text/ (accessed on 25 September 2025).

European Commission. (2022). *Open science policy.* Available online: https://research-and-innovation.ec.europa.eu/strategy/strategy-research-and-innovation/our-digital-future/open-science_en (accessed on 25 September 2025).

Kramer, B., & Ross, G. (2024). *DIAMAS survey on Institutional Publishing–aggregated data.* Available online: https://zenodo.org/records/10590503 (accessed on 13 October 2025).

OPERAS. (2021). *Transforming research through innovative practices for linked interdisciplinary exploration (TRIPLE): GoTriple.* Available online: https://project.gotriple.eu/ (accessed on 13 October 2025).

Royal Irish Academy and Trinity College Dublin. (2023). *Publish OA Ireland.* Available online: https://www.ria.ie/publishing-house/publishoa// (accessed on 13 October 2025).

UNESCO. (2021). *UNESCO recommendation on open science.* Available online: https://www.unesco.org/en/open-science (accessed on 25 September 2025).

publications

MDPI

Article

Diamond Open Access Landscape in Croatia: DIAMAS Survey Results †

Jadranka Stojanovski [1,*] and Danijel Mofardin [2]

1 University of Zadar, 23000 Zadar, Croatia
2 Research Library, University of Zadar, 23000 Zadar, Croatia; dmofardi1@unizd.hr
* Correspondence: jadranka.stojanovski@irb.hr

† Developing Institutional Open Access Publishing Models to Advance Scholarly Communication.

Abstract: As open science initiatives address the crisis in scholarly communication driven by commercialisation, diamond open access publishing—promoting equity for authors and readers—has emerged as a focal point in open access scholarly publishing. This study examines the landscape of institutional publishing in Croatia, focusing on the community-owned diamond open access model. Through the DIAMAS project survey, which targeted 251 institutional publishers and achieved a response rate of 77, the research identifies the distinct features of Croatian institutional publishing. Institutional publishers are characterised by governance structures, funding challenges, voluntary staffing, and alignment with open science principles. Notable traits include reliance on public funding, use of the national open access journal platform, and a strong diamond open access publishing tradition. Key findings emphasise the critical role of national infrastructure, services, and multilingual publishing. Persistent challenges include meeting indexing criteria, advancing open science practices, and ensuring metadata quality. This study provides a comprehensive mapping of Croatian institutional publishers, offering insights into their strengths and weaknesses while proposing strategies for improvement. The findings underscore the importance of national policy frameworks, capacity building, and international collaboration to ensure the sustainability and visibility of Croatian institutional publishing.

Keywords: diamond open access; scholarly publishing; editorial quality; open science

1. Introduction

In addition to promoting high-quality research, the core values of the open science movement include universal open access (OA) and collective welfare. These principles dictate that scientific practices should be inclusive, sustainable, and equitable, ensuring fairness among researchers (UNESCO, 2021). While open access has significantly increased the availability of research methods and results, the current business models employed by major publishers do not provide equal publication opportunities for scientists, nor do they uphold the same levels of integrity for scientific publications from smaller or less developed countries. This situation suggests an ongoing colonisation of scientific publishing and open access (Khanna et al., 2022).

Research suggests that many journals from these countries remain unindexed in prominent databases (Raza et al., 2024). To advance global equity and foster epistemological diversity in knowledge production and consumption, a shift from the gold open access model—characterised by high publication fees (Borrego, 2023)—to the diamond model (Druelinger & Ma, 2023) is essential. While the diamond model is commonly understood as one in which neither authors nor readers pay fees, its implementation is more complex.

https://doi.org/10.3390/publications13010013

In some regions, the diamond model is deeply embedded in the publishing tradition, while in others, it has only recently been introduced as the primary publishing method (Mahony, 2024). Meanwhile, some countries are still experimenting with this approach. These varying levels of adoption have resulted in diverse characteristics in diamond publishing, such as governance structures, cost-sharing arrangements, workforce requirements, editorial management, alignment with open science principles, publication languages, visibility, and technical support services.

Moreover, the success of the diamond model is closely tied to the research assessment systems in place. Despite its clear advantages, diamond open access publications are often undervalued in research evaluations (Liu, 2024). Addressing all these complexities at the 2nd Diamond Open Access Conference, seven key facets of diamond open access were identified: (1) equity, (2) knowledge as a public good, (3) community-driven initiatives, (4) diversity, (5) transitioning to diamond, (6) research assessment and recognition, and (7) multi-level cooperation (Saenen et al., 2024). Thus, studies that examine the intricate nature of diamond publishing are highly valuable.

Locally published scholarly journals play a crucial role in small and developing countries, primarily by safeguarding the quality of locally relevant research, as outlined in the Leiden Manifesto (Hicks et al., 2015). They foster the development of non-English terminology in various scientific disciplines. They promote using the native language in scientific discourse, facilitating access to research findings for the broader local community without language barriers. Although research shows that non-English journals generally have a lower global impact in terms of citation counts (Yoon et al., 2023), prioritising linguistic accessibility enhances scholarly communication and knowledge dissemination within local contexts, thereby fostering greater stakeholder engagement and understanding.

Furthermore, they offer invaluable support to early career researchers by providing closer editors' guidance and collaboration throughout the publishing process, actively contributing to the enrichment of research and academic culture, bolstering the reputation of the local scholarly community and shaping the criteria for assessment in the academic sphere. These journals also highlight the significance of impact beyond mere citation numbers, allowing scientists to disseminate their work without the exorbitant fees often associated with prestigious "gold" journals (Druelinger & Ma, 2023). Local scholarly publications bridge the divide between scientific advancements and societal applications by emphasising ethical considerations and research integrity.

Croatian scholarly publishing has a long history, dating back to the first scholarly journal, "Arkiv za povjestnicu jugoslavensku" (Archives of South Slavic History) in 1851 (Hebrang Grgić, 2018). The specifics of the Croatian publishing landscape set it apart from the prevailing models in journal publishing, which are often characterised by profit-driven approaches, high prices, monopolies, paywalls, digital divides, and English language dominance. In Croatia, scholarly journals are primarily published by universities and learned societies committed to a diamond, non-profit business model, a critical factor in the early adoption of open access principles. This commitment led to the founding of the Portal of Croatian Scientific and Professional Journals (HRČAK) in 2006, a comprehensive national platform hosting Croatian open access journals.

As of the writing of this article, HRČAK hosts more than 500 Croatian scholarly, professional, and popular open access journals, including more than 400 active journals, which collectively store almost 300,000 published articles. State subsidies to journals support the diamond open access publishing model, which is contingent on open access and the inclusion of the subsidised journal in HRČAK. Only a few Croatian journals utilise the 'article processing charges' (APC) model, underscoring the community's dedication to the unrestricted dissemination of knowledge. Although state subsidies are insufficient to cover all publication costs, a significant share of volunteer work and institutional support enables the publication of many scholarly journals.

In contrast to Croatia's thriving open access journal scene, the transition towards OA publication of books and monographs has been more cautious, with only a limited number of active academic publishers engaged in this endeavour. Unlike journal publishing, state book subsidies do not typically incentivise open access. A possible explanation is that these subsidies are often directed towards small commercial publishing houses, which heavily rely on such financial support for their sustainability, regardless of their OA policies. Nonetheless, certain universities have initiated establishing publishing platforms dedicated to releasing open access books and conference proceedings.

Despite various studies examining Croatian journals, the focus has predominantly been on bibliometric analyses of individual journals (Silva de Araújo et al., 2020; Marijan, 2019; Dabić et al., 2021; Wang et al., 2020) or a set of journals (Moslavac, 2022), with limited research covering the analysis of state subsidies (Sambunjak et al., 2008; Macan & Stojanovski, 2008). To our knowledge, comprehensive research on the Croatian open access publishing landscape appears absent, indicating gaps in understanding and documentation. Therefore, this paper aims to map the Croatian publishing landscape, focusing on institutional publishers and the diamond open access model. The main research question was what are the key characteristics of Croatian institutional publishers and service providers (IPSPs) regarding governance, funding, staff, services, publications, and open science practices, and how do these impact editorial quality and management, technical services efficiency, and visibility?

This question was further divided into the following subquestions:

1. What types of institutions and governance models are predominant among Croatian institutional publishers, and how active are they in local and international professional circles?
2. What are the primary funding sources for Croatian institutional publishers, and how many staff members do they employ?
3. What range of services, types of publications, and languages do Croatian institutional publishers offer and use?
4. To what extent do Croatian institutional publishers implement open science practices?
5. How do Croatian institutional publishers ensure editorial quality and uphold research integrity?
6. What technical services do Croatian institutional publishers provide, and what are their main challenges?
7. What strategies do Croatian institutional publishers employ to improve the visibility and impact of their publications?

As part of the Developing Institutional Open Access Publishing Models to Advance Scholarly Communication (DIAMAS) project, a thorough survey was conducted across 45 European countries, including Croatia, garnering significant participation from institutional publishers and editors (Armengou et al., 2023). Primary survey outcomes specific to Croatia have been detailed in this paper, with the broader findings integrated into the comprehensive reports "Institutional Publishing in the ERA[1]: Results from the DIAMAS survey" (Armengou et al., 2023) and "Institutional Publishing in the ERA: Full Country Reports" (Agnoloni et al., 2024).

Croatian organisations participating in the DIAMAS project are the University of Zadar and the University of Zagreb Faculty of Humanities and Social Sciences.

2. Materials and Methods

DIAMAS IPSP survey was conducted between 29 March and 10 May 2023. The survey focused on institutional publishers and service providers (IPSPs) as a target group rather than on individual journals. Two complementary types of IPSP are distinguished: institutional publishers (IPs), who carry legal, ethical, or scientific responsibility for academic publishing, and service providers (SPs), who have more limited responsibility for specific activities in the publishing process (Armengou et al., 2023). Both types can be integrated into a single IPSP. DIAMAS defined institutions as research-performing institutions, research-funding institutions, scholarly/learned societies, and academies (Bargheer et al., 2023).

The survey questions were structured in nine groups as follows (DIAMAS, 2024):

1. Introductory questions—identification;
2. Introductory questions—demographics;
3. Funding;
4. Ownership and governance;
5. Open access and open science practices;
6. Editorial quality, editorial management, and research integrity;
7. Technical service efficiency;
8. Visibility, including indexation;
9. Equity, Diversity, Inclusion, and Belonging (EDIB): multilingualism, gender equity, and accessibility.

Before dissemination, limited face validity and full testing were conducted to check questions' clarity and collect feedback. According to the testing results, some questions were corrected, and one-third were deleted to avoid a high dropout rate. To ensure the best possible accessibility and to receive as many responses as possible, the final English version of the survey (DIAMAS, 2024), containing 59 questions in nine groups, was translated into Croatian by corresponding project members.

The survey invitations were distributed via Qualtrics, an online survey tool, between 29 and 31 March 2023. Croatian project members also sent individual invitations to identified IPSPs, followed by two reminders. Additionally, the survey was disseminated through existing Croatian mailing lists, targeting editors, publishers, and libraries. It remained open until 10 May 2023. Informed consent was obtained from all participants through an integrated statement in the introductory section of the survey, as documented in the Survey Questions Data Description within the available dataset (Kramer & George, 2024).

The DIAMAS survey targeted 251 Croatian IPSPs and achieved a response rate of 77, the second-highest among the 45 ERA countries participating in the DIAMAS study. Croatian project partners identified contacts for 228 IPSPs using data from the HRČAK platform and 23 from external resources. While service providers (SPs) can be distinct entities from institutional publishers (IPs), most respondents identified themselves as institutional publishers that also provide services. Consequently, IPSPs were treated as the unit of analysis without differentiating between IPs and SPs.

Several limiting factors necessitate caution when generalising the findings to the broader population of IPSPs. These include the relatively low response rate compared to the number of invitations sent, ambiguities in question wording, and challenges in translating the survey content from English to Croatian. This data collection, analysis, and report serve as a foundational effort, offering essential insights and highlighting areas for further investigation and improvement.

3. Results

3.1. IPSP Profiles, Governance, and Membership

We gathered identifying information from introductory identification and demographic responses such as IPSP official names in Croatian, translated names, contact and respondent names and email addresses, respondent function, website URLs, and contact permissions. This information allowed us to access IPSP identification and additional data collection by checking their websites. Among 77 respondents, we identified five types of IPSPs: university/faculty (21, including 4 universities with dedicated web pages for their publishing activities), learned society/association (18), research institute (6), library (3), and museum (3). Still, 22 respondents identified themselves as a single journal. The rest of the respondents reported that national publishing platforms (1), library repositories (1), and publishing houses (1) were IPSP types. The responses on the respondent's function revealed seven types of staff who have filled out the survey: editor (40), librarian (11), publishing representative (9), society/association representative (9), administration/management (6), director of the publishing house (1), and SP representative (1) (Table 1).

Table 1. IPSPs' and respondents' profiles.

IPSP Profile		Respondent Profile	
university/faculty	21	editor (editor-in-chief, editor, technical editor, associate editor)	40
learned society	18	librarian	11
research institute	6	IP publishing representative (president of the publishing committee, head of the publishing service)	9
library	3	society representative (president, treasurer, chairman)	9
museum	3	administration/management (professors, deans, vice-deans, assistant directors)	6
single journal	22	director of the publishing house	1
national publishing platform	1	SP representative	1
publishing house	1		
library repository	1		
error (personal web page)	1		
Total	77	Total	77

The survey revealed that Croatian IPSPs predominantly operate under public entities, such as universities and research institutes (66%), while 25% are private, non-profit organisations (Table 2). Five respondents chose the 'other' category, including two non-governmental organisations, two professional societies, and one 'society of associations' ('savez udruga' in Croatian). The one respondent who self-identified as a company (a small one, in a category of 2–5 employees and publishing 2–5 journals and up to 50 books and conference outputs a year) is a service provider to institutional publishing.

Table 2. IPSPs' or parent organisations' type of legal entity.

Parent Organisation's Type	# of IPSPs
Public organisation (e.g., university, research institute, laboratory, research organisation)	51
Private, not-for-profit organisation (e.g., charity, foundation, learned society, or association)	19
Other (please describe)	5
Company (owned by directors; limited liability)	1
Don't know	1
Total	77

The governance model of IPSPs is primarily based on a governing board, with 44 out of 65 respondents reporting their use. In contrast, management offices and external audits are less common, cited by 22 out of 56 and 16 out of 57 respondents. Other governance structures include publishing committees, councils, teams for digital collections management, offices, editors-in-chief, editorial boards, and faculty management. Formal documentation of IPSP activities is predominantly in the form of statutes, by-laws, and articles of association, while external legislation, requirements, and policies are less frequently referenced. One respondent identified a university senate decision as the primary formal document.

To promote collaboration and enhance institutional publishing quality, it is crucial for Croatian IPSPs to participate in professional circles and join relevant associations and initiatives. One-third of surveyed IPSPs are members of the Croatian Association of Scholarly Communication (CROASC/ZNAK). The European Association of Science Editors (EASE) is well-represented in Croatia, supported by an active regional chapter. While many IPSPs adhere to the guidelines of the Committee on Publication Ethics (COPE) (COPE, n.d.), only a small fraction hold formal COPE membership. None of the respondent IPSPs are affiliated with the Coalition for Advancing Research Assessment (CoARA), and only a few have endorsed the Helsinki Initiative on Multilingualism in Scholarly Communication or the TOP Guidelines.

3.2. Funding and Staff

Over half of the respondents (42 out of 77) reported starting each year with the approved budget. A survey revealed that excluding one IPSP with an annual budget exceeding EUR 1 million (a government-funded national publishing house), the average annual budget for IPSPs, based on data from 31 respondents who disclosed their budgets, is approximately EUR 30,000, with many operating on less than EUR 10,000 (Table 3).

Table 3. IPSPs' annual budgets.

Annual Budget (in Thousands of EUR)	# of IPSPs
<1	2
1–10	9
11–50	13
51–100	7
101–500	0
501–1000	0
>1000	1
Do not wish to disclose	2
Don't know	8
Total	42

IPSPs closely monitor their expenses, with 61 out of 77 respondents indicating active oversight, particularly when receiving government subsidies. They are also required to submit annual financial reports. Parent organisations frequently provide in-kind support, such as facilities (69%), IT services (63%), and staff salaries (51%) (Table 4). However, support for human resource management, financial services, and legal services is typically absent. Notably, one respondent in the "Other" category stated, "All of the above in-kind contributions are provided not by our parent organisation but by the IPSP itself".

Table 4. In-kind support from the parent institution.

Does Your Parent Organisation Provide the IPSP with In-Kind Support, Either in the Form of Labour, Facility Costs or Other (Excluding Peer Review)?	
In-Kind Support Type	**# of IPSPs**
Facilities and premises	24
Service-specific IT services	22
General IT services (email, hardware, etc.)	19
Salaries of permanent staff	18
Salaries of temporary staff	6
Other (please specify)	3
N/A	4
Don't know	1
HR management, general financial and legal services	0
Total	42

The survey question concerning paid staff revealed that IPSPs are significantly supported by voluntary efforts, with 54% indicating an absence of paid staff. Among the rest, 26% have a staff of 2–5, 14% have less than two, and less than 6% have a staff of 6–10 or more than 30 employed or contracted staff involved in publishing (Table 5).

Table 5. IPSPs' paid staff.

How Many Paid Staff Are Directly Employed or Contracted by the IPSP (i.e., Editorial, Production and Operational Staff in Full-Time Equivalent (FTE))?	
Staff Directly Employed or Contracted by the IPSP	**# of IPSPs**
None	41
Less than two	11
2–5	20
6–10	2
More than 30	2
Total	76

3.3. Services, Publications, and Publication Language

Publishing relies on a wide array of services, including editorial, production, IT, communication, administrative, legal, financial services, and training (Table 6). Editorial services, such as manuscript processing, are typically provided voluntarily or as in-kind contributions, whereas production and IT services are predominantly outsourced. Communication, administrative, legal, financial services, and training are less commonly used and were frequently marked as "None/N/A" in the survey. Additionally, some IPSPs outsource specific services, such as printing, CrossRef DOI registration, and translations, which were categorised under "Other".

Croatian IPSPs mainly publish academic journals, books, and conference outputs. Many also publish media and digital products and professional journals. On average, an IPSP publishes 1–5 scholarly journals, 11–100 scholarly articles per year, 1–10 academic books, and 1–20 conference proceedings (Table 7). Although IPSPs predominantly come from the social sciences and humanities (21 and 19, respectively, out of 43) and have a multidisciplinary approach (24 out of 43), they are also represented across various disciplines (natural sciences: 16; engineering and technology: 11; medical and health sciences: 10), with a smaller presence in agricultural sciences (7 out of 43). Three respondents selected "non-academic" as a discipline.

Table 6. Types of external services in terms of funding requirements.

	Voluntary Work	In-Kind Contributions	Outsourced	None/Not Applicable	Don't Know
Editorial services	24	16	6	16	0
Production services	9	15	35	7	0
IT services	10	17	26	11	2
Communication services	14	14	4	22	3
Administrative, legal and financial services	3	16	12	21	3
Training, support and/or advice on publishing policies and best practice	16	13	4	21	4
Other	0	1	2	4	1

Total number of IPSPs using external services: 61. Multiple answers were allowed.

Table 7. Number of publications by type.

Which of the Following Does the IPSP Publish or Provide a Service for?			
Scholarly Journals in 2022	**# of IPSPs**	**Academic Books in 2022**	**# of IPSPs**
1	28	1–10	36
2–5	31	11–20	9
6–10	7	21–50	3
11–20	3	51–100	0
21–50	1	>100	0
51–100	0		
>100	1		
Scholarly Articles in 2022	**# of IPSPs**	**Conference Outputs in 2022**	**# of IPSPs**
1–10	6	1–20	39
11–50	40	21–50	7
51–100	10	51–100	4
101–200	7	101–200	1
201–500	3	>500	0
>500	2		

Croatian IPSPs publish 5.3 journals, 75 articles, 9.2 books, and 21.8 conference outputs annually.

Among the surveyed IPSPs, only three exclusively publish content in Croatian, while an additional 37 predominantly publish in Croatian and also venture into other languages (the number of IPSPs that publish in Croatian, English, and another language is indicated with a plus sign and a specific language in Table 8).

Respondents were prompted to rank languages by their prevalence, underscoring that Croatian is the primary publication language for 59% of responding IPSPs (Table 8). Conversely, 11 IPSPs exclusively publish in English. This indicates that 14 IPSPs confine their publications to Croatian or English, while 55 surveyed IPSPs are committed to multilingual publishing.

Table 8. Publication languages.

Language	# of IPSPs
Croatian	3
English	11
Croatian—English	26
+German	25
+Serbian	9
+French	8
+Slovenian	8
+Italian	11
+Russian	4
+Bosnian	3
+Spanish	2
+Hungarian	2
+Czech	1
One language	14
Two languages	26
Three languages	5
Four languages	3
Five languages	21

3.4. Open Science Practices

The DIAMAS survey addressed several aspects of open science practices, like the sharing of OA publications, OA/OS policies, copyright and licensing, open peer review, research data sharing and data availability policies, and new approaches towards research assessment. Some questions used a sliding scale ranging from 0 to 100, which some respondents misinterpreted.

Responses related to open science practices among Croatian IPSPs revealed that nearly all journals and a significant number of books and conference proceedings are published in open access (OA). Most IPSPs have institutional repositories for archiving and publishing OA content. Of 59 respondents to this question, 49 indicated 100% OA for journals, and nine IPSPs claimed 100% OA for books.

Croatia has a history of OA publishing since the 1990s but lacks a comprehensive national open access/open science (OA/OS) policy. Nevertheless, support exists through national laws, such as mandates for journals to be OA on the HRČAK portal for government subsidies. Furthermore, many IPSP parent institutions have OA/OS policies. Despite no formal national policy, the integration of OA principles within the scholarly domain remains strong. IPSPs' OA/OS policies mainly address copyright, self-archiving, and open licences (Table 9). Most IPSPs use Creative Commons licences for all journals, or at least for some. We can observe that 16 IPSPs reported using CC licences for books despite the immaturity of the OA book landscape. Among Creative Commons licenses, CC BY, CC BY-NC-ND, and CC BY-NC are often used, with some IPSPs using multiple licenses.

Croatian IPSPs encourage authors to share published content through academic networks like ResearchGate. Allowing self-archiving in repositories is also common, and the embargo is imposed only by a few respondents. However, many IPSPs are not accepting submissions shared as preprints (Table 10). Many respondents are unaware of their policies regarding specific statements, as indicated by the substantial number of participants who selected "I Don't Know" or "N/A."

Table 9. The issues addressed by the open science/open access policy.

Does the IPSP's Open Science/Open Access Policy Address the Following Issues?		
Open Science/Open Access Policy Issues Addressed	**# of IPSPs**	**%**
Copyright	56	86
Self-archiving	41	63
Use of open licences	29	45
Use of identifiers	24	37
Metadata rights	17	26
Third-party copyright	9	14
Embargoes	7	11
Publication of negative research results	3	5
Other	4	6
Don't know	6	9

Other (please specify): "This journal provides immediate open access to its content on the principle that making research freely available to the public supports a greater global exchange of knowledge. The journal content is published under the Creative Commons CC-BY-SA licence that allows others to share the work with an acknowledgement of the work's authorship and initial publication in this journal"; "The policies of the national platform HRČAK". Total number of respondents: 65.

Table 10. OA/OS principles adopted by IPSPs.

Please Consider the Following Statements and Mark Those That Are Implemented at IPSP Level						
	Yes, for Books	**Yes, for All Journals**	**Yes, for Some Journals**	**No**	**I Don't Know**	**N/A**
Use Creative Commons (or other open licences)	16	44	10	5	4	6
Make references openly available according to the principles of I4OC (Initiative for Open Citations)	11	32	4	12	13	7
Allow self-archiving of your published content in open repositories (subject-specific or institutional)	17	49	4	4	5	7
Impose embargo periods for self-archiving	3	2	1	38	11	12
Accept submissions that have been publicly shared as a preprint or working paper before or on submission	6	14	9	24	12	7
Encourage or allow sharing the full text of your published content via academic sharing services (such as Academia.edu or ResearchGate)	12	49	4	4	5	8

Total number of respondents: 75.

Thirty-two IPSPs reported having references openly available per I4OC principles, though this should be verified cautiously. A notable share of respondents was unsure about I4OC compliance, embargoes, and preprint acceptance.

Regarding open peer review, most responses were "No, (we are not enabling any form of open peer review)". Still, ten IPSPs reported on already implemented open peer review, two are experimenting with it, and seventeen plan to implement it later.

Research data sharing is still developing, with most IPSPs needing corresponding policies. Despite the prevalence of negative responses (23 out of 75), we recorded 13 out of

75 cases of inclusion of data sharing in OS/OA policies, 20 out of 75 IPSPs implementing research data sharing at the journal level, and 4 at the publisher level.

The contributorship model, distinguishing between contributor roles, is not widely implemented, with many respondents unaware of it. According to the responses, only 12 IPSPs distinguished between contributor roles in their publications, while 28 responded negatively. As many as 24 IPSPs marked "Don't know", which could indicate their lack of knowledge about the contributorship model.

3.5. Editorial Quality, Editorial Management, and Research Integrity

The survey results revealed the significant involvement of Croatian IPSPs in the editorial management of their publications, which is also true for the whole DIAMAS sample, with around 70% of IPSPs saying they participate in the editorial management of publications (Armengou et al., 2023). Expectedly, IPSPs are involved mainly in recruiting and managing the editorial board members. According to the responses, they are also significantly involved in other tasks like sourcing reviewers, coordinating the peer review process, performing basic checks, and doing plagiarism scans. Only a few IPSPs have no tasks in editorial management. Similarly, a substantial number of IPSPs are engaged in managing editorial quality. Among them, over half of IPSPs create guidelines and instructions, define quality criteria and ensure compliance.

Croatian IPSPs predominantly employ double-anonymised peer reviews with anonymous authors and reviewers. Single-anonymised peer review, where authors do not know who the reviewers are but the reviewer knows the author's identity, is used less. Some IPSPs indicate they practice open peer review, with few implementing open identities and one using open review reports. Eight IPSPs use editorial reviews.

More than half of the surveyed IPSPs have a policy on research integrity or publication ethics, slightly less than the whole DIAMAS sample, with around 63% of IPSPs having these policies in place. Still, 27 do not have such a policy, and some IPSPs are unaware of its existence.

3.6. Technical Service Efficiency

Responses regarding technical services provided by Croatian IPSPs indicate that most offer a full editorial workflow (55%), hosting (45%), and end-user interface (41%). Metadata and quality control (33%), software (27%), and partial editorial workflow (25%) are less common (Table 11).

Table 11. Technical services provided by IPSP.

What Technical Services Does the IPSP Provide?	
Technical Services	**# of IPSPs**
Hosting	34
Software	20
Full editorial workflow	41
Partial editorial workflow	19
Metadata and quality control	25
End-user interface	31
Other (Please specify)	3

Other: "Hrčak", "web page", "does not provide". Total number of respondents: 75.

Technical services are primarily maintained in-house by dedicated publishing departments (25 out of 30 respondents) and IT departments or personnel (21 out of 35). The technical infrastructure is managed in-house by IT departments (24 out of 35), while some services are partially, mainly, or fully outsourced (8, 13, and 1 respondent(s), respectively, out of 20).

The predominant publishing system used to support editorial workflows in Croatia is the Open Journal System (OJS), followed by customised or self-developed open-source solutions. Other systems include Open Monograph Press (OMP) and WordPress, while commercial software options, such as Editorial Manager, Scholar One, Indigo, and Manuscript Manager, were rarely mentioned.

Persistent Identifiers (PIDs) are assigned by the majority of IPSPs (57 out of 75). The most commonly implemented PIDs include CrossRef-DOI, ISSN, and ISBN.

Standard international publishing practices include releasing metadata in a standardised format under an open license or Public Domain Dedication. Among Croatian IPSPs, 36% share metadata under CC BY or another Creative Commons license (Table 12). However, many do not release metadata this way (27%), and a significant portion (25%) are still determining. Other (please specify) (Table 12) answers were as follows: "Yes, but not under a public license"; "Yes, but without the licence"; "Just starting with JATS XML for the journal"; and "Yes, UNIMARC".

Table 12. Sharing metadata.

Does the IPSP Release Its Metadata Openly with a Standard Metadata Description Schema (MARC, MODS, DC, ONIX, JATS, TEI)?	
Sharing Metadata Status	**# of IPSPs**
Yes, under Creative Commons Public Domain Dedication (CC0)	4
Yes, under CC BY or another Creative Commons licence	27
No	20
Don't know	19
Other (please specify)	4

Regarding content formats, PDF is the prevalent format (99%), likely due to current international publishing practices, HRČAK's previous lack of support for other formats and the ongoing presence of printed publications.

Almost two-thirds of respondents have archiving and backup policies in place, and 73% actively preserve published content through the Croatian National and University Library, the national infrastructure provided by the University of Zagreb, the University Computing Centre (SRCE), and institutional libraries or infrastructures.

The main technical challenges faced by Croatian IPSPs in providing adequate infrastructure and services include financial constraints (48 out of 67 respondents) and a lack of human resources (33 out of 67). The shortage of personnel also impacts key areas such as metadata quality (33 out of 67), interoperability (28 out of 67), and preservation (24 out of 67). Additionally, technical limitations in the existing infrastructure present challenges across all technical services.

While a lack of expertise is another significant issue, it appears to be evenly distributed across technical services and is less frequently addressed. Similarly, administrative constraints remain a less prominent focus in addressing these challenges.

3.7. Visibility, Communication, Marketing, and Impact

More than half of Croatian IPSPs prioritise better indexing. Beyond Web of Science Core Collection and Scopus, they seek indexing in Directory of Open Access Journals (DOAJ), Directory of Open Access Books (DOAB), ERIH PLUS, PubMed, Google Scholar, Google Books, and Open Access Publishing in European Networks (OAPEN). Almost half of IPSPs are satisfied with their current indexing status. Still, the main challenge for

Croatian IPSPs in achieving better indexing is meeting the technical participation criteria. Non-technical criteria, metadata requirements, membership fees, and recurring charges pose significant challenges.

Publicly displaying metrics is less common, with fewer than half of IPSPs doing so (31 out of 75). The prevalent metrics include data about submissions, acceptance, and publication dates (27 out of 31); article-level usage metrics, like visits, views, and downloads (18 out of 31); publication-level usage metrics, such as Journal Impact Factor (17 out of 31); and publication-level usage metrics, such as visits, views, and downloads (12 out of 31) (Table 13). It is expected that IPSPs are more aware of the article- and publication-level metrics provided for their journals by the national HRČAK platform. Citation badges provided by Dimensions are not known to IPSPs, and the widget showing geographical spread of visitors is used only by one IPSP.

Regarding communication, many IPSPs maintain a newsletter, social media, or networking profile (43 out of 75) to keep their community informed.

Table 13. Publicly displayed metrics.

Type of Metrics	# of IPSPs
Submission, acceptance, and publication dates	27
Article-level usage metrics, such as visits, views, and downloads	18
Publication-level usage metrics, such as visits, views, and downloads	12
Article-level impact metrics, such as citation counts	9
Publication-level impact metrics, such as Journal Impact Factors	17
Rejection rates	3
Altmetrics, such as Altmetric and Plum X Metrics	2
Dimensions citation badges	0
Widget showing geographical spread of visitors	1

Other (please specify): "This differs depending on the type of publication (it is not the same for the articles and for the journals, not even for all journals)".

4. Discussion

The results highlight the strengths and weaknesses of Croatian institutional publishers in advancing the diamond open access model. It should be noted that the significant representation of journals and journal editors in the survey could weaken the representation of other types of publications issued by IPSPs, resulting in skewed results towards journals' practices.

RQ1: What types of institutions and governance models are predominant among Croatian institutional publishers? Are they present in local and international professional circles?

Croatian IPSPs predominantly operate under public entities, such as universities and research institutes, and private, non-profit organisations, such as learned societies. These findings are consistent with the whole DIAMAS sample, where two-thirds of IPSPs are public organisations (such as most universities), and together with private but not-for-profit organisations (such as most societies and associations), over 85% of responding IPSPs are indeed not for profit (Armengou et al., 2023). Governance structures are varied, with many IPSPs employing governing boards, but formalised management practices remain limited.

The national professional circle of Croatian IPSPs is strong, largely due to the active efforts of the Croatian Association for Scholarly Communication (CROASC/ZNAK), which plays a pivotal role in major activities related to promoting and implementing open science principles. Croatian publishers and editors also benefit from their connection through the HRČAK platform.

In contrast, international engagement is significantly weaker and Croatian IPSPs rarely participate in major initiatives, learned societies, or professional networks. For instance, while many Croatian IPSPs follow the COPE guidelines to promote research and publication integrity, formal COPE membership is almost non-existent. Similarly, the CoARA, which aims to reform research assessment systems, is particularly relevant for small diamond publishers but sees no involvement from Croatian IPSPs. Some respondents were uncertain about their institution's membership status, indicating a need for increased awareness and transparency. An exception is the Croatian EASE Regional Chapter, a valuable link between Croatian IPSPs and the broader international publishing community, providing an avenue for greater global integration and collaboration.

RQ2: What are the primary funding sources for Croatian institutional publishers, and how many staff members are employed?

The dominance of public entities reflects a non-profit approach aligned with diamond open access principles. The Croatian government is the primary funder, with national ministries being the leading contributors, followed by counties, national foundations, cities, universities, private companies, and state agencies. However, a firm reliance on government subsidies, in-kind contributions from parent institutions, and volunteer work poses significant challenges and risks to sustainability (Yoon et al., 2024; Dufour et al., 2023). The results revealed that despite this reliance on government subsidies and institutional support, many IPSPs start the year without an approved budget. Croatian IPSPs are primarily driven by voluntary efforts, with over half indicating no paid staff. Stable funding mechanisms, such as multi-year grants, could alleviate financial uncertainty.

Survey responses to open-ended questions highlight several key challenges in funding, which we categorised accordingly:

- Continuity: Ensuring permanent, stable income is crucial for uninterrupted publication and development;
- Regularity: Delays in funding from ministries complicate financial planning;
- Sufficiency: Many IPSPs report insufficient state support and seek increased funding for essential services and development;
- Unexpected Changes: Sudden changes in public financing systems pose risks.
- Financial Literacy: Improved knowledge and skills in financial sustainability are needed;
- High Costs: Rising costs for copy-editing, printing, and online submission systems are a concern;
- Printing: Balancing the costs of print editions with the need for visibility in open access is challenging;
- Voluntary Work: Reliance on unpaid labour makes it difficult to retain skilled personnel;
- Dependency on Parent Institutions: Additional stable funding sources are necessary for further development.

Interestingly, according to the collected data, most respondents consider fixed and permanent subsidies from the parent organisations and permanent public and government funding stable or very stable. Delays and remittances did not influence the perception of the reliability of government funds. In contrast, IPSPs consider voluntary contributions, content and print sales, and article processing charges highly unstable.

During the past decades, Croatian journals were funded mainly by the Ministry of Science and Education as the main funder and the Ministry of Culture. Recently, the Ministry of Science and Education changed its subsidy policy and started distributing the finances for scholarly publications through programme agreements with public universities and research institutes as a part of institutional subsidy for research infrastructure. Although we can consider such an approach positive for several reasons (institutions' support for their own scientific publishing can result in better communication and improvement of funding criteria, encouraging an increase in quality), it remains to be seen how it will reflect on the development of diamond scientific publishing in Croatia.

According to the survey results, IPSPs consider the changes in modalities for government funding without timely announcements and public consultations a severe challenge. They also face an increase in the price of printing, copy-editing, and securing an appropriate online submission system. Even though print sales are very unstable, most Croatian IPSPs still print their journals. The possible reasons for this could be the unclear wording in one of the Ministry's funding criteria and the vague reluctance of IPSPs to switch to an exclusively online version.

The survey question concerning paid staff revealed that IPSPs are significantly supported by voluntary efforts, with over half indicating an absence of paid staff, compared to the whole DIAMAS sample, where only around one-quarter of IPSPs reported having no paid staff. When talking about different regions from the DIAMAS survey, Croatian results are mostly comparable to those from the Southern Europe region (Armengou et al., 2023).

RQ3: What range of services, types of publications, and languages do Croatian institutional publishers provide?

The distinction between in-house services used for IPSP publishing activities, services provided by IPSPs to other publishing organisations (within or outside their parent institution), and external services from third-party providers proved to be more complex than anticipated in the survey. Respondents faced challenges in categorising the type of services they use or offer, reflecting academic institutions' intricate and multi-layered organisational structures, where publishing activities are often distributed across various levels (Armengou et al., 2023). Despite these complexities, the collected data provide valuable insights into the range of services utilised and offered by IPSPs.

IPSPs also provide in-house services for editors, authors, reviewers, and readers. IPSPs primarily offer editorial services, including manuscript selection and peer review. They also provide production services like copy-editing, proofreading, typesetting, and metadata management. About half offer IT services, including submission systems and websites; communication services like marketing and dissemination; and administrative, legal, and financial services. Some IPSPs offer training, support, or counsel on publishing policies and best practices. Compared to the whole DIAMAS sample, the services Croatian IPSPs provide are comparable, except for the training, support, and/or advice services, which are provided considerably less often (Armengou et al., 2023).

External services often rely on nationally or internationally provided infrastructure like HRČAK or the national DOI Office at the Croatian National and University Library. Editorial services, including manuscript selection and peer review, are typically provided voluntarily or as in-kind contributions, while production and IT services are mostly outsourced.

The publication language practices among surveyed IPSPs in Croatia reveal a diverse multilingual landscape. While some IPSPs exclusively focus on publishing content in Croatian or English, most engage in multilingual publishing efforts. Over half of respondents disseminate content in multiple languages, with many providing bilingual or sequential versions across various documents or journals.

Multilingualism extends to abstracts, with many IPSPs offering abstracts in different languages, predominantly translating them into English if the source language differs. Moreover, several IPSPs extend translation services to metadata and language-check assistance for authors, showcasing a dedication to inclusive and accessible communication.

The Croatian language is among numerous languages spoken by small national groups, considered low-resource languages with a lack of training data (Begoli et al., 2024), causing a slower advancement of machine translation tools. Therefore, a reliance on human translators persists, highlighting additional costs for IPSPs. Although emerging tools offer potential, IPSPs still predominantly support a limited number of languages, underscoring the need for continued exploration and adaptation to technological advancements.

RQ4: To what extent do Croatian institutional publishers implement open science practices?

The survey results reveal a strong foundation for open science practices among Croatian IPSPs, particularly related to open access publishing. Croatian IPSPs demonstrate a well-established tradition of OA publishing, with nearly all journals and a notable proportion of books and conference proceedings available in OA. This aligns with Croatia's history of OA initiatives dating back to the 1990s, despite the absence of a comprehensive national OA/OS policy. The reliance on the HRČAK platform and institutional OA/OS policies has supported the widespread adoption of OA practices, further incentivised by government subsidies contingent on OA compliance. However, while OA for journals is nearly universal in Croatia, the OA book landscape is still underdeveloped, as reflected in the small share of OA books and modest use of Creative Commons (CC) licenses.

Most IPSPs have adopted OA/OS policies addressing copyright, self-archiving, and open licensing. However, compared to the whole DIAMAS sample, the use of open licences is addressed in fewer instances in the open science/open access policies of Croatian IPSPs (Armengou et al., 2023). In addition, less than half of the IPSPs address critical issues such as metadata rights, use of persistent identifiers, or third-party copyright.

The survey indicates that open peer review remains largely unexplored, with only a few IPSPs reporting implementation or plans to adopt it. This finding is consistent with the broader challenges of integrating transparency into peer review systems. Similarly, preprint sharing is not yet widely adopted, with many IPSPs explicitly not accepting submissions shared as preprints.

Research data sharing is still in its infancy among Croatian IPSPs. While a few respondents reported data-sharing policies at the journal or publisher level, most lacked such frameworks. This gap reflects broader challenges in aligning Croatian IPSPs with global open science initiatives emphasising data availability and reproducibility.

The contributorship model, which provides a more nuanced distinction of contributor roles supporting new ways of research assessment, has not been widely adopted. The high number of uncertain responses suggests limited awareness of this model.

While Croatian IPSPs are active in OA publishing, with a strong tradition and institutional support, there are gaps in understanding and implementing broader OS practices, especially in preprint sharing, open peer review, and the contributorship model. Increased training and capacity building could enhance these practices.

RQ5: How do Croatian institutional publishers ensure and manage editorial quality and research integrity?

The survey results underscore the active role of Croatian IPSPs in editorial management and quality assurance, reflecting trends observed across the DIAMAS sample. While the involvement of IPSPs in tasks such as recruiting and managing editorial board members is expected, without an insight into the structure of the respondents (mainly editors), tasks such as sourcing reviewers, coordinating the peer review process, performing basic editorial checks, and conducting plagiarism scans would undoubtedly surprise us.

Double-anonymised peer review is the predominant peer review method, ensuring anonymity for both authors and reviewers. Single-anonymised peer review is less commonly employed, and while some IPSPs are experimenting with open peer review practices, its adoption remains limited. This aligns with broader hesitancy to embrace more transparent peer review processes, which may require additional training and infrastructure support.

Over half of the surveyed IPSPs have established guidelines and instructions, quality criteria, and mechanisms for compliance to manage editorial quality effectively. However, the adoption of research integrity and publication ethics policies, while present in the majority, leaves room for improvement.

The relationship between publishers and editors is essential and should be clearly defined, adhering to ethical norms in scientific publishing. Publishers should handle recruiting and managing editorial board members, providing financial support, space, equipment, necessary tools, and training to ensure quality and independent editorial work. Editors, on the other hand, should manage the content, including the peer review process.

RQ6: What technical services do Croatian institutional publishers provide, and what are the main challenges?

Croatian IPSPs offer a range of technical services primarily maintained in-house, with publishing and IT departments managing most of the infrastructure. This internal management depicts a reliance on institutional resources rather than outsourcing, which is used only to a limited extent. The predominant use of the Open Journal System (OJS) as a publishing platform reinforces the role of open-source solutions in supporting editorial workflows from submission to publication (Dufour et al., 2023). Other open-source tools, such as Open Monograph Press (OMP), further demonstrate a preference for adaptable and cost-effective systems, although some IPSPs employ commercial software. The central installations of OJS and OMP maintained by SRCE, which are freely available to all Croatian IPSPs, undoubtedly enhance the popularity and usage of open-source tools.

Persistent Identifiers (PIDs) are widespread among Croatian IPSPs, with most of them assigning PIDs to their publications. However, the adoption of standardised metadata practices is uneven. While 36% of IPSPs release metadata under Creative Commons licenses, 27% do not share metadata openly, and 25% are uncertain about their metadata policies. Although its policy resembles the CC BY license, the national platform HRČAK has not clearly defined its metadata terms under a Creative Commons license or Public Domain Dedication. Clarifying HRČAK's metadata policy would benefit other IPSPs. The open comments suggest that some IPSPs are in the early stages of adopting standardised metadata schemas.

Currently, the assignment of Persistent Identifiers (PIDs) in Croatia is relatively complex and could be easily improved. While a national Digital Object Identifier (DOI) office within the National and University Library only serves journal publications and assigns DOIs solely to original scientific articles, publishers needing DOIs for other types of content must seek individual memberships in CrossRef (for publications) or Datacite (for datasets). Although using CrossRef DOI is common among Croatian IPSPs, not all IPSPs assign PIDs to all published content. Given the importance of DOIs for enhancing discoverability, this area needs attention.

PDF remains the dominant content format. Compared to Croatia, the whole DIAMAS sample uses other formats more, with 41% of IPSPs using HTML to display content and another 20% using the XML format (Armengou et al., 2023). Efforts made by Croatian IPSPs to adopt HTML and XML formats are underway, and their representation should be increased.

Most IPSPs have archiving and backup policies and actively preserve published content using national infrastructure, such as the Croatian National and University Library and the University Computing Centre (SRCE).

Financial constraints and lacking human resources are the most pressing challenges for Croatian IPSPs. These limitations impact critical areas such as metadata quality, interoperability, and long-term preservation. Additionally, technical limitations in existing infrastructure create barriers across all technical services, underscoring the need for infrastructure upgrades. While a lack of expertise is also a challenge, it appears less frequently addressed than financial and staffing issues.

RQ7: What strategies do Croatian institutional publishers use to enhance the visibility and impact of their publications?

Indexing in prestigious databases and directories, such as Web of Science Core Collection, Scopus, DOAJ, and ERIH PLUS, remains a top priority for over half of Croatian IPSPs. However, technical participation criteria, including metadata requirements and compliance, emerge as the most significant barriers to achieving broader indexing. Non-technical factors, such as membership fees and recurring charges, further complicate the process.

Publicly displaying metrics is not yet widespread, with fewer than half of the IPSPs providing such data. Among those that do, the most common metrics are operational statistics (e.g., submission, acceptance, and publication dates), followed by article-level usage metrics (e.g., visits, views, and downloads) and publication-level impact metrics (e.g., Journal Impact Factor). However, advanced metrics such as citation counts, altmetrics (e.g., Altmetric or PlumX), and tools like Dimensions citation badges remain largely unexplored.

This lack of adoption could indicate limited awareness or resource constraints. For example, while HRČAK provides article- and publication-level usage metrics (e.g., visits and downloads) for all journals, not all IPSPs leverage these data effectively. Additionally, the geographic visitor widget is used by only one respondent, suggesting unused potential in showcasing the reach and impact of publications.

In terms of communication strategies, many IPSPs actively maintain newsletters, social media profiles, or other networking tools to engage with their communities. With many respondents using these platforms, it is evident that digital communication is a key strategy for IPSPs to increase visibility and foster connections with stakeholders. Further leveraging these tools for targeted marketing and dissemination could enhance the reach and impact of their publications.

5. Conclusions

This study underscores the pivotal role of Croatian institutional publishers and service providers (IPSPs) in advancing diamond open access publishing and promoting equitable scholarly communication. Strengths include a strong tradition of diamond OA journal publishing, reliance on public funding, and commitment to multilingualism, supported by platforms like HRČAK and open-source systems for editorial management such as OJS.

Croatian IPSPs mainly operate under community-owned public or non-profit entities and rely heavily on voluntary work, with many lacking paid staff. Financial and human resource constraints challenge their ability to meet all technical requirements, improve metadata quality, and adopt more advanced open science practices. While OA journal publishing is widespread, OA books remain underdeveloped.

Editorial quality is supported by guidelines and peer review processes, with double-anonymised peer review prevailing. However, open peer review and contributorship models are underexplored. Research data-sharing policies are limited, reflecting broader gaps in aligning with global OS standards.

Technical infrastructure, predominantly managed in-house, relies on open-source solutions, with PIDs and archiving policies being common. However, existing infrastructure requires upgrades to address interoperability and preservation challenges. Indexing in major databases like Scopus and Web of Science Core Collection remains a priority, but IPSPs face barriers such as compliance with metadata standards. Metrics tracking is limited, with advanced tools like citation counts and altmetrics rarely employed.

To ensure sustainability, national open science policies, sufficient funding, and infrastructure upgrades are essential. International collaborations, training programs, and technical support can resolve some skill gaps and elevate Croatian IPSPs' global visibility. Strengthening capacity for OA books, improving editorial workflows, and advancing research integrity policies will further position Croatian IPSPs as leaders in equitable and accessible knowledge dissemination.

Author Contributions: Conceptualisation, J.S.; methodology, J.S. and D.M.; formal analysis, J.S.; writing—original draft preparation, J.S. and D.M.; writing—review and editing, J.S. and D.M. All authors have read and agreed to the published version of the manuscript.

Funding: This research was part of the Developing Institutional Open Access Publishing Models to Advance Scholarly Communication (DIAMAS) project funded by the European Union's Horizon -WIDERA-2021-ERA-01 research and innovation programme, grant number 101058007.

Data Availability Statement: Aggregated data from the DIAMAS survey are stored on ZENODO and available at https://doi.org/10.5281/zenodo.10590503 (accessed on 26 February 2025) (Kramer & George, 2024).

Acknowledgments: We sincerely thank Iva Melinščak Zlodi for her invaluable contribution to the DIAMAS Country Report Croatia. We want to thank our colleagues from all DIAMAS partner institutions who participated in the DIAMAS landscape study. A special mention goes to Jan Erik Frantsvåg for successfully leading this demanding work package and providing continuous support and to George Ross, Bianca Kramer, and Jeroen Bosman for curating data.

Conflicts of Interest: The authors declare no conflicts of interest.

Note

1 European research area.

References

Agnoloni, T., Bargheer, M., Bosman, J., Caliman Fontes, L., de Pablo Llorente, V., Franczak, M., Frantsvåg, J. E., Klaus, T., Kramer, B., Manista, F., Melinščak Zlodi, I., Pellin, E., Peruginelli, G., Rooryck, J., Schima, J., Stojanovski, J., Stone, G., Wnuk, M., Angelaki, M., ... Ševkušić, M. (2024). *Institutional publishing in the ERA: Complete country reports*. Zenodo. [CrossRef]

Armengou, C., Aschehoug, A., Ball, J., Bargheer, M., Bosman, J., Brun, V., de Pablo Llorente, V., Franczak, M., Frantsvåg, J. E., Hersperger, O., Klaus, T., Kramer, B., Kuchma, I., Laakso, M., Manista, F., Melinščak Zlodi, I., Mounier, P., Pölönen, J., Pontille, D., ... Wnuk, M. (2023). *Institutional publishing in the ERA: Results from the DIAMAS survey*. Zenodo. Available online: https://zenodo.org/records/10022184 (accessed on 31 August 2024).

Bargheer, M., Bosman, J., Drahomira, C., Frantsvåg, J. E., Klaus, T., Kramer, B., Laakso, M., Manista, F., Melinščak Zlodi, I., Peruginelli, G., Proudman, V., Rooryck, J., Souyioultzoglou, I., Stojanovski, J., Stone, G., & Verheusen, A. (2023). *D2.1 IPSP scoping report_approved by the EC*. Zenodo. [CrossRef]

Begoli, E., Mahbub, M., & Srinivasan, S. (2024, August 15). *Rosetta Balcanica: Deriving a "gold standard" neural machine translation (NMT) parallel dataset from high-fidelity resources for western Balkan languages*. Seventh Workshop on Technologies for Machine Translation of Low-Resource Languages (LoResMT 2024), Bangkok, Thailand.

Borrego, Á. (2023). Article processing charges for open access journal publishing: A review. *Learned Publishing, 36*(3), 359–378. [CrossRef]

Committee on Publication Ethics (COPE). (n.d.). *Guidance*. Available online: https://publicationethics.org/guidance (accessed on 31 August 2024).

Dabić, M., Švarc, J., Vlačić, B., & Lažnjak, J. (2021). Internationalisation in scholarly publishing in croatia through the lens of bibliometric overview of the journal *Društvena Istraživanja*. *Društvena Istraživanja: Časopis Za Opća Društvena Pitanja, 30*(4), 807–829. [CrossRef]

DIAMAS. (2024). *DIAMAS survey questionnaire and glossary*. Zenodo. [CrossRef]

Druelinger, D., & Ma, L. (2023). Missing a golden opportunity? An analysis of publication trends by income level in the directory of open access journals 1987–2020. *Learned Publishing, 36*(3), 348–358. [CrossRef]

Dufour, Q., Pontille, D., & Torny, D. (2023). Supporting diamond open access journals. *Nordic Journal of Library and Information Studies, 4*(2), 35–55. [CrossRef]

Hebrang Grgić, I. (2018). *Kratka povijest knjižnica i nakladnika: S kodovima i aplikacijom*. Naklada Ljevak.

Hicks, D., Wouters, P., Waltman, L., de Rijcke, S., & Rafols, I. (2015). Bibliometrics: The Leiden Manifesto for research metrics. *Nature, 520*(7548), 429–431. [CrossRef] [PubMed]

Khanna, S., Ball, J., Alperin, J. P., & Willinsky, J. (2022). Recalibrating the scope of scholarly publishing: A modest step in a vast decolonization process. *Quantitative Science Studies, 3*(4), 912–930. [CrossRef]

Kramer, B., & George, R. (2024). *DIAMAS survey on institutional publishing—Aggregated data* (Version 1.0) [Data set]. Zenodo. [CrossRef]

Liu, M. (2024). When diamond is still a luxury: An early career researcher perspective. *Dutch Journal of Applied Linguistics, 13*. [CrossRef]

Macan, B., & Stojanovski, J. (2008). Analiza novčane potpore Ministarstva znanosti, obrazovanja i športa hrvatskim znanstvenim časopisima. *Kemija u Industriji: Časopis Kemičara i Kemijskih Inženjera Hrvatske, 57*(3), 115–122. Available online: https://hrcak.srce.hr/20932 (accessed on 31 August 2024).

Mahony, J. (2024). Towards an all-Ireland diamond open access publishing platform: The PublishOA.ie Project—2022–2024. *Publications, 12*(3), 19. [CrossRef]

Marijan, Z. J. (2019). Pedeset godina Časopisa za suvremenu povijest: Bibliometrijska analiza (1969–2018). *Časopis za Suvremenu Povijest, 51*(1), 59–96. [CrossRef]

Moslavac, A. (2022). Bibliografska, bibliometrijska i scientometrijska analiza znanstvenih časopisa Filozofskog fakulteta Sveučilišta u Rijeci za razdoblje od 2010. Do 2020. godine. *Bosniaca: Časopis Nacionalne i univerzitetske biblioteke Bosne i Hercegovine, 27*(1), 192–215. [CrossRef]

Raza, M. Z., Rafiq, M., & Saroya, S. H. (2024). Status of open access scholarly journal publishing in Pakistan. *Journal of Librarianship and Information Science, 56*(2), 415–423. [CrossRef]

Saenen, B., Ancion, Z., Borrell-Damián, L., Mounier, P., Oliva Uribe, D., Papp-Le Roy, N., & Rooryck, J. (2024, December 8–14). *2nd diamond open access conference report*. 2nd Diamond Open Access Conference, Toluca, Mexico. [CrossRef]

Sambunjak, D., Ivaniš, A., Marušić, A., & Marušić, M. (2008). Representation of journals from five neighboring European countries in the journal citation reports. *Scientometrics, 76*(2), 261–271. [CrossRef]

Silva de Araújo, R., Fernandes Porto, N. V., Carvalho Laureano, I. C., Farias, L., Cabral Cavalcanti, A. F., Goncharuk-Khomyn, M., & Leite Cavalcanti, A. (2020). Bibliometrijska analiza časopisa *Acta Stomatologica Croatica*: Od 2009. do 2018. *Acta Stomatologica Croatica: International Journal of Oral Sciences and Dental Medicine, 54*(2), 186–193. Available online: https://hrcak.srce.hr/239056 (accessed on 31 August 2024). [CrossRef] [PubMed]

UNESCO. (2021, November 9–24). *UNESCO recommendation on open science*. UNESCO General Conference, Paris, France. [CrossRef]

Wang, X., Xu, Z., & Škare, M. (2020). A bibliometric analysis of *Economic Research-Ekonomska* Istraživanja (2007–2019). *Economic Research-Ekonomska Istraživanja, 33*(1), 865–886. [CrossRef]

Yoon, J., Kim, N., & Chung, E. (2023). Characteristics of scholarly journals published in non-English-speaking countries: An analysis of library and information science SCOPUS journals. *Learned Publishing, 36*(1), 14–24. [CrossRef]

Yoon, J., Ku, H., & Chung, E. (2024). The road to sustainability: Examining key drivers in open access diamond journal publishing. *Learned Publishing, 37*(3), e1611. [CrossRef] *publications*

MDPI

Case Report

FAIR as a Journey: Lessons Learned from Building the GoTriple Discovery Platform for Social Sciences and Humanities

Luca De Santis

Net7 Srl, 56124 Pisa, Italy; desantis@netseven.it

Abstract: This report describes the experience in implementing the FAIR principles for the GoTriple Discovery Platform for Social Sciences and Humanities (SSH). It shows how adherence to FAIR should be considered as a continuous process throughout the entire lifespan of any information management system, including GoTriple, rather than a static goal with decisions only made at the design time. This report presents an introduction highlighting the importance of the FAIR principles, indicating how they can be assessed in data management systems. Then, the GoTriple case is presented, with a general overview of this discovery platform before describing some of the implemented practices in support of FAIR. The Discussion Section shows, on the one hand, some virtuous reuse of GoTriple data, together with one major pitfall in the platform's FAIR implementation. In this sense, this report serves as a case study that can offer insights and actionable advice for those implementing information systems aligned, from the very outset, with the FAIR principles.

Keywords: FAIR principles; open science; Social Sciences and Humanities (SSH); information and data management systems; discovery platforms for SSH research; OPERAS services

1. Introduction: FAIR as a Journey

To obtain the maximum value from information, it is essential that both the data and associated metadata respect the characteristics of being Findable, Accessible, Interoperable, and Reusable (henceforth, FAIR). FAIR was introduced for the first time in 2016 with the seminal article by Wilkinson and colleagues [1]. Their *FAIR Guiding Principles for scientific data management and stewardship* highlighted the "urgent need to improve the infrastructure supporting the reuse of scholarly data".

FAIR is now a pillar of open science, albeit the road to reach FAIRness is paved with obstacles and difficulties.

Moreover, while it is advisable that information management systems are designed from the very beginning to be FAIR, it is common that adjustments are performed along the way to improve or even implement technical solutions to respect or increase their FAIRness compliance, as long as new data are ingested and managed.

Therefore, it makes perfect sense to think of "FAIR as a journey", as specified in the *Recommendations on FAIR metrics for EOSC* of the European Commission [2], and not simply as a static requirement. It should be seen as a road to take and never steer away from. In [2], it is claimed that "...if FAIR is not seen as a continuum, we risk alienating communities who are not well advanced in sharing their data in a FAIR way, or indeed in data sharing at all. We also risk losing advanced communities for whom the effort to attain optional indicators outweighs the expected benefit".

Therefore, it is advisable to approach FAIR using a "continuous improvement" process, like those used by modern agile project management systems such as SCRUM [3] for software development or FitSM [4] for IT service management.

Assessing FAIR compliance has become possible thanks to the guidelines specified in the previously mentioned *The FAIR Guiding Principles* article [1] and in *Recommendations on FAIR metrics for EOSC* of the European Commission [2]. The *FAIR Data Maturity Model*

Specification and Guidelines of the FAIR Data Maturity Model Working Group [5] also provide actionable indicators to measure FAIRness.

The former presents the 15 principles that must guide every implementation of FAIR.

The European Commission's document includes seven recommendations on the definition and implementation of metrics for FAIR data. While focusing on the context of the European Open Science Cloud (EOSC), that report provides useful indications for anyone interested in the FAIRness of data, including the already cited concept of considering "FAIR as a journey" (Recommendation 2.2). Finally, the latter provides a complete list of indicators for verifying adherence to the FAIR principles. It consists of 41 criteria that easily allow us to assess FAIR compliance both for data and for their associated metadata, specifying for each one of them three possible levels of implementation priority (essential, important, useful).

By analysing these principles, it is evident how technical support from IT specialists (in-house developers/sysadmins or external consultants/system integrators) is mandatory to ensure the success of the FAIRness strategy. Think, for example, of the indicators RDA-F4-01M ("Metadata is offered in such a way that it can be harvested and indexed") or RDA-A1-04D ("Data is accessible through standardised protocol") in [5]. It is evident that they cannot be fully achieved without strict collaboration with the technical team in charge of the development, operation, and maintenance of an information management system. At the same time, FAIR is a real philosophy of data management that cannot be just dismissed as a set of technical issues to implement or solve.

The experience of developing GoTriple, a discovery platform for the Social Sciences and Humanities, serves as a good example of how FAIR must be intended as a continuous journey, of which this report represents a sort of logbook. Here, the solutions provided, the good practices put in place, and also the pitfalls of the implementation of FAIR for GoTriple are presented. Many of these strategies proved to be quite solid and stood real tests, with virtuous examples of reuse that are described herein. At the same time, other choices turned out to be weak and quite expensive to correct.

This report is intended as a guide for those planning to develop a data management system, offering hints that, if followed, can make the road to FAIR less arduous. In the following section (Section 2), the experience with FAIR for the GoTriple.eu website is described. After a general presentation of GoTriple (Section 2.1), the actual solutions implemented to adhere to the FAIR principles are described (Sections 2.2–2.5), with explicit references to the "FAIR Guiding Principles", as defined in Wilkinson et al.'s article [1], to facilitate understanding. Section 3 shows how the FAIR principles have been translated into practice, highlighting both the effective reuse of GoTriple data and a major pitfall in the platform's FAIR implementation. The conclusions provide a summary and suggest possible directions for GoTriple's implementation roadmap, particularly concerning FAIR compliance.

2. Detailed Case Description: FAIR in GoTriple

2.1. Introducing GoTriple

GoTriple (https://gotriple.eu, accessed on 20 August 2024) is a multilingual discovery platform for the Social Sciences and Humanities. It is the main outcome of the TRIPLE research project [6], which received funding from the European Union's Horizon 2020 Research and Innovation action (funding scheme INFRAEOSC-02-2019 "Prototyping new innovative services"). The project, whose full name is "Transforming Research through Innovative Practices for Linked Interdisciplinary Exploration", ran between October 2019 and March 2023. It was coordinated by CNRS and featured 22 partners from 15 different European countries.

GoTriple provides a central access point that allows users to explore, find, access, and reuse materials such as articles, datasets, project descriptions, and author profiles at the European scale.

It is one of the Discovery Services of OPERAS [7], the Research Infrastructure that supports open scholarly communication in the Social Sciences and Humanities in the European Research Area.

At its heart, GoTriple has a search engine whose indexes are fed by a configurable harvesting and processing pipeline, which continuously imports and processes publication and project metadata from multiple sources (about 1400), including large aggregators (BASE, DOAJ, OpenAire, Isidore) and national repositories alike (Hrčak, Biblioteka Nauki, ZRC Sazu, EKT, Recyt or Pombaline).

Recently, the support of MARC21 XML data sources has been implemented in GoTriple, which allowed for the ingestion of metadata from over 1.7 million documents in the German National Library (DNB) [8].

Innovative services are integrated into the platform to improve user experience with personalised recommendations, interactive visualisations, and the possibility to use a web annotation tool to take notes on material found in GoTriple.

Finally, users can register to the platform to create a personal profile, claim ownership of the documents published in the indexes, and find and connect with other SSH authors and researchers.

2.2. Findability

The requirement of making a digital asset "findable" is expressed by the four principles mentioned in Table 1.

Table 1. FAIR guiding principle: findability.

To Be Findable	
F1.	(meta)data are assigned a globally unique and persistent identifier
F2.	data are described with rich metadata
F3.	metadata clearly and explicitly include the identifier of the data they describe
F4.	(meta)data are registered or indexed in a searchable resource

The first one (F1) requires that each data resource is assigned a unique and persistent identifier. GoTriple respects this requirement by identifying each resource with a Uniform Resource Identifier (URI), which is the URL of its landing page. From a theoretical viewpoint, this requirement is fully respected, as this identifier is unique and persistent (at least as long as GoTriple exists). As a matter of fact, this design choice proved to be a pitfall in the global GoTriple implementation, which will be commented on in depth in Section 3 (Discussion: FAIR Principles in Practice within GoTriple).

The F2 principle indicates the importance of describing data assets with rich metadata. In this sense, GoTriple fully respects this requirement by providing a detailed vision for its data model, whose main structures are shown in Figure 1. It consists of three main asset types, i.e., document, profile, and project, which were initially designed by using standard ontologies like Schema.org and SIOC to describe their attributes.

It reflects the type of metadata that can be harvested from the available data sources. In particular, every publication creates an entry in the document index, while its authors are stored in the profile index, with a link between them. Projects, on the other hand, have so far been harvested from sources without meaningful associated research publications, or where it was difficult to determine whether the mentioned persons are simply administrators or actual SSH researchers. This explains the lack of relationships between the project index and the document and profile indexes.

The F3 principle requires that "metadata clearly and explicitly include the identifier of the data it describes". All original identifiers are retrieved during the harvesting process of GoTriple content and shown in their descriptive pages of the website, as shown in Figure 2.

Figure 1. TRIPLE data model.

Figure 2. GoTriple document page. The original identifiers of the resource are maintained and shown.

Finally, F4 requires that a searchable index is required to access the resources easily. As indicated, search is one of the main features of GoTriple, which offers an intuitive faceted interface for further filtering the list of results.

2.3. *Accessibility*

Accessibility demands that data and metadata are retrievable by both humans and machines through well-defined, open, and universally implementable protocols. Table 2 shows in detail the accessibility requirements.

All GoTriple data are accessible via the open and standard HTTP protocol (principles A1. and A1.1), providing interfaces both for humans (the website GoTriple.eu) and software programs, the latter in the form of REST APIs, accessible publicly or only after previous authentication (A1.2). APIs' documentation is available through a link on the GoTriple website [9]. GoTriple's document metadata are also accessible for harvesting through the standard OAI-PMH [10] protocol. Finally, in its local indexes, GoTriple copies the metadata of the original assets, guaranteeing their preservation even if the data in the original source, for example, the full text of an article, are no longer accessible (A2.).

Table 2. FAIR guiding principle: accessibility.

To Be Accessible	
A1.	(meta)data are retrievable by their identifiers using a standardised communications protocol
A1.1	the protocol is open, free, and universally implementable
A1.2	the protocol allows for an authentication and authorisation procedure, where necessary
A2.	metadata are accessible, even when the data are no longer available

Beyond the FAIR guiding principles of accessibility indicated above, it is important to highlight a strategic decision taken in GoTriple to enhance users' access to data. As a multilingual platform, with articles written in many different languages, to improve readability, GoTriple always provides an English translation of the text of its assets, by resorting, when necessary, to eTranslation [11], an automatic neural machine translation service provided by the European Commission.

2.4. Interoperability

Interoperability in FAIR is based on the assumption that to facilitate the exchange of information amongst systems, data and metadata should be defined by following standard formats, using shared vocabularies and providing references to other resources. Its guiding principles are presented in Table 3.

Table 3. FAIR Guiding Principle: interoperability.

To Be Interoperable	
I1.	(meta)data use a formal, accessible, shared, and broadly applicable language for knowledge representation.
I2.	(meta)data use vocabularies that follow FAIR principles
I3.	(meta)data include qualified references to other (meta)data

Over time, the GoTriple data model has been formally defined through the TRIPLE Ontology [12] (see principle I1.). This allowed for not only providing a semantic web-compliant, machine-understandable description of the three main asset types of the platform but also the controlled vocabularies used to specify the values of the "license", "conditions of access", "document type", and "discipline" attributes (see principles I2.).

The former two simply provide the list of the admitted identifiers used in GoTriple.

"Document type" on the other hand provides a linked data description of the 20 admitted types by linking them to the corresponding resource types of the COAR Controlled Vocabularies for Repositories [13].

The "disciplines" controlled vocabulary is again a linked data resource that uses the SKOS ontology [14] to provide a formalisation of the SSH domain in 27 fields of study. This formalisation is one of the outcomes of the TRIPLE project and exploits the vision of a former EU-funded research project (MORESS [15]). In this vocabulary, each discipline is linked to one or more corresponding concepts of other widely known classification systems, including the Library of Congress Subject Headings, Wikidata, and the Dewey Decimal Classification. Finally, the vocabulary is also multilingual, with concepts available in English, Italian, French, and German.

GoTriple also makes use of automatic classification systems by which all the content ingested is assigned to one or more disciplines and "tagged" with concepts belonging to TRIPLE vocabulary [16]. The latter consists of a rich controlled vocabulary of over 3370 linked data SSH-related concepts. This is another significant outcome of the TRIPLE project: it has been formalised in SKOS and provides translations in 11 languages.

The presence of a formal description of its assets, along with several linked data attributes, improves interoperability and enables better reuse of GoTriple's content (see principle I3.)

2.5. Reusability

Reusability, whose guiding principles are indicated in Table 4, ensures that data and associated metadata are well-documented and licensed in a clear and accessible manner, to enable their future use by others with minimal restrictions.

Table 4. FAIR guiding principle: reusability.

To Be Reusable	
R1.	meta(data) are richly described with a plurality of accurate and relevant attributes
R1.1	(meta)data are released with a clear and accessible data usage license
R1.2	(meta)data are associated with detailed provenance
R1.3.	(meta)data meet domain-relevant community standards

GoTriple's entity descriptions proved to be complete and accurate (see R1.). As a result, the original metadata fetched from external sources normally can only match a part of the platform's data model. This is especially true for the majority of the harvested sources, where metadata are imported using the OAI-PMH harvesting protocol and described in Dublin Core, which provides only a limited set of metadata elements.

Licenses and conditions of access for using the imported metadata are preserved and republished on GoTriple using a controlled vocabulary (see Section 2.4), provided they were specified at the source (see R1.1).

A detailed explanation of the origin of the documents in the platform's index is also provided (R1.2). By clicking on a link on the presentation page of a document, the user can distinguish the attributes coming from the original source from those produced by the GoTriple processing pipeline through the curation and enriching phase.

Finally concerning R1.3, as mentioned previously, GoTriple's controlled vocabularies are carefully defined by linking them to widely recognised standards. It is also worth mentioning the possibility for users to export document metadata easily in a variety of standard formats, including BibTeX, JSON, and JSON-LD.

3. Discussion: FAIR Principles in Practice within GoTriple

In the previous section, GoTriple's compliance with the FAIR principles was described. Beyond the mere declaration of commitment, it is useful to see how all the choices made and presented above translate into practice. Most of these measures proved to be useful and beneficial for the research community at large, as they enabled data interoperability and reuse in several contexts.

The first example is provided by VERA [17], OPERAS' service for participatory research. VERA is a web-based platform that enables laypersons and researchers to collaborate on SSH-related citizen science initiatives. Projects in VERA are defined by a set of descriptive attributes, including "Academic subjects", for which GoTriple's disciplines have been used. Additionally, a VERA project can be automatically published on GoTriple (see the "EcoVoce" VERA project as an example [18]), and the use of this shared classification not only ensures its correct presentation on the Discovery Platform but also helps create connections with other initiatives in the same field of study.

GoTriple open APIs also facilitated the reuse of GoTriple's content on various occasions. For example, a team of the AGH University of Krakow, led by professor Mikołaj Leszczuk, used GoTriple APIs for research on identifying similar illustrations in scientific publications [19]. Using APIs, they collected over 5600 scientific papers for which their full texts in PDF were available. This enabled the team to extract almost 65,000 images, which helped them to develop and fine-tune the software methodology at the core of their research.

Finally, through a collaboration between the University of Pisa and the Italian company Net7 [20], an Artificial Intelligence-driven chatbot was implemented on GoTriple's content. In a similar way, the full texts of over 1000 articles of a specific SSH discipline were retrieved and used to implement an interactive assistant, able to respond to actual research questions and to provide references of the sources used.

It is also important to highlight that despite full compliance with FAIR principles, not all of GoTriple's design and implementation choices have proved to be valid. One pitfall worth mentioning is the implementation of Persistent Identifiers (PIDs). The importance of PIDs is emphasised by the fact that all related indicators in [5] are marked as "essential".

As mentioned, in GoTriple, a PID consists of the URL of the presentation page of an entity. This URL is created by merging GoTriple's domain name with the original identifier of the content from the remote source, which is usually. the first one returned during the harvesting phase. An example is provided below.

https://www.gotriple.eu/documents/<PRIMARY_ID>

For example, the PID of a GoTriple document is as follows:

https://www.gotriple.eu/documents/oai:revues.org:bergsoniana/1748, accessed on 20 August 2024.

In general, using URLs for IDs is a bad idea. Some research (see [21], for example) mentions that over a long period, a significant percentage of URLs (over 50%) become inaccessible. Also, linking an external identifier so strictly to GoTriple's ID is risky. In fact, when harvesting sources, it is common to receive multiple IDs for the same resource, and the first one taken is not always the one intended to be persistent. It might be an internal ID that can change over time, provided that, if present, the persistent ID (e.g., a DOI) is maintained.

Unfortunately, this consideration was realised too late in the implementation of GoTriple, after millions of records had already been ingested and published. Fixing this problem by creating PIDs with a more solid logic for both new and existing content is one of the goals for the next phase of GoTriple's implementation. One interesting approach to consider is the one used by OpenAIRE for the entities of its graph [22]. Here, the PIDs are created by merging an identifier of the source and a hash code generated by processing the content's original identifier, privileging, for this operation, those known to be persistent (DOI, Handle System identifiers, ISBN). Of course, this operation in GoTriple must be planned with great care in order to maintain backward compatibility with the current platform's identifiers.

Finally, it must be noted that most of the effort in designing and implementing GoTriple's FAIR support has been devoted to documents that represent the majority and possibly the most valuable content of the Discovery Platform. While the TRIPLE Ontology has recently been expanded to support projects and profiles, some other FAIR-related features, such as the accessibility of content through standard harvesting protocols like OAI-PMH, are currently only available for documents.

4. Conclusions

The journey towards FAIR must be intended as a continuous endeavour, and the GoTriple case study is exemplary in this regard. The current development plan for the platform aims not only to enhance existing achievements (such as fixing Persistent Identifiers and increasing FAIRness for projects and profiles) but also to improve the quality of metadata and the general alignment of GoTriple vocabularies with other relevant SSH-related ontologies.

This effort is being pursued under the ATRIUM research project [23], funded by the European Union under the call HORIZON-INFRA-2023-SERV-01. Here, some of the original partners of the TRIPLE project (Coimbra University, Foxcub, IBL-PAN, Net7) collaborate with the OPERAS infrastructure to advance GoTriple, also enhancing its FAIRness.

Funding: This research was funded by the European Union, grant agreement numbers 863420 (TRIPLE [6]) and 101132163 (ATRIUM [22]).

Data Availability Statement: Data sharing not applicable—no new data generated.

Acknowledgments: The author wants to thank the Pubmet2023 team at the University of Zadar, in particular, Jadranka Stojanovski and Drahomira Cupar, whose friendship honours him.

Conflicts of Interest: The author declares no conflicts of interest.

References

1. Wilkinson, M.D.; Dumontier, M.; Aalbersberg, I.J.; Appleton, G.; Axton, M.; Baak, A.; Blomberg, N.; Boiten, J.W.; da Silva Santos, L.B.; Bourne, P.E.; et al. The FAIR Guiding Principles for scientific data management and stewardship. *Sci. Data* **2016**, 3. [CrossRef] [PubMed]
2. Genova, F.; Aronsen, J.M.; Beyan, O.; Harrower, N.; Holl, A.; Hooft, R.W.; Principe, P.; Slavec, A.; Jones, S. *Recommendations on FAIR Metrics for EOSC*; Publications Office of the European Union, 2021. Available online: https://op.europa.eu/en/publication-detail/-/publication/ced147c9-53c0-11eb-b59f-01aa75ed71a1/language-en (accessed on 1 April 2024). [CrossRef]
3. Scrum.org Web Site. Available online: https://www.scrum.org (accessed on 1 April 2024).
4. FitSM Web Site. Available online: https://www.fitsm.eu/ (accessed on 1 April 2024).
5. FAIR Data Maturity Model Working Group. *FAIR Data Maturity Model. Specification and Guidelines*; Zenodo.org, 2020. [CrossRef]
6. TRIPLE Project Web Site. Available online: https://project.gotriple.eu/ (accessed on 1 April 2024).
7. OPERAS Web Site. Available online: https://operas-eu.org/ (accessed on 1 April 2024).
8. Deutsche Nationalbibliothek (DNB) Web Site. Available online: https://www.dnb.de/ (accessed on 1 April 2024).
9. De Santis, L. *TRIPLE Deliverable: D6.6 API's Development-RP3*; Zenodo.org, 2022. [CrossRef]
10. Open Archives Initiative Protocol for Metadata Harvesting (OAI-PMH). Available online: https://www.openarchives.org/pmh/ (accessed on 1 April 2024).
11. eTranslation. Available online: https://commission.europa.eu/resources-partners/etranslation_en (accessed on 1 April 2024).
12. TRIPLE Ontology. Available online: https://www.gotriple.eu/ontology/triple (accessed on 1 April 2024).
13. COAR Controlled Vocabularies for Repositories: Resource Types 3.1. Available online: https://vocabularies.coar-repositories.org/resource_types/ (accessed on 1 April 2024).
14. SKOS—Simple Knowledge Organization System. Available online: https://www.w3.org/2009/08/skos-reference/skos.html (accessed on 1 April 2024).
15. MORESS—Mapping of Research in European Social Sciences and Humanities. Available online: https://cordis.europa.eu/project/id/HPSE-CT-2002-60060 (accessed on 1 April 2024).
16. TRIPLE Vocabulary. Available online: https://www.semantics.gr/authorities/vocabularies/SSH-LCSH/vocabulary-entries?language=en (accessed on 1 April 2024).
17. VERA—Virtual Ecosystem for Research Activation. Available online: https://vera.operas-eu.org/ (accessed on 1 April 2024).
18. EcoVoce Project in GoTriple. Available online: https://gotriple.eu/projects/vera:82-ecovoce (accessed on 31 July 2024).
19. Leszczuk, M.; Dziula, P. Implementation of Software for Searching Similar Illustrations in Scientific Publications. In Proceedings of the Opening Collaboration for Community-Driven Scholarly Communication (OPERAS2024), Zadar, Croatia, 24 April 2024; Zenodo.org. 2024. [CrossRef]
20. Bertozzi, A.; Abbamonte, M.L.; Abaza, A.; De Santis, L. From Words to Search: GoTriple's AI ChatBot for Efficient Research Engagement. In Proceedings of the Opening Collaboration for Community-Driven Scholarly Communication (OPERAS2024), Zadar, Croatia, 24 April 2024; Zenodo.org. 2024. [CrossRef]
21. Stojanovski, J. PIDs in the SSH—Current state and upcoming challenges. In Proceedings of the TRIPLE Booksprint—The role of Open Metadata in the SSH Scholarly Communication, Konstancin-Jeziorna, Poland, 7–9 September 2022.
22. OpenAIRE Graph Documentation. PIDs and Identifiers. Available online: https://graph.openaire.eu/docs/data-model/pids-and-identifiers (accessed on 1 April 2024).
23. Advancing fronTier Research in the Arts and hUManities (ATRIUM) Web Site. Available online: https://atrium-research.eu/ (accessed on 1 April 2024).

publications

MDPI

Review

Benefits of Citizen Science for Libraries

Dolores Mumelaš and Alisa Martek *

National and University Library in Zagreb, 10000 Zagreb, Croatia; dmumelas@nsk.hr
* Correspondence: amartek@nsk.hr

Abstract: Participating in collaborative scientific research through citizen science, a component of open science, holds significance for both citizen scientists and professional researchers. Yet, the advantages for those orchestrating citizen science initiatives are often overlooked. Organizers encompass a diverse range, including governmental entities, non-governmental organizations, corporations, universities, and institutions like libraries. For libraries, citizen science holds importance by fostering heightened civic and research interests, promoting scientific publishing, and contributing to overall scientific progress. This paper aims to provide a comprehensive understanding of the specific ways in which citizen science can benefit libraries and how libraries can effectively utilize citizen science to achieve their goals. The paper is based on a systematic review of peer-reviewed articles that discuss the direct benefits of citizen science on libraries. A list of the main benefits of citizen science for libraries has been compiled from the literature. Additionally, the reasons why it is crucial for libraries to communicate the benefits of citizen science for their operations have been highlighted, particularly in terms of encouraging other libraries to actively engage in citizen science projects.

Keywords: benefits for libraries; citizen science; libraries; open science

1. Introduction: Citizen Science and Its Benefits for the Society and Its Participants

Open science is an umbrella term used to denote the concepts of openness, transparency, repeatability, replication, and the accumulation of knowledge, which are also fundamental features of scientific endeavors [1]. Open science instigates societal, cultural, and technological transformations by emphasizing transparency in the processes of designing, conducting, documenting, and evaluating research. Irreversible trends such as open data tools, open access platforms, open peer review methods, and public engagement initiatives are influencing all participants in the scientific community and possess the capacity to expedite the research cycle [2]. Open science is one of the political priorities of the European Union, which categorizes open science into eight pillars within the "Open Science Policy Platform". The last pillar relates to citizen science, asserting that the broader public should be able to make a significant contribution to scientific research and be recognized as a "creator" of scientific knowledge [3]. Citizen science, like open science, facilitates and encourages widespread participation in science and scientific research, with a highlighted role assigned to libraries in promoting the potential of citizen science. It is emphasized that libraries play a role in handling and preserving research data and metadata, enabling the organization, skills, and collaboration necessary for citizen science [4]. The convergence of open science and citizen science is evident in their shared emphasis on transparency, public engagement, and the inclusive contribution of the broader community to scientific research.

The term "citizen science" originated in the mid-1990s, and it was first mentioned by Alan Irwin, who explained that citizen science is science that serves the interests of citizens, simultaneously involving scientific activities performed by citizens [5]. Richard Booney described citizen science as scientific projects where "amateurs" contribute observational data to scientists. In return, they gain new scientific skills, creating a reciprocal exchange, a "two-way street" [6]. Citizen science is a concept that encompasses various interpretations, but the fundamental and simplest definition characterizes it as scientific research conducted in whole or in part by members of the broader public, typically amateur non-professional scientists. Participants collect, share, analyze, or transcribe data and observations, often over large geographic areas or extended periods, generally utilizing mobile applications and the internet. Citizen science is also known as community science, crowd-supported science, cloud science, volunteer monitoring, or simply public participation in scientific research [7]. Citizen science participants have the opportunity to participate in various aspects of the scientific process, including formulating research questions, collecting data, analyzing information, making conclusions, and sharing findings [8]. In 2013, Muki Haklay identified levels of citizen science based on participant involvement, spanning from 'citizens as sensors' (crowdsourcing) and 'citizens as interpreters' (distributed intelligence) to higher levels where participants actively contribute to defining problems and collection protocols (participatory science), or are deeply involved in the entire scientific process development (extreme citizen science) [9]. Citizen science offers numerous opportunities for scientific research, harnessing the collective power of individuals from diverse backgrounds. This approach not only expands the scope of scientific investigations but also brings research closer to the public, fostering a sense of shared responsibility and engagement in scientific discovery. Additionally, it promotes a deeper understanding of complex issues and encourages collaboration between citizens and professional scientists, ultimately benefiting society as a whole.

Citizen science has the ability to connect scientific subjects with people's daily experiences, transforming them into inquiries that relate to their everyday life. By prioritizing the methods and procedures over the final results, citizen science offers a dynamic and adaptable approach to communication, one that aligns with the project's specific circumstances and remains open to shifts within that framework [10]. Nevertheless, it is crucial to observe that numerous empirical scientific articles across various disciplines have addressed research questions using data derived from citizen science. Many studies have also affirmed the high quality of citizen science data, thereby contributing valuable information to scientific outcomes [11]. Engaging in citizen science enhances the relevance and practicality of results across various fields. Although citizen science may not always result in high-profile academic papers or traditional forms of academic success, it can generate outcomes that significantly impact the lives of those at the core of the research. Citizen science contributes to improved research both technically, by considering a broader range of factors, and ethically, as it promotes greater equity [12].

The key participants in citizen science prominently include citizen scientists and professional researchers. There are an abundance of data available concerning the benefits that participants derive from engaging in citizen science. Jones, M. G. et al. conducted an extensive study that included a literature review on this topic, where they identified benefits for citizen scientists such as social engagement, interaction, improvements in knowledge, skills, and attitudes, as well as changes in behaviors [13]. Additionally, research by Pateman, M., Dyke, A., and Elizabeth, S. also listed benefits such as greater employability, stress reduction, formation of new relationships and communities, social learning, and better understanding of the scientific process [14]. Regarding the benefits of citizen science for scientists, Veeckman et al. state that increased research capacity, newly acquired data and information, more innovative research, and more societally relevant research are bridging the gap between scientists and science and diversity in science [15]. Besley, Oh, and Nisbet indicate that scientists are motivated by the desire to improve the public's favorable perception of science, raise awareness about scientific concepts, and persuade the public about the significance of the scientists' contributions [16]. Citizen science offers benefits by engaging citizens in scientific endeavors, providing valuable data for researchers, fostering public understanding of science, and enhancing the collaboration between the scientific community and the general public.

2. Citizen Science and Benefits for Libraries

As stated by Ignat, Cavalier, and Nickerson, facilitators in citizen science could also be libraries. These spaces offer secure environments with access to information, resources, and communities. The collaboration between citizen science and libraries requires a close coordination among researchers, libraries, and the public [17]. There are numerous ways in which libraries can provide support for citizen science. Ignat et al. noted some examples like ensuring access to citizen scientists' contributions and the research outcomes they contribute to, promoting and nurturing literacy skills, establishing partnerships with entities, and facilitating local engagement and dissemination [18]. All types of libraries can be involved in citizen science, but this work will focus on public libraries and research libraries given that more research has been found in the literature on these types of libraries.

A public library offers entry to information, lifelong learning, and creative works using various resources and services. It is open to all community members, irrespective of race, nationality, age, gender, religion, language, disability, economic and employment status, and educational attainment. This institution is established and sustained by the community, either through local, regional, or national government support or through other community organizations. The main objective of the public library is to offer a diverse range of resources and services across various media, catering to the educational, informational, and personal development needs of both individuals and groups, encompassing recreation and leisure as well [19]. Citizen science initiatives can be effectively executed within public libraries, and there is potential for these libraries to be "leaders and innovators in citizen science" [20]. Engaging public libraries in citizen science has the potential to offer alternative learning opportunities. When combined with heightened social cohesion, this collaboration may create fresh insights into public libraries, transforming them into spaces where knowledge is not just shared but also collaboratively constructed in a horizontal manner [21]. In accordance with the mentioned paragraphs, public libraries, characterized by inclusivity and a wide array of resources, have the potential to take a leading role in citizen science. This involvement may contribute to collaborative knowledge construction through alternative learning experiences and increased social cohesion.

A research library is a library that houses a comprehensive assortment of materials focused on one or multiple subjects. Typically, it encompasses a thorough compilation of materials related to specific topics and it is created to address the requirements of scholarly investigations, ensuring they are equipped with genuine materials comprising high-quality content [22]. Research libraries are primarily affiliated with research-intensive universities and possess extensive collections dedicated to scholarly research. Interestingly, it is noteworthy to mention that LIBER has formulated its own definition of a research library because of the change in the landscape of European universities. Those changes are marked by the establishment of new universities, university mergers, and an increased collaboration among higher education institutions [23]. LIBER's proposed 'Endorsement Proposal' emphasizes that research libraries wishing to join should adhere to LIBER's values. LIBER's values are as follows: providing excellent services to library and information users, ensuring intellectual freedom, fostering collaboration with various partners, responsibly managing collections and resources, demonstrating leadership and innovation, and promoting inclusivity, equality, and the realization of potential are key principles to be embraced [24]. The concept of citizen science is gaining popularity, with various hubs emerging at European universities to support it. Research libraries have the potential to play a pivotal role in promoting both citizen science and open science [25].

It is interesting to note that some studies have shown that scientists do not perceive the benefits of citizen science. For instance, Golumbic and colleagues published a study revealing that many scientists find it challenging to accept the idea that the public can make actual contributions to science. Although the scientists acknowledge the advantages of citizen participation for the public, they express no desire to actively engage with the public and prefer to conduct traditional studies without involving the public [26]. In a study conducted by Riesch and Potter, scientists pointed out key issues in citizen science from scientist´s perspective, including concerns about the quality of data, how their work is perceived by the broader scientific community, and the ownership aspects related to publication [27]. In their study on Flemish scientists, Duerinckx et al. point out additional disadvantages such as the challenge of securing long-term commitment from participants in the project, increased administrative workload, and issues related to financing, as well as legal, ethical, and privacy aspects [28]. Libraries have the opportunity to examine such and similar views of scientists on citizen science and shape specialized programs and education related to citizen science. Despite some scientists holding negative opinions about citizen science, libraries can leverage this insight to tailor their programs and education to the needs of scientists. This approach allows libraries to build a bridge between scientists and citizen science, identifying and addressing specific biases or concerns scientists may have.

Although libraries consistently emphasize the importance of their involvement in citizen science in terms of benefits for participants (both citizen scientists and researchers), it is worth noting that libraries themselves can derive certain benefits. Clearly, due to their mission and vision, they are oriented towards societal well-being, and their own benefits are seldom highlighted. However, more frequent acknowledgment of the direct benefits for libraries engaged in citizen science may encourage other libraries to join. The following text will examine literature from which an attempt will be made to compile a list of benefits of citizen science for libraries.

3. Materials and Methods: Literature Review

For the compilation of the list of benefits of citizen science for libraries, articles by experts from various types of libraries were analyzed, as well as those by other facilitators who organized citizen science activities in collaboration with libraries. Google Scholar was used as a tool for information retrieval. The key words used for the search were 'citizen science' and 'libraries', with the addition of the word 'benefits' and its synonyms such as 'advantages', 'perks', 'pluses', 'opportunities', 'gains', and 'positives'. Publications on public and research libraries were included in the search.

A descriptive review of the literature was chosen for its ability to provide a general overview of the available literature on the topic and present different perspectives and viewpoints, rather than conducting a detailed analysis or synthesis of results. Since the aim was to compile a list of benefits of citizen science for libraries, a descriptive review of literature provided an appropriate approach for gaining a general insight into various aspects of the topic. Additionally, Google Scholar provides a wide range of literature from various sources, which was useful for encompassing the diversity of perspectives and information in this literature review. Google Scholar is a freely accessible database, which is consistent with the transdisciplinary ethos of citizen science.

3.1. Public Libraries

The goals of citizen science are in harmony with those of public libraries and numerous community organizations. Public libraries and citizen science shared objectives include promoting fair access to information, expanding knowledge, fostering participatory lifelong learning opportunities, and cultivating and supporting diverse communities [29]. Goulding, in her review paper on community engagement activities in public libraries, concluded that the role of the public library extends beyond being a space for borrowing or reading books, and even beyond accessing digital materials. Instead, she emphasizes that the public library is evolving into a vital community resource and facility. It serves not only as a venue for community events but also as a hub that facilitates connections between individuals. The library acts as a conduit linking people to their local communities and fostering connections between communities and the broader society [30]. Maroto stated that the benefits of citizen science for public libraries include access to materials, instruments, and resources, raising awareness of innovation, building relationships with scientists and researchers, and engaging patrons [31]. Citizen science aligns with the goals of public libraries and community organizations by promoting equitable access to information, expanding knowledge, and fostering diverse communities.

Senabe et al. argue that, based on the views of librarians, integrating public libraries into citizen science could facilitate unconventional learning opportunities. This, combined with enhanced social cohesion, has the potential to cultivate fresh outlooks on public libraries, transforming them into spaces where knowledge is not merely shared but also collaboratively constructed in a horizontal manner [32]. This assertion can be extended to all types of libraries, not just public libraries.

Cigarini et al. explored the potential of public libraries to become hubs for citizen science. In this context, the authors surveyed librarians. The respondents emphasize some of the benefits: the initiative attracted new library users and fostered new local connections; citizen science brought additional resources to the library while strengthening social networks in the community; librarians emphasized the opportunity the activity provided for them to acquire new skills and practices and citizen science enhances social cohesion and improves the perception of the library's societal value [21]. The next project discusses the benefits for libraries from the perspective of collaborators in the implementation of a citizen science project. The authors, Lasky et al., presented the project "North Carolina Candid Critters". Project leaders acknowledged that collaborating with local libraries enabled them to establish more direct connections with rural communities. Libraries played a crucial role in distributing equipment, a task that would have been impractical on such a large scale from a single facility without additional funds [33]. Citizen science projects demonstrate the transformative role of public libraries, attracting new users, building community connections, and enhancing resources. Collaboration with libraries proves pivotal in establishing direct links with diverse communities and efficiently distributing equipment, showcasing the broader societal value of libraries.

3.2. Research Libraries

From broader perspective, Cohen et al. stated that by linking researchers with citizen scientists, the library serves as a channel for citizen science initiatives and functions as an intellectual center—a space for both accessing scientific knowledge and actively participating in scientific pursuits [34]. This also means that libraries can be recognized as institutions that can support scientific research, which is not always the primary mission of libraries.

Ignat et al. stated that with the help of citizen science, libraries could enrich their collections and make them more accessible [17]. Mumelaš explained it further and stated that depending on the project type, libraries can encourage citizen scientists to use sources more frequently, whether in the form of printed or online materials. Examining successfully implemented projects reveals that participants, with prior education and clear instructions, can swiftly and effectively supplement and enhance, for example, digitized collections by participating in their description and tagging. In addition to raising awareness about the sources and collections the library possesses, citizen scientists also assist in the execution of library processes [35]. Bonney and Dickison have argued that citizen science influences scientific communication and encourages the publication of research results in open access. Libraries can facilitate broader access to published scientific papers [36]. One of the benefits of citizen science projects for libraries are the development of new competencies and professional advancement. Ridge states that such projects encourage library staff to acquire additional skills, including community engagement methods, project management, communication of scientific topics, and improved business process management [37]. According to the research by Kaarsted et al., research librarians already possess the skills necessary for integrating citizen science, which they can further enhance. In the mentioned study, survey respondents were asked questions aimed at understanding the skills available in their libraries. More than three-quarters of respondents indicated they have skills in advocacy, organizing events, facilitating workshops, teaching, and communications. Between 50 and 74% of the respondents reported skills in seven areas: project coordination, project management, evaluation, research data management, publishing FAIR (findability, accessibility, interoperability, and reusability) data, preservation of data and protocols, and General Data Protection Regulation (GDPR). The only areas with less than 50% of the respondents indicating competencies were writing grant proposals and others [25]. The LERU advice paper highlights additional advantages of citizen science for universities, and these benefits can also be relevant to research libraries. One advantage involves supporting the educational and societal goals of universities by nurturing interest and active participation in science across various demographics, especially among teachers and students, through their involvement in research projects. Additionally, there is a reinforcement of the connection between universities and society by directly engaging citizens in research that holds significant implications for their local environments. The encouragement of collaboration with a diverse array of stakeholders who can provide valuable insights, suggestions, and ideas to improve existing research activities is another noteworthy benefit. Furthermore, the utilization of non-anonymized data from consenting citizen scientists can play a pivotal role in exploring new research inquiries, particularly in areas such as health and socio-economics [38]. Research libraries stand to benefit significantly from the integration of citizen science initiatives. By leveraging citizen science, libraries can enrich their collections, improve accessibility, and raise awareness about their holdings. Additionally, participation in citizen science projects contributes to the development of new competencies among library staff, fostering professional advancement and enhancing skills in areas such as community engagement, project management, and scientific communication.

If we look at papers that analyze specific examples of specific libraries and citizen science projects conducted in libraries or with library support, we can also observe some directly mentioned benefits. Overgaard and Kaarsted, in their work presenting the citizen science project "A Healthier Funen", explained how, through collaboration with the media, they managed to reach a large audience/citizen scientist. They also emphasized the importance of partnerships with other stakeholders. As a direct consequence of the success of the "A Healthier Funen" citizen science project, the authors mentioned the establishment of a citizen science network between the university and the hospital [39]. Ayris and Ignat argue that if research organizations can foster both collaboration and competition as integral components of their research activities, positive outcomes will ensue. They suggest that a practical method for implementing citizen science at the institutional level involves establishing a single citizen science point of contact, referred to as BESPOC (Broad Engagement in science, Point in Contact). As an example, they point to UCL Library Services, which has identified key priorities for citizen science activities and intends to integrate them into a comprehensive UCL program. The aim is to seamlessly integrate outreach activities to new communities into the library's regular operations. Additionally, they propose the creation of a virtual office for open science, serving as a central hub for BESPOC [40]. Wiederkehr presented the benefits of conducting citizen science activities within the ETH Library. Similarly to previous authors, he addresses the advantages in terms of increased media visibility for libraries through citizen science projects. Additionally, implementing citizen science projects within the library (in the case of this library, it was a crowdsourcing based on their Map Collection) has spurred the development of new library programs and tools. It was also emphasized that the ETH Library "had become a recognized competent partner in citizen science projects" [41].

The authors Opryshko and Nazarovets describe the project "Grinchenko's Dictionary and Modernity", which emerged as a product of a previously established citizen science project, the Dictionary of Borys Grinchenko. This confirms how libraries, based on implemented citizen science projects, can introduce new similar initiatives and additional programs. The authors also emphasized the importance of partnerships within the institution (in their case, Borys Grinchenko Kyiv University) as another benefit of citizen science for libraries [42]. About the experience of the University Library "Svetozar Marković" and their projects "Wiki Marathons" and "Transcribathon" wrote Mumelaš, Martek and Mučnjak. As benefits of conducted citizen science activities for the library, there is emphasized robust collaboration and outreach across diverse institutions throughout Serbia, integration of Wiki articles into the faculty curriculum, heightened visibility of materials in cultural institutions, the enhancement of library staff knowledge, and the establishment of robust business connections with libraries in Serbia [43]. Holley, in her review article, discusses the benefits of crowdsourcing for libraries, and in addition to those mentioned, she also adds advantages such as "building new virtual communities and user groups, improving the quality of data, adding value to data, and making it discoverable for diverse audiences". The author also mentions benefits such as "gaining first-hand insight into user desires, and encouraging a sense of public ownership and responsibility towards cultural heritage collections" [44].

In examining papers that analyze the benefits of citizen science for research libraries, several overarching advantages become apparent. Citizen science initiatives facilitate the broadening of audience reach, enhancing visibility and engagement with diverse communities. The establishment of collaborative networks and partnerships emerges as a significant benefit, fostering connections within and outside the institution. The seamless integration of citizen science into regular library operations is highlighted, enabling libraries to efficiently incorporate outreach activities. Furthermore, citizen science activities contribute to increased media visibility, emphasizing libraries as active contributors to scientific endeavors.

It is necessary to emphasize that there are likely additional benefits for libraries that engage in or support citizen science activities. Only peer-reviewed papers that are mentioning direct benefits were considered. It should be noted that some libraries involved in citizen science do not share their experiences through written papers. Moreover, those that do often focus on the benefits for the local and scientific community.

4. Discussion—List of Benefits

Based on the reviewed literature, benefits of citizen science for libraries have been identified. The benefits were determined based on their direct mention in the literature and are depicted in Figure 1. The investigated benefits are divided into two categories: external and internal. External benefits refer to the library's impact on the broader community, including partnerships with other organizations, attracting new users, and creating visibility in the media. On the other hand, internal benefits focus on improving internal processes and capacities of the library, such as collection development, leveraging employee expertise, and their personal development.

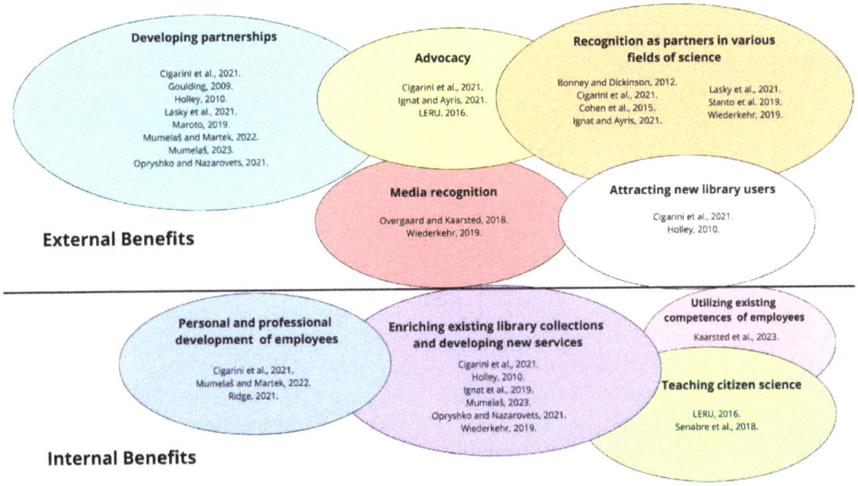

Figure 1. Benefits of citizen science for libraries [17,21,25,30–44].

Each category is visually represented in a specific size corresponding to how many times different authors have mentioned it. It can be seen that the most frequently mentioned benefits are developing partnerships, recognition as partners in various fields of science, and enriching existing library collections and developing new services. The least mentioned benefits are utilizing existing competences of employees, media recognition, and teaching citizen science. Some authors have mentioned multiple different benefits, so they appear in multiple places.

Based on the literature review shown in Figure 1, a list of benefits of citizen science for libraries is proposed:

(a) Recognition as partners in various fields of science.
(b) Advocacy.
(c) Teaching citizen science.
(d) Developing partnerships.
(e) Attracting new library users.
(f) Media recognition.
(g) Enriching existing library collections and developing new services.
(h) Utilizing existing competences of employees.
(i) Personal and professional development of employees.

Libraries have the potential to be acknowledged as collaborative partners in a range of scientific disciplines. Through active participation in citizen science initiatives, libraries position themselves as valuable contributors and supporters, engaging with diverse scientific fields and fostering collaborative efforts. This recognition stems from their role in providing access to research materials, contributing to data management practices, and advocating for open access principles. By aligning with these activities, libraries strengthen their position as essential partners in advancing scientific knowledge across various domains.

By advocating for citizen science, libraries support the idea that the public can contribute to scientific research. This approach promotes active citizen participation in research, resulting not only in increased data accessibility but also in the development of shared responsibility for scientific topics. Libraries, as advocates of this model, position themselves as promoters of inclusivity in knowledge creation, thereby reinforcing their role as relevant and progressive institutions in society.

Engaging in citizen science provides a valuable opportunity for education within the library setting. By actively participating in citizen science initiatives, libraries contribute to the education of librarians, scientists, and citizen-scientists alike. Furthermore, the establishment of a dedicated unit such as BESPOC within the library framework can serve as a focal point for organizing and delivering targeted educational programs. Through BESPOC, libraries can offer specialized training sessions, workshops, and resources designed to enhance the understanding of citizen science principles and practices. This tailored education can benefit librarians by equipping them with the expertise needed to effectively support and guide citizen science initiatives.

Engaging in citizen science initiatives enables libraries to cultivate partnerships both within their organizational structure (internal) and with external entities. Internally, libraries can forge collaborations among different departments or teams within the library, fostering a multidisciplinary approach to citizen science projects. Externally, libraries can establish partnerships with external organizations, research institutions, community groups, or other stakeholders involved in citizen science. Kaarsted et al. recommend that (research) libraries actively pursue partnerships by engaging with established working groups, organizations, networks, or project consortia. Alternatively, they can take the initiative to create new collaborations. The suggested partners encompass universities, civil society, government entities, the education sector, the private sector, etc. [25]. These collaborative efforts contribute to the library's ability to support and enhance citizen science activities, broaden its network, and create a more robust ecosystem of shared knowledge and resources.

By actively participating in citizen science initiatives, libraries have the potential to draw in and attract new users. Citizen science projects often involve the community in scientific research, creating an opportunity for individuals who may not traditionally use library services to engage with the library. The appeal of citizen science, which encourages active participation in scientific activities, can serve as a gateway for people to discover and utilize the resources and services offered by the library. In this way, libraries can broaden their user base and reach individuals who are interested in both scientific exploration and the diverse offerings provided by the library.

Citizen science initiatives can contribute to gaining recognition from the media for libraries. When libraries actively participate in citizen science projects, they engage in collaborative and impactful activities that are often of interest to the broader community. The media may find these initiatives noteworthy, leading to coverage and visibility for the library's involvement in citizen science. This recognition can take the form of news articles, interviews, or features that highlight the library's role in supporting scientific research and community engagement. By leveraging citizen science projects, libraries have the potential to enhance their visibility in the media, thereby strengthening their public image and raising awareness about the valuable contributions they make to scientific endeavors and community involvement.

Citizen science participation can contribute to the enrichment of a library's existing collections and services. Through citizen science projects, libraries often involve the community in activities that generate new knowledge, materials, or resources. The outcomes of these projects, such as data, research findings, or tangible artefacts, can be incorporated into the library's collections, enhancing the diversity and relevance of available materials. Moreover, citizen science engagement may inspire the development of new services that align with the interests and needs of the community involved in these projects. Citizen science serves as a means for libraries to actively augment their collections and adapt their services to better reflect the evolving interests and contributions of the community they serve.

In their research, Kaarsted et al. identified the acknowledgment of transferable skills that are well-suited for citizen enhanced open science. Research libraries have the opportunity to assess the existing skill set and concentrate on enhancing competencies in areas that may be lacking [25]. Leveraging existing competences is a significant benefit when integrating citizen science into library initiatives. Libraries inherently possess a diverse pool of skills and competences among their staff, ranging from information management to community engagement. By aligning these existing competences with the collaborative nature of citizen science, libraries can efficiently contribute to scientific projects while maximizing the utilization of their internal expertise.

The involvement of library employees in citizen science can yield positive effects on their personal and professional development. Engaging in citizen science projects offers employees opportunities to develop and enhance a variety of skills, such as project coordination, project management, evaluation, and research data management. These experiences contribute to the enrichment of their professional skill set and may lead to increased competence in handling diverse aspects of library work. Additionally, participating in citizen science can broaden the horizons of library staff, exposing them to new challenges and fostering a deeper understanding of the collaborative nature of scientific inquiry. This exposure not only contributes to their professional growth but also adds a valuable dimension to their personal development by fostering a sense of accomplishment and engagement with meaningful, community-oriented work. Overall, citizen science initiatives in libraries provide a platform for continuous learning and development for library employees.

Why is it important to talk about the benefits of citizen science for libraries? Firstly, it sheds light on the valuable contributions that libraries can make to scientific endeavors through citizen science initiatives. This recognition is crucial in highlighting the evolving role of libraries beyond traditional information repositories. Secondly, emphasizing these benefits serves to inspire and encourage other libraries to engage in citizen science. By showcasing the positive outcomes, such as increased visibility, enriched collections, and community engagement, it encourages a broader adoption of citizen science practices within the library community. Furthermore, discussing these benefits contributes to a broader understanding of the societal impact of libraries. It underscores their role not only as information providers but as active participants in community-driven scientific activities. This can enhance the public perception of libraries, positioning them as dynamic institutions that contribute actively to the advancement of knowledge and community well-being.

5. Conclusions

Today, the concept of citizen science is positioned within the broader field of open science, and citizen science is recognized as a grounded and valid approach to scientific research [45]. Participation in citizen science activities presents a multifaceted opportunity for libraries, transcending their conventional roles as repositories of knowledge. Engaging in citizen science not only positions public and research libraries as active contributors to scientific endeavors but also fosters dynamic partnerships across diverse fields.

This literature review, which explored the benefits of citizen science for public and research libraries, identified the following advantages: recognition as partners in various fields of science, advocacy, teaching citizen science, developing partnerships, attracting new library users, media recognition, enriching existing library collections and developing new services, utilizing existing competences and personal and professional development of employees. Those benefits are divided into two groups: external and internal.

Through active participation in citizen science initiatives, libraries position themselves as valuable contributors and supporters, engaging with diverse scientific fields and fostering collaborative efforts. This recognition stems from their role in providing access to research materials, contributing to data management practices, and advocating for open access principles. By aligning with these activities, libraries strengthen their position as essential partners in advancing scientific knowledge across various domains. To leverage the potential of being recognized as partners in various scientific fields, libraries should actively promote their involvement in citizen science projects. Additionally, they need to continue supporting open access to research materials and develop initiatives that enhance collaboration with the research community. Educating stakeholders about the benefits of their role in citizen science projects could also contribute to increasing the recognition of libraries as key players in scientific research.

By actively advocating for citizen science, libraries endorse the notion that the public can play a crucial role in scientific research. This advocacy encourages active citizen involvement in research, leading to not only enhanced data accessibility but also the cultivation of shared responsibility for scientific endeavors. With advocacy, libraries position themselves as advocates for inclusivity in knowledge creation, thereby strengthening their role as pertinent and forward-thinking institutions in society. Encouraging community involvement and fostering partnerships with educational institutions can further promote the inclusivity of citizen science initiatives. Additionally, libraries can collaborate with policymakers to integrate citizen science principles into broader scientific strategies, emphasizing the importance of diverse perspectives in shaping the future of research.

The engagement of libraries in citizen science presents a valuable opportunity for education within the library setting. Actively participating in citizen science initiatives allows libraries to contribute to the education of librarians, scientists, and citizen-scientists alike. The establishment of a dedicated unit, such as BESPOC, within the library framework serves as a central hub for organizing and delivering targeted educational programs. Through BESPOC, libraries can provide specialized training sessions, workshops, and resources designed to enhance the understanding of citizen science principles and practices. This tailored education is advantageous for librarians, equipping them with the expertise needed to effectively support and guide citizen science initiatives. Collaborating with educational institutions and citizen science organizations can broaden the reach of these programs.

Engaging in citizen science initiatives empowers libraries to develop partnerships both internally and externally. Internally, libraries can foster collaborations among different departments or teams, encouraging a multidisciplinary approach to citizen science projects. Externally, libraries can establish partnerships with organizations, research institutions, community groups, and other stakeholders involved in citizen science. They can also partner with working groups, organizations, networks, project consortia, civil society, government entities, etc. To further develop partnerships, libraries should proactively engage with diverse internal departments and teams to promote a collaborative approach to citizen science initiatives. External partnerships can be expanded by actively participating in established networks and seeking out potential collaborators in universities, government entities, and the private sector. Additionally, documenting and sharing successful partnership models can inspire other libraries to pursue similar collaborations.

Active engagement in citizen science initiatives positions libraries to draw in and attract new users. Citizen science projects, involving the community in scientific research, provide an opportunity for individuals who may not typically use library services to interact with the library. The allure of citizen science, promoting active participation in scientific activities, acts as a gateway for people to discover and utilize the resources and services offered by the library. In this manner, libraries can expand their user base, reaching individuals interested in both scientific exploration and the diverse offerings provided by the library. To further attract new users, libraries should actively promote their involvement in citizen science projects through targeted outreach and marketing efforts. Collaborating with community organizations, schools, and local media can enhance visibility and awareness of library initiatives. Libraries can also consider tailoring specific programs and services to cater to the interests of the diverse audience engaged through citizen science projects.

Participating in citizen science initiatives provides libraries with an avenue to gain recognition from the media. When libraries actively engage in collaborative and impactful citizen science projects, these activities often capture the interest of the broader community. The media may find such initiatives noteworthy, resulting in coverage and visibility for the library's involvement in citizen science. This recognition can manifest through news articles, interviews, or features that highlight the library's role in supporting scientific research and community engagement. To continue gaining media recognition, libraries should proactively share information about their citizen science projects through press releases, social media, and other communication channels. Building relationships with local journalists and media outlets can facilitate coverage of library initiatives. Regularly assessing the media coverage and adapting communication strategies accordingly will further contribute to sustaining and expanding the library's presence in the public eye.

Citizen science participation plays a crucial role in enriching a library's existing collections and fostering the development of new services. This not only contributes to the diversity of content within the library but also highlights the community's ability to participate in shaping and expanding the cultural heritage preserved by the library. Furthermore, citizen science engagement has the potential to inspire the creation of new services that align with the interests and needs of the community involved in these projects. To continue enriching collections and developing services through citizen science, libraries should actively seek out projects that align with the diverse interests of their community. Libraries can also explore innovative approaches, such as virtual resources or interactive platforms, to make citizen science outcomes more accessible to the community and seamlessly integrate them into their collections and services.

Utilizing existing competences of library employees emerges as a significant advantage for libraries when integrating citizen science into their initiatives. Libraries have a diverse pool of skills and competences among their staff, spanning from information management to community engagement. By aligning these competences with the collaborative nature of citizen science, libraries can efficiently contribute to scientific projects while maximizing the utilization of their internal expertise. To further leverage existing competences, libraries should conduct a thorough assessment of the skills within their staff and identify areas for enhancement. Establishing interdisciplinary teams within the library can facilitate the collaborative utilization of diverse competences.

The involvement of library employees in citizen science projects yields positive effects on both their personal and professional development. Engaging in these initiatives offers employees opportunities to develop and enhance various skills, including project coordination, project management, evaluation, and research data management. These experiences contribute to the enrichment of their professional skill set, potentially leading to increased competence in handling diverse aspects of library work. Additionally, participating in citizen science broadens the horizons of library staff, exposing them to new challenges and fostering a deeper understanding of the collaborative nature of scientific inquiry. Providing opportunities for skill-building workshops, training sessions, and mentoring programs can enhance the capabilities of library staff. Recognizing and celebrating the achievements of employees involved in citizen science initiatives can foster a positive and supportive organizational culture.

Future research endeavors can delve into the specific benefits derived from individual citizen science projects within the context of libraries. Examining the outcomes and impacts of particular initiatives can provide nuanced insights into the effectiveness of citizen science engagement at the project level. Researchers may explore how different types of projects contribute to community empowerment, scientific knowledge advancement, and the overall mission of libraries.

Author Contributions: Conceptualization, D.M. and A.M.; methodology, D.M.; validation, D.M. and A.M.; formal analysis, D.M.; data curation, A.M.; writing—original draft preparation, D.M.; writing—review and editing, A.M.; visualization, D.M. All authors have read and agreed to the published version of the manuscript.

Funding: This research received no external funding.

Conflicts of Interest: The authors declare no conflict of interest.

References

1. Vazire, S. Implications of the credibility revolution for productivity, creativity, and progress. *Perspect. Psychol. Sci.* **2018**, *13*, 411–417. [CrossRef]

2. Vicente-Saez, R.; Martinez-Fuentes, C. Open Science now: A systematic literature review for an integrated definition. *J. Bus. Res.* **2018**, *88*, 428–436. [CrossRef]
3. European Commission. Open Science. 2019. Available online: https://research-and-innovation.ec.europa.eu/system/files/2019-12/ec_rtd_facts-heet-open-science_2019.pdf (accessed on 15 October 2023).
4. Ayris, P.; Bernal, I.; Cavalli, V.; Dorch, B.; Frey, J.; Hallik, M.; Hormia-Poutanen, K.; Labastida i Juan, I.; MacColl, J.; Ponsati Obiols, A.; et al. LIBER Open Science Roadmap. *Zenodo* **2018**, 1–27. [CrossRef]
5. Irwin, A. *Citizen Science: A Study of People, Expertise, and Sustainable Development*; Routledge: London, UK; New York, NY, USA, 1995.
6. Booney, R. Citizen science: A Lab Tradition. *Living Bird* **1996**, *15*, 7–15.
7. Schoenenberger, N.; Zenzerović, P.; Tolić, A. *Handbook of Citizen Science [Priručnik za Građansku Znanost]*; IRIM: Zagreb, Croatia, 2020. (In Croatian)
8. Land-Zandstra, A.; Agnello, G.; Gültekin, Y.S. Participants in citizen science. In *The Science of Citizen Science*; Vohland, K., Land-Zandstra, A., Ceccaroni, L., Eds.; Springer: Cham, Switzerland, 2021. [CrossRef]
9. Haklay, M. Citizen science and volunteered geographic information: Overview and typology of participation. In *Crowdsourcing Geographic Knowledge: Volunteered Geographic Information (VGI) in Theory and Practice*; Sui, D., Elwood, S., Goodchild, M., Eds.; Springer: Berlin/Heidelberg, Germany, 2013; pp. 105–122.
10. Wagenknecht, K.; Woods, T.; Nold, C.; Rüfenacht, S.; Voight-Heucke, S.; Caplan, A.; Hecker, S.; Vohland, K. A question of dialogue? Reflections on how citizen science can enhance communication between science and society. *J. Sci. Commun.* **2021**, *20*, A13. [CrossRef]
11. Finger, L.; van den Bogaert, V.; Schmidt, L.; Fleischer, J.; Stadtler, M.; Sommer, K.; Wirth, J. The science of citizen science: A systematic literature review on educational and scientific outcomes. *Front. Educ.* **2023**, *8*, 1226529. [CrossRef]
12. Nature. The best research is produced when researchers and communities work together. *Nature* **2018**, *562*, 7. [CrossRef] [PubMed]
13. Jones, M.G.; Childers, G.; Andre, T.; Corin, E.N.; Hite, R. Citizen scientists and non-citizen scientist hobbyists: Motivation, benefits, and influences. *Int. J. Sci. Educ. B* **2018**, *8*, 287–306. [CrossRef]
14. Pateman, M.; Dyke, A.; Elizabeth, S. The Diversity of Participants in Environmental Citizen Science. *Citiz. Sci. Theory Pract.* **2021**, *6*, 1–16. [CrossRef]
15. Veeckman, C.; Keersmaekers, F.; Verbrugge, K.; Livémont, E. *Citizen Science Starters Kit: Online Citizen Science Training Materials*; Vrije Universiteit Brussel: Ixelles, Belgium, 2022. [CrossRef]
16. Besley, J.C.; Oh, S.H.; Nisbet, M. Predicting scientists' participation in public life. *Public Underst. Sci.* **2023**, *22*, 971–987. [CrossRef]
17. Ignat, T.; Cavalier, D.; Nickerson, C. Citizen Science and Libraries: Waltzing towards a collaboration. *Mitteilungen Ver. Österr. Bibl.* **2019**, *72*, 328–336. [CrossRef]
18. Ignat, T.; Ayris, P.; i Juan, I.L.; Reilly, S.; Dorch, B.F.; Kaarsted, T.; Overgaard, A.K. Merry work: Libraries and citizen science. *Insights* **2018**, *31*, 1–10. Available online: https://insights.uksg.org/articles/10.1629/uksg.431 (accessed on 18 November 2023). [CrossRef]
19. Koontz, C.; Gubbin, B. *IFLA Public Library Service Guidelines*; De Gruyter Saur: Berlin, Germany; New York, NY, USA, 2010.
20. Bridgeman, M. Public Libraries Can Be Open Science Laboratories for Citizen Science Projects. *Evid. Based Libr. Inf. Pract.* **2023**, *18*, 84–88. [CrossRef]
21. Cigarini, A.; Bonhoure, I.; Vicens, J.; Perelló, J. Public libraries embrace citizen science: Strengths and challenges. *Libr. Inf. Sci. Res.* **2021**, *43*, 101090. [CrossRef]
22. Young, H. *ALA Glossary of Library and Information Science*; American Library Association: Chicago, IL, USA, 1983.
23. Hormia-Poutanen, K.; Matheson, A. *LIBER Definition of Research Library: Background Paper*; LIBER: Hague, The Netherlands, 2017. Available online: https://libereurope.eu/wp-content/uploads/2020/12/Mar2017Mail_DefinitionofResearchLibrariesBackgroundPape pdf (accessed on 5 January 2024).
24. LIBER. Libraries Joining LIBER: Endorsement Proposal. 2017. Available online: https://libereurope.eu/wp-content/uploads/2020/12/Mar2017Mail_EndorsementProposal.pdf (accessed on 25 January 2024).
25. Kaarsted, T.; Blake, O.; Nielsen, K.H.; Alving, B.; Rasmussen, L.T.; Overgaard, A.K.; Hansen, S.M.B. How European Research Libraries Can Support Citizen-Enhanced Open Science. *Open Inf. Sci.* **2023**, *7*, 20220146. [CrossRef]
26. Golumbic, Y.N.; Orr, D.; Baram-Tsabari, A.; Fishbain, B. Between vision and reality: A study of scientists' views on citizen science. *Citiz. Sci. Theory Pract.* **2017**, *2*, 6. [CrossRef]
27. Riesch, H.; Potter, C. Citizen science as seen by scientists: Methodological, epistemological and ethical dimensions. *Public Underst. Sci.* **2014**, *23*, 107–120. [CrossRef]
28. Duerinckx, A.; Hens, C.; Kerckhoffs, S.; Van Laer, J.; Verstraelen, K. *The Citizen in Flemish Citizen Science: Demography, Motives, and Experiences*; Scivil: Leuven, Belgium, 2021. [CrossRef]
29. Cavalier, D.; Nickerson, C.; Salthouse, R.; Stanto, D. The Librarian's Guide to Citizen Science. 2019. Available online: https://s3-us-west-2.amazonaws.com/orrery-media/misc/CitSci_Librarians_Guide_02_22_r1.pdf (accessed on 17 October 2023).
30. Goulding, A. Engaging with community engagement: Public libraries and citizen involvement. *New Libr. World* **2009**, *110*, 37–51. [CrossRef]
31. Maroto, N. Citizen Science in public libraries: En experience in linguistics. In Proceedings of the Presentation from Open Science International Staff Week, Madrid, Spain, 6–8 November 2019. Available online: https://e-archivo.uc3m.es/bitstream/handle/10016/29285/citizen_maroto_OSISW_2019.pdf?sequence=1 (accessed on 19 October 2023).

32. Senabre, E.; Ferran-Ferrer, N.; Perelló, J. Participatory design of citizen science experiments [Diseño participativo de experimentos de ciencia ciudadana]. *Comun. Media Educ. Res. J.* **2018**, *26*, 29–38. [CrossRef]
33. Lasky, M.; Parsons, A.; Schuttler, S.; Mash, A.; Larson, L.; Norton, B.; Pease, B.; Boone, H.; Gatens, L.; Kays, R. Candid critters: Challenges and solutions in a large-scale citizen science camera trap project. *Citiz. Sci. Theory Pract.* **2021**, *6*, 4. [CrossRef]
34. Cohen, C.; Cheney, L.; Duong, K.; Lea, B.; Pettway Unno, Z. *Identifying Opportunities in Citizen Science for Academic Libraries*; ISTL: Atsugi, Japan, 2015. [CrossRef]
35. Mumelaš, D. Citizen science and libraries as its implementers [Građanska znanost i knjižnice kao njezini provoditelji]. *Vjesn. Bibl. Hrvat.* **2023**, *66*, 105–138.
36. Bonney, R.; Dickinson, J.L. Overview of Citizen Science. In *Citizen Science: Public Participation in Environmental Research*; Cornell University Press: New York, NY, USA, 2012; pp. 19–26.
37. Ridge, M. *Why Get Involved in Citizen Science? A Research Library Perspective*; INOS Project Introductory Lecture; LIBER: Hague, The Netherlands, 2021. [CrossRef]
38. Wyler, D.; Grey, F.; Maes, K.; Frölich, J. *Citizen Science at Universities: Trends, Guidelines and Recommendations*; League of European Research Universities: Leuven, Belgium, 2016.
39. Overgaard, A.K.; Kaarsted, T. A New Trend in Media and Library Collaboration within Citizen Science? The Case of 'A Healthier Funen'. *Liber Q.* **2018**, *28*, 1–17. [CrossRef]
40. Ignat, T.; Ayris, P. Built to last! Embedding open science principles and practice into European universities. *Insights UKSG J.* **2021**, *33*, 9. [CrossRef]
41. Wiederkehr, S. Open data for the crowd: An account of citizen science at ETH Library. *Liber Q.* **2019**, *29*, 1–10. [CrossRef]
42. Opryshko, T.; Nazarovets, S. Case study: Citizen Science in digital humanities context. In *DHW 2021: Digital Humanities Workshop, Kyiv, Ukraine, 23 December 2021*; ACM: New York, NY, USA, 2021; pp. 198–203.
43. Mumelaš, D.; Martek, A.; Mučnjak, D. *Upscaling Collaboration between Academic and Public Libraries for CeOS in SE Europe*; LIBER: Hague, The Netherlands, 2022. Available online: https://zenodo.org/records/7414551 (accessed on 18 November 2023).
44. Holley, R. Crowdsourcing: How and why should libraries do it? *D-Lib Mag.* **2010**, *16*, 1–21. [CrossRef]
45. Ivanjko, T.; Zlodi, G.; Horvat, Z. *Građanska Znanost*; Faculty of Humanities and Social Sciences, FF-Press: Zagreb, Croatia, 2024; Available online: https://openbooks.ffzg.unizg.hr/index.php/FFpress/catalog/book/172 (accessed on 23 February 2024).

publications

MDPI

Article

FAIRness of Research Data in the European Humanities Landscape

Ljiljana Poljak Bilić [1,2,*] and Kristina Posavec [3]

1 Department of Information Sciences, University of Zadar, 23 000 Zadar, Croatia
2 University of Split Library, University of Split, 21 000 Split, Croatia
3 Data Management Department, University of Zagreb University Computing Centre SRCE, 10 000 Zagreb, Croatia; kristina.posavec@srce.hr
* Correspondence: lpoljak@unizd.hr

Abstract: This paper explores the landscape of research data in the humanities in the European context, delving into their diversity and the challenges of defining and sharing them. It investigates three aspects: the types of data in the humanities, their representation in repositories, and their alignment with the FAIR principles (Findable, Accessible, Interoperable, Reusable). By reviewing datasets in repositories, this research determines the dominant data types, their openness, licensing, and compliance with the FAIR principles. This research provides important insight into the heterogeneous nature of humanities data, their representation in the repository, and their alignment with FAIR principles, highlighting the need for improved accessibility and reusability to improve the overall quality and utility of humanities research data.

Keywords: datasets; humanities; FAIR; repositories; openness; licencing; research data

1. Introduction

Research data play a crucial role in the development of the scientific communication landscape since sharing and reusing data are considered key activities in the transition to open science at the European level. Research data in the humanities are the most diverse of all scientific disciplines because almost any data on human activity can be considered research data, including newspapers, photographs, diaries, church records, court files, etc. [1]. Given the confusion surrounding the definition of data, Borgman believes that it is more relevant to question when something becomes data rather than what data are, because it "usually involves the process by which a scientist recognises that an observation, object, record, or other entity can be used as evidence of phenomena, and then collects, acquires, presents, analyses, and interprets these entities as data" [2].

Data sharing is essential in enabling the transparency, validation, and reproducibility of the research process, and further discovery based on reused data [3]. Therefore, it is possible to say that "the value of data lies in their use" [2]. To enable reuse, data must be shared in a way that is primarily FAIR (Findable, Accessible, Interoperable, Reusable), which ensures their finding, availability, interoperability, and reuse. The FAIR principles provide guidelines for the publication of digital resources in a way that makes them findable, accessible, interoperable, and reusable, and describe a continuum of characteristics, attributes, and behaviours that will bring digital resources closer to this goal [4].

The aim of this paper is to examine and answer three research questions related to datasets in the field of humanities: what types of research data are represented in the humanities? (1), to what extent are datasets in repositories in the field of the humanities represented by openness and under what licence? (2), and to what extent do research data align with the FAIR principles? (3).

In the literature, there is still no consensus on the definition of research data in the humanities, so they are often used as a broad term that includes different types of research sources. This paper aims to determine the most prevalent data types in the humanities found in repositories.

To evaluate the FAIRness of datasets, this study used Wilkinson et al.'s [5] FAIR guidelines principles and Routledge Open Research data guidelines [6]. The F-UJI tool was used to assess the FAIRness level of datasets. This tool evaluates all FAIR elements using the URL or persistent identifier of a dataset [7]. Using tools to assess the FAIRness of data helps the future improvement of data FAIRness and, therefore, their reuse [8]. The use of the F-UJI tool is already acknowledged in scientific research [9,10]. Petrosyan et al. [9] used the F-UJI tool for the FAIR assessment of agriculture datasets and proposed a methodology that integrates the process of obtaining datasets and their subsequent evaluation, which can be used to investigate the degree of FAIRness of datasets in different disciplines.

2. Review of the Literature

The concept of research data in the humanities is still vague, especially in comparison to data-driven fields like STEM. This is due to the unique nature of humanities scholarly primitives [11], which refer to the basic functions that are common in scholarly activity across various disciplines. However, to participate effectively in current research practices, there is a need for a clearer understanding of what research data mean in the humanities.

Research data are often determined by definition as a set of symbols, that is, quantitative or qualitative, and by type, i.e., numerical, textual, and similar (definitions by Baretto, Burrel, Oppenheim) [12]. These characteristics describe research data, i.e., data that have been collected, recorded, or generated for analysis to obtain new, original research results. Each scientific field interprets and groups research data differently, most often according to the method of collection [13] and the level of processing [14].

According to DARIAH-DE [15], research data are all sources, materials, and results that have been collected, recorded, or evaluated in the context of research and answers to research questions in the field of humanities and culture, as well as computer-processed data for permanent storage, citation, and further processing. The definition is deliberately broadened to encompass the particular characteristics of humanities research, as well as the heterogeneous nature of research data [15]. Since there is no consensus on the definition, research data in the humanities field are often used as an umbrella term that includes different types of sources for research instead of the specific material that needs to be researched using quantitative tools [16]. Research data can also differ according to different perspectives, so we distinguish between artefacts intentionally created by people; texts, which are subject to interpretation; and information that is machine-processable and can be quantitatively analysed. However, such a division does not allow for the distinction of research data from research sources. Perhaps the most significant specificity of the humanities, in the context of scientific research data, are the unclear boundaries between data and publications. They are often used as equals, so primary sources are considered research data in the humanities [17]. Borgman describes this in the example of an old book, which can be considered not only a publication, but also a data source for retrieving names, places, and events [1]. According to the results of research by Allen and Hartland [18], in some fields, especially in history, researchers do not even recognise that they use data. It is often not considered a weakness, but a resistance to using the general term "data" when there is a more developed and accepted terminology, such as primary and secondary sources, bibliographies, and notes, and it is possible to describe research processes using them [18]. But quite often, they are not autonomous products of research, but are part of the cultural and social practices of the institutions that preserve, curate, and (co)produce them, such as libraries, museums, and archives [19]. Thus, another particularity of the humanities in this context is that they are not only devoted to physical entities, as in other disciplines, but also to abstract entities that include work as a physical and intellectual manifestation.

2.1. Humanities Scientists on Data

In contrast to other disciplines, there is not much research on the perception of research data and generally on the management of research data among scientists in the humanities field. Thoegersen [20] conducts research on research data and its management among scientists in the humanities field, and the results indicate that respondents consider research materials as data and equate them with information. Some distinguish between information and data, in that information is considered everything they have, while data are numerical, that is, quantitative. They believe that when information is used in research, it becomes data, that is, research information. Although the research is interesting, limitations are apparent. The very small sample of nine respondents is perhaps the most significant limitation, so these results can be used as encouragement for further research on this topic. Hauf and coauthors [3], in their research on research data and their storage and use in the social sciences and humanities, intentionally use the term data instead of research data, because this phrase could refer too much to the STEM field and lead respondents (scientists in the social sciences and humanities) on the wrong track. The results indicate that the respondents most often use numerical data, including statistical and other quantitative data; scientific publications are in the second place, surveys and interviews in the third, and digital artefacts are in the fourth place. The correlation between the type of reused data and the discipline has been proven and the use of digital artefacts in the fields of archaeology, art, history, and literature is statistically significant. The fact that scientists from the social sciences and humanistic fields are involved in research partially explains the fact that numerical data are used most often, but it is necessary to investigate this in more detail. Gualandi, Pareschi, and Peroni [4] conducted research with the objective of defining research data in the humanities; that is, to define what that term includes and to provide an overview of current data practices. The research methodology was based on the previously mentioned research conducted by Thoegersen [20] and involved a sample of 19 scientists in the humanities field at the University of Bologna. The research resulted in a list of 13 types of research data, including publications, that is, primary and secondary sources. The respondents viewed the term "data" broadly, encompassing everything necessary for their research, and were not inclined to limit this term. Unlike the results of the research conducted by Thoegersen [20], the respondents did not consider the term "data" problematic and considered it relevant to their research context.

Limited research is available on how humanists conceptualise research data, and the studies that have been conducted are characterised by small sample sizes, making it hard to draw any conclusions. It should be noted that the term data itself is often problematic in the context of humanistic research.

2.2. Previous Research on FAIRness in Humanities

Quite often, the particularities regarding research data in the humanities make the implementation of the FAIR principles challenging. Kalinin and Skvortsov [21] identified four key characteristics of humanities data usage: 1. Research objects are collected, not created [22,23]; 2. Analogue data are critical; 3. Licence restrictions are imposed by data owners (libraries, galleries, and museums, not scientific institutes); 4. Context is of great importance [22]. Therefore, research data come in various forms, making it challenging to interpret and reuse them in other research once they are removed from their initial context.

The FAIR concept was the subject of research in different humanities areas. Calamai and Frontini [24] examined current data science and archiving practices in the area of speech and oral archives in the humanities. All FAIR principles were analysed and explained from the oral and speech archive perspective, i.e., the FAIR principles were applied to the CLARIN RI. Furthermore, de Jong et al. [25] further demonstrated the compliance of the CLARIN infrastructure with the FAIR concept through its data architecture. Strange, Gooch, and Collinson [26] investigated the question of data sustainability and existing repository services on the institutional level at the University of Oxford. Hiebel et al. [27] presented an approach to creating FAIR data for prehistoric mining archaeology based on ontology and semantic web standards. They demonstrated that the creation of FAIR data concerns all the sub-principles and particularities of the field. One of the main implications for practice is that the demonstrated approach is generic and can be applied to any archaeological investigation carried out in Austria. Some cross-domain research studies aimed to incorporate research data from various fields, including the humanities [18,21]. Despite accounting for critical differences between disciplines, such as the diversity of data types, research infrastructures (RI), and attitudes towards sharing and perceived individual benefits [18], field particularities and lack of representation have resulted in positioning the humanities, understood as non-STEM areas such as the Social Sciences and Humanities (SSH) [3,28] and Arts and Humanities, as an area of science unrepresented in cross-disciplinary research [21].

Tóth-Czifra [22] found that the FAIRness of humanities research data is based on particularities of humanities compared to other fields: "First, scholarly data or metadata are digital by nature, second, scholarly data are always created and therefore owned by researchers, and third, there is a wide community-level agreement on what can be considered scholarly data. The problems around such assumptions in arts and humanities are cornerstones in reconciling disciplinary traditions with FAIR data management. By addressing them one by one, our aim is to contribute to a better understanding of discipline-specific needs and challenges in data production, discovery, and reuse".

From previous research on the FAIR concept in the humanities, it can be observed that most of the research is focused or limited to Ris (e.g., CLARIN, DARIAH, SDS Oxford University services), with an emphasis on the infrastructure that supports FAIRification [29], not on the data themselves. But the importance of reaching a consensus around the notion of "data" [2,19,20] is a stepping stone for representable humanities research data in the open science landscape.

The question of determining what data are in the humanities is very current, reflecting challenges in distinguishing between data and publications. In addition to this problem, there are other specificities of research data in the humanities which need to be further investigated. The literature notes a lack of research on data in the humanities, including their definition and the adequacy of general concepts such as the FAIR principles.

3. Materials and Methods

The purpose of this paper is to gain insight into the humanities research data landscape, with a focus on the current data types, their representation in repositories, and alignment with the FAIR principles.

(1) Since consensus on the definition has not yet been reached, research data in the humanities are often used as an umbrella term that includes different types of sources for research. For this research, the DARIAH-DE definition of research data is used to determine the types of data represented in the humanities. An analysis of datasets published in institutional and thematic repositories in the field of humanities was performed using Digital Academic Archives and Repositories (DABAR), CROSSDA, and OpenAIRE. This research question aimed to determine the most common types of data found in open and/or closed access repositories in the humanities;

(2) In a study on the storage of research data in repositories, Buddenbohm et al. [30] found that a culture of sharing and reusing research data has not yet been established. Despite some data being stored in repositories, they are often difficult to find. The second research question is set up to examine the representation of humanities datasets published in open access sources and the licencing conditions under which they are published;

(3) Given the available number of open access datasets, this research question aims to investigate the extent to which the datasets align with the FAIR principles and, therefore, are appropriate for further use. The evaluation of FAIRness was conducted using F-UJI, a web service that enables the assessment of datasets. It is based on the metrics proposed by the RDA FAIR Data Maturity Model Working Group and developed by

the FAIRsFAIR project "Fostering FAIR Data Practices in Europe". The tool performs a FAIR assessment "based on aggregated metadata; this includes metadata embedded in the data (landing) page, metadata retrieved from a PID provider (e.g., Datacite content negotiation), and other services (e.g., re3data)" [31]. By inputting the URL or persistent identifier of a dataset into the tool interface, F-UJI assesses the dataset and categorises its FAIRness assessment into four levels: incomplete, initial, moderate, and advanced. Each FAIR element is evaluated on the metrics presented in Table S1. Each FAIR principle in the F-UJI tool has a maximum score that every dataset can reach. The maximum score for Findable is 7, for Accessible 3, for Interoperable 4, and for Reusable 10.

This research was conducted in humanities fields, including philosophy, theology, philology, history, art history, art science, archaeology, ethnology and anthropology, religious studies, and interdisciplinary humanities science [32]. The Croatian Social Science Archive (CROSSDA) [33], Digital Academic Archives and Repositories (DABAR) [34], and institutional repositories providing OpenAIRE Explore [35] were selected as data sources due to their search and filter functionalities that enable the breakdown of datasets by subject category. Other repositories, e.g., Zenodo, were not used due to the lack of search and filter functionalities as they could not provide the information needed for conducting this research.

Data were analysed using a deductive or "a priori" coding approach in which initial codes come from the literature or key variables from the conducted research [36]. For data analysis, attribute coding was used as the method in which information about sample data is recorded in the form of a framework matrix [37]. For each dataset in the sample, the following values were applied: name of the repository, scientific field, data type, openness, licences, file format, and FAIR assessment (Findable score (FS), FS FAIR level, Accessible score (AS), AS FAIR level, Interoperable score (IS), IS FAIR level, Reusable score (RS), RS FAIR level, FAIR level in general). This was performed using the F-UJI tool [34]. The aforementioned values were analysed to answer the research questions: the scientific field provided information about humanities fields, the data type and file format gave information about the specific types of datasets stored in repositories, licences gave information about the openness of the datasets, and the F-UJI tool conducted a FAIR assessment and provided information about the FAIR level of datasets.

4. Results

RQ1: What types of research data are represented in the humanities?

Although the question of defining research data in the humanities is still under discussion, for this research, we chose the DARIAH DE definition of research data, which includes various types of research data, such as text samples, tables, images, maps, databases, etc. However, based on this definition, research data are not a publication or research article.

From the research sample, the authors collected 123 objects (108 from OpenAire, 13 from DABAR, 2 from CROSSDA) stored as datasets, but only 20% were actual datasets, and the rest were research papers. Among the 26 actual datasets retrieved, the majority were mixed (55.6% were numeric and textual data). Figure 1 shows the types of repositories where it is evident that the largest types of dataset are mixed data that contain both numerical and textual data. The second dataset represented in the repository are textual data with 16.7% and audio data with 11.1%. With the same percentage of 5.6%, repositories represented databases, software, and applications.

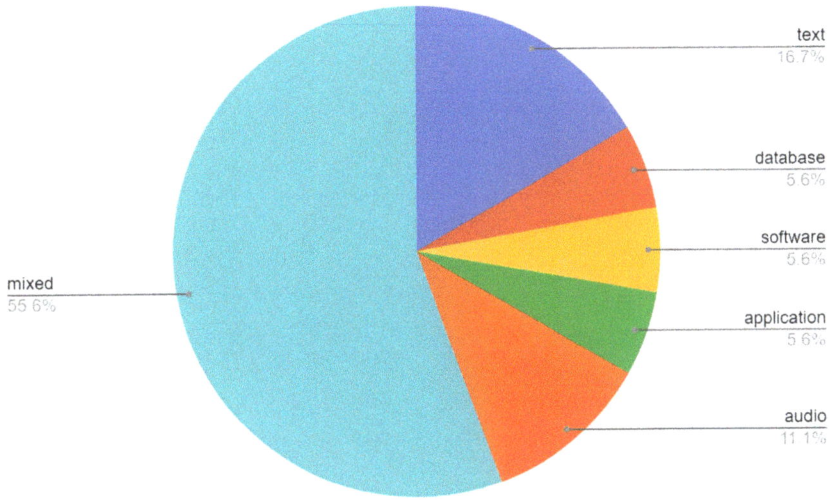

Figure 1. Representation of the type of dataset (n = 26).

The majority of datasets were from the interdisciplinary humanities (38.5%) and philology (30.8%); archaeology represented 23.1%, and art history and theology 3.8%.

Each dataset stored in the repositories consisted of several files with different data. The results indicate that 47.5% of the data are stored as spreadsheets or tabular files, e.g., .xlsx, .csv, .tab, .r, .tsv, .rda. The second category, representing 22% of the total, are text files, for example .docx, .txt, .pdf, .md. The third place, at 11.9%, is jointly shared by the categories of compressed files (.zip, .gz) and files for storing software code (.json, .mat, .loch, .es3). The research results showed that the least common formats for datasets stored in repositories are database formats (.sql), with 3.4%, and multimedia (.dcf), and audio files (.mp3) each with 1.7%.

RQ2: To what extent are datasets in repositories in the field of humanities represented by openness and under what licence?

Almost all data are openly accessible (88.5%); 3.8% of the data have limited access, and 7.7% of the data are not openly accessible. Although most of the datasets are open access, there are still some restrictions on reuse. Figure 2 shows a representation of the licences assigned to the repository datasets that were analysed. Most datasets have copyright licence with all rights reserved (34.62%). CC BY is one of the least restrictive licences, represented in 20% of the datasets and the second most popular licence in this sample, with 19.23%. Only 11.54% of the datasets are marked with CCO, which serves as a public domain dedication tool and is the most suitable for research data. The CC BY NC ND, CC BY NC, CC BY ND, and CC BY NC SA licences are represented in 7.69% of the datasets, while GPL-3.0 is assigned to 3.85% of the datasets.

RQ3: To what extent do research data align with the FAIR principles?

The analysis of the datasets included in this research showed that the average score for the Findable principle is 5.36 and the mode value is 5, which equals a moderate level of findability. None of the datasets has scores 1 and 3. One dataset had a score of 2, five datasets had a score of 4, ten datasets had a score 5, five datasets had a score of 6, and five datasets had a score of 7, representing an advanced level of findability. Based on this, most of the datasets have a moderate level of findability (n = 17), one dataset has a basic level, and eight datasets have an advanced level.

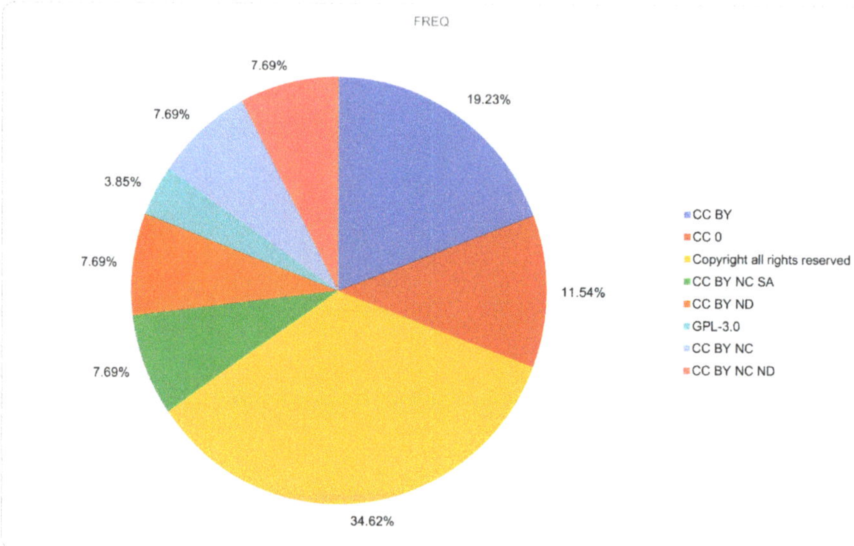

Figure 2. Licences assigned to the datasets (n = 26).

The average score for the Accessible principle is 1.3 and the mode value is 1, which equals a basic level of accessibility. Most datasets had a score of 1 (n = 20), five datasets had a score of 2, and one dataset had a score of 3, which represents an advanced level of accessibility. Based on this, most of the datasets have a basic level of accessibility (n = 20), one dataset has an advanced level, and five datasets have a moderate level.

The average score for the Interoperable principle is 1.56 and the mode value is 0, which equals an incomplete level of interoperability. Most of the datasets did not score any points; they scored 0 (n = 12) out of 4. One dataset had a score of 1, three datasets had a score of 2, eight datasets had a score of 3, and two datasets had a score of 4, which represents an advanced level of interoperability. Based on this, most of the datasets have an incomplete level of interoperability (n = 12), one dataset has a basic level, ten datasets have a moderate level, and three datasets have an advanced level.

The average score for Reusable principle is 2.32 and the mode value is 1, which indicates a basic level of reusability. None of the datasets has scores of 10, 9, 8, 7, or 5. Most of the datasets had a score of 1 (n = 13), three datasets had a score of 2, four datasets had a score of 3 and 4, and two datasets had a score of 6. Based on this, the majority of datasets have a basic reusability level (n = 23), two datasets have a moderate level, and one dataset has an advanced level.

Based on these results, the FAIR principles with the lowest scores were reusability and accessibility. Most datasets (88.5%) are at a basic FAIR level regarding the reusability principle and the accessible principle with 76.9%. The Findable principle reached the best score, with one dataset at the moderate level and 30.8% at the advanced level. The lowest FAIR principle was Interoperable, because 46.2% of the datasets were at the incomplete level.

Table 1 presents the number of datasets classified by the FAIR levels that the datasets achieved during testing with the F-UJI tool.

Table 1. Number of datasets ($n = 26$) classified by FAIR levels.

	Incomplete	Initial	Moderate	Advanced
Findable	0	1	17	8
Accessible	0	20	5	1
Interoperable	12	1	10	3
Reusable	0	14	10	2
Total FAIR level	-	14	10	2

The assessment of each dataset provides information about the overall percentage of datasets on each FAIR level. The analysis of the results reveals that most of the datasets are at a basic level of FAIRness ($n = 14$), with an average score of 28.86%; ten datasets are at a moderate FAIR level, with an average of 55.55%; and two datasets are at an advanced FAIR level, with an average of 79%. Based on this, the average score of the overall FAIR level for the datasets is 43.72% and the mode value is 29, which is equal to a basic FAIR level, which means that the average percentage of datasets is at a moderate level and the most frequent FAIR level percentage is 29, which is equal to the basic level. Only one dataset had the highest FAIR level, at 83%, and the lowest FAIR level was 25%. Overall, 53.8% of the datasets are at a basic level of FAIRness, 38.5% of the datasets are at a moderate level of FAIRness, and only 7.7% of the datasets are at an advanced level of FAIRness.

Based on the analysis of FAIRness, datasets in the DABAR system have an average score of 28.38%, which equals a basic FAIR level, the datasets in CROSSDA have an average score of 59%, which equals a moderate FAIR level, and the datasets in OpenAIRE have an average score of 57.71%, which equals a moderate FAIR level.

5. Discussion

This article highlights several key findings regarding the state of research data in the humanities, emphasising their significance in the context of open science and the need for improvements in their accessibility and reusability. It confirms that humanities data are diverse, and the line between data and publications is still unclear, since most of the datasets stored in repositories are research articles rather than datasets. This implies that more education and training related to research data management and the principles of FAIRness is needed.

According to Tóth-Czifra [38], the reusability of research data in the humanities is equal to their sustainability, and the problem is not openness but a lack of transparency and proper documentation of research data. This research confirms Tóth-Czifra's [38] findings, because most datasets were openly available, but there was a lack of metadata documentation. This research has also confirmed that the culture of sharing and reusing data has not yet been established [30]. While research data are stored in repositories, they are difficult to find due to the lack of functionalities such as subject categories for filtering datasets on platforms and repositories. The analysis of the dataset confirmed that there is a need to improve the existing platform and repository interfaces with more functional search and filter options, allowing users to obtain the information they need. Although Tóth-Czifra [38] equals reusability and sustainability, it does not mean that reusability is unimportant in the humanities. Based on our results, it is challenged by the fact that the majority of the research data are licenced with copyright or restrictive Creative Commons licences (CC BY NC ND, CC BY NC, CC BY ND, CC BY NC SA). These licenses pose requirements or restrictions that make future reuse challenging.

Within the scientific community, repositories have an important role in developing and disseminating standards such as the FAIR concept, as they "often bridge the data sharing gap between the individual researcher collecting data, funding agencies, publishers, and standards authorities" [39]. This research has shown that all datasets tested using the F-UJI tool adhere to the FAIR principles. However, most of these datasets are only at a basic FAIRness level. The reusability and accessibility principles need improvement, as the datasets scored the lowest on these FAIR principles. These findings are consistent with previous research conducted by Petrosyan et al. [9], whose investigation showed that the principles of reusability and interoperability have the lowest FAIR assessment score. Another study by Dumontier [10] also found that the interoperability principle had the lowest score, which can be attributed to the focus of F-UJI on structure and not metadata and data measurements.

This study has provided several recommendations for improving the FAIR level of datasets. Comprehensive and standardised metadata for each dataset must be ensured to enhance findability. This can be achieved by providing detailed descriptions of the data, keywords, and relevant contextual information in the form of a Readme file that is stored in the repository along with the dataset. To improve accessibility, datasets should be clear and detailed, including information on data structure, methodology, and any specific considerations for usage. To enhance interoperability, standardised and widely accepted data formats are recommended, e.g., CSV, DOCX, JSON, etc. In addition, it would be useful to represent metadata using a formal knowledge representation language, using semantic resources, or establishing links between data and related entities [9]. To promote reusability, datasets need to adequately address aspects such as whether the metadata actually specify the content of the data, whether they include information on licences, or whether both the data and metadata use standards and formats recommended by the scientific discipline to which they belong [9], to ensure that they are not only accessible but also reliable and usable for subsequent research. In addition, a clear and permissive licensing practice needs to be cultivated regarding the reusability of datasets, such as the use of licenses like Creative Commons (CC) that promote reuse while respecting intellectual property rights. To improve the level of FAIRness, the integration of FAIR assessment tools such as F-UJI into the data publication workflow is recommended. Furthermore, researchers should be provided with support and resources to self-assess and improve the FAIRness of their datasets.

According to Wilkinson et al. [40], FAIRmetrics and FAIRness are focused on metrics that cover various aspects of the FAIR principles and apply to all types of digital objects. These metrics should be universal but flexible enough to adapt to a specific community's needs. They must adhere to the FAIR principles and be open standards to encourage the development of assessment tools. Various methods for FAIR assessment, such as self-assessment, task forces, crowd-sourcing, and automation, should be enabled. However, scalability for assessing billions or even trillions of diverse digital objects is crucial. FAIRness assessments must be continuously updated, revised, timestamped, and publicly accessible. A simple visualisation of a "FAIRness grade" can be a powerful way to inform users and guide resource producers. The assessment process should be designed to encourage digital resource providers to participate and improve based on these assessments. Furthermore, Wilkinson et al. [40] state that FAIRmetrics should have the following qualities: clear, so that anyone can understand the purpose metric; realistic, so it should not be complicated for a resource to comply with the metric; the discriminating metric should measure something important for FAIRness; measurable, which means that the assessment can be made in an objective, quantitative, machine-interpretable, scalable, and reproducible manner, ensuring transparency about what is being measured and how; and universal, so that metrics apply to digital resources. For an improvement in FAIR level, the integration of FAIR assessment tools such as F-UJI into the data publication workflow is recommended because it could provide support and resources for researchers to self-assess and improve the FAIRness of their datasets.

Community engagement is one of the ways to promote FAIRness, e.g., through the organisation of workshops and training sessions to educate researchers, repository managers, and other stakeholders about the FAIR principles. Establishing a feedback mechanism to allow users to provide input on dataset quality and FAIRness is useful and can drive continuous improvement.

6. Conclusions

This study is significant because of the ambiguity surrounding humanities research data and the lack of research in this field. The findings reveal a high level of uncertainty in the definition of research data, with most of the analysed datasets being research articles, underscoring a crucial distinction between data as evidence and publications as a source in the humanities. Although the datasets align with the FAIR principles, most are at a basic FAIR level, indicating the need for improvement in terms of compliance. Research data play a fundamental role in the European open science landscape, making it necessary to ensure openness and FAIRness for effective sharing and reuse. In general, this study emphasises the need for enhanced accessibility and reusability to improve the quality and utility of humanities research data.

The limitations of this research study relate to a few main issues. Since we only used the F-UJI tool and considered three repositories, additional data collection and the use of different tools could have provided different results. The identified limitations signal a continuing commitment to advancing the understanding of humanities data to foster openness, accessibility, and reusability in the field.

Future research could be conducted on a broader scale, including more databases and repositories in the analysis. To gain a complete understanding of FAIRness, future research could benefit from using several similar tools on a sample.

This research covers the FAIR principles in digital objects and questions the fundamental principles of open science in humanities. This study can be useful to open science service providers in the humanities field, policymakers, various scholarly or professional interest groups, and researchers. The quest for functional, FAIR, and reusable research data in the humanities depends on their shared understanding, and this research contributes to it.

Supplementary Materials: The following supporting information can be downloaded at: https://www.mdpi.com/article/10.3390/publications12010006/s1, Excel S1: Percentage of datasets by FAIRness level; Table S1: FAIR levels of assessment.

Author Contributions: Conceptualisation, L.P.B. and K.P.; Data curation, K.P.; Formal analysis, L.P.B. and K.P.; Investigation, L.P.B. and K.P.; Methodology, L.P.B. and K.P.; Resources, L.P.B. and K.P.; Software, K.P.; Validation, L.P.B. and K.P.; Visualisation, K.P.; Writing—original draft, L.P.B. and K.P.; Writing—review and editing, L.P.B. and K.P. All authors have read and agreed to the published version of the manuscript.

Funding: This research received no external funding.

Data Availability Statement: The original contributions presented in the study are included in the article/Supplementary Materials, further inquiries can be directed to the corresponding author/s.

Conflicts of Interest: The authors declare no conflicts of interest.

References

1. Borgman, C.L. Data, Disciplines, and Scholarly Publishing. *Learn. Publ.* **2008**, *21*, 29–38. [CrossRef]
2. Borgman, C.L. *Big Data, Little Data, No Data: Scholarship in the Networked World*; MIT Press: Cambridge, MA, USA, 2015; ISBN 978-0-262-02856-1.
3. Hauf, N.; Fürholz, A.; Klaas, V.C.; Morger, J.; Šimukovič, E.; Jaekel, M. *Data Reuse in the Social Sciences and Humanities: Project Report of the SWITCH Innovation Lab "Repositories & Data Quality"*; ZHAW Zürcher Hochschule für Angewandte Wissenschaften: Winterthur, Switzerland, 2021. [CrossRef]
4. Gualandi, B.; Pareschi, L.; Peroni, S. What Do We Mean by "Data"? A Proposed Classification of Data Types in the Arts and Humanities. *J. Doc.* **2022**, *79*, 51–71. [CrossRef]
5. Wilkinson, M.D.; Dumontier, M.; Aalbersberg, I.J.; Appleton, G.; Axton, M.; Baak, A.; Blomberg, N.; Boiten, J.-W.; da Silva Santos, L.B.; Bourne, P.E.; et al. The FAIR Guiding Principles for Scientific Data Management and Stewardship. *Sci. Data* **2016**, 3, 160018. [CrossRef]

6. Open Data and Accessible Source Materials | Routledge Open Research. Available online: https://routledgeopenresearch.org/for-authors/data-guidelines?utm_source=google&utm_medium=sem&utm_campaign=JRE28264&gad_source=1&gclid=CjwKCAiAvJarBhA1EiwAGgZl0Jp_SEnDs-9Tf7yH8tnZkwn11k8qZy_AbxVbmFsg9btZRiMq5y40GRoCd0IQAvD_BwE (accessed on 28 November 2023).
7. Devaraju, A.; Huber, R.; Mokrane, M.; Cepinskas, L.; Davidson, J.; Herterich, P.; L'Hours, H.; de Vries, J.; White, A. *FAIRsFAIR Data Object Assessment Metrics*; European Commission: Brussels, Belgium, 2020. [CrossRef]
8. Krans, N.A.; Ammar, A.; Nymark, P.; Willighagen, E.L.; Bakker, M.I.; Quik, J.T.K. FAIR Assessment Tools: Evaluating Use and Performance. *NanoImpact* **2022**, *27*, 100402. [CrossRef]
9. Petrosyan, L.; Aleixandre-Benavent, R.; Peset, F.; Valderrama-Zurián, J.C.; Ferrer-Sapena, A.; Sixto-Costoya, A. FAIR Degree Assessment in Agriculture Datasets Using the F-UJI Tool. *Ecol. Inform.* **2023**, *76*, 102126. [CrossRef]
10. Sun, C.; Emonet, V.; Dumontier, M. A Comprehensive Comparison of Automated FAIRness Evaluation Tools: 13th International Conference on Semantic Web Applications and Tools for Health Care and Life Sciences. *Semant. Web Appl. Tools Health Care Life Sci.* **2022**, *3127*, 44–53.
11. Unsworth, J. Scholarly primitives: What methods do humanities researchers have in common, and how might our tools reflect this. In Proceedings of the Symposium on Humanities Computing: Formal Methods, Experimental Practice, London, UK, 13 May 2000; King's College: London, UK; p. 5-00.
12. Zins, C. Conceptual Approaches for Defining Data, Information, and Knowledge. *J. Am. Soc. Inf. Sci. Technol.* **2007**, *58*, 479–493. [CrossRef]
13. National Science Board. *Long-Lived Digital Data Collections Enabling Research and Education in the 21st Century*; Technical Report NSB-05-40; National Science Foundation: Arlington, VA, USA, 2005.
14. Celjak, D.; Dorotić Malič, I.; Matijević, M.; Poljak, L.J.; Posavec, K.; Turk, I. *Istraživački Podaci—Što s Njima? Priručnik o Upravljanju Istraživačkim Podacima*; Sveučilište u Zagrebu, Sveučilišni Računski Centar: Zagreb, Croatia, 2020.
15. Forschungsdaten—DARIAH-DE. Available online: https://de.dariah.eu/en/forschungsdaten (accessed on 28 November 2023).
16. Pawlicka, U. Data, Collaboration, Laboratory: Bringing Concepts from Science into Humanities Practice. *Engl. Stud.* **2017**, *98*, 526–541. [CrossRef]
17. Owens, T. Defining Data for Humanists: Text, Artifact, Information or Evidence? *J. Digit. Humanit.* **2011**, *1*, 325–341.
18. Allen, R.; Hartland, D. *FAIR in Practice—Jisc Report on the Findable Accessible Interoperable and Reuseable Data Principles*; Zenodo: Geneva, Switzerland, 2018. [CrossRef]
19. Edmond, J.; Tóth-Czifra, E. *Open Data for Humanists, A Pragmatic Guide*; Digital Research Infrastructure for the Arts and Humanities (DARIAH): Dublin, Germany, 2018. [CrossRef]
20. Thoegersen, J.L. "Yeah, I Guess That's Data": Data Practices and Conceptions among Humanities Faculty. *Portal* **2018**, *18*, 491–504. [CrossRef]
21. Kalinin, N.A.; Skvortsov, N.A. Difficulties of FAIR Principles Implementation in Cross-Domain Research Infrastructures. *Lobachevskii J. Math.* **2023**, *44*, 147–156. [CrossRef]
22. Tóth-Czifra, E. *The Risk of Losing Thick. Description: Data Management Challenges Arts and Humanities Face in the Evolving FAIR Data Ecosystem*; Open Book Publishers: Cambridge, UK, 2019; p. 29.
23. Tóth-Czifra, E.; Błaszczyńska, M.; Gelati, F.; Admiraal, F.; Blümm, M.; Buelinckx, E.; Chiquet, V.; Gautschy, R.; Gietz, P.; Király, P.; et al. *Research Data Management for Arts and Humanities: Integrating Voices of the Community*; Fachhochschule Potsdam: Potsdam, Germany, 2023.
24. Calamai, S.; Frontini, F. FAIR Data Principles and Their Application to Speech and Oral Archives. *J. New Music. Res.* **2018**, *47*, 339–354. [CrossRef]
25. de Jong, F.; Maegaard, B.; De Smedt, K.; Fišer, D.; Van Uytvanck, D. CLARIN: Towards FAIR and Responsible Data Science Using Language Resources. In Proceedings of the Eleventh International Conference on Language Resources and Evaluation (LREC 2018), Miyazaki, Japan, 7–12 May 2018; European Language Resources Association (ELRA): Miyazaki, Japan, 2018.
26. Strange, D.; Gooch, M.; Collinson, A. Equality, Findability, Sustainability: The Challenges and Rewards of Open Digital Humanities Data. *Int. J. Perform. Arts Digit. Media* **2023**, 1–21. [CrossRef]
27. Hiebel, G.; Goldenberg, G.; Grutsch, C.; Hanke, K.; Staudt, M. FAIR Data for Prehistoric Mining Archaeology. *Int. J. Digit. Libr.* **2021**, *22*, 267–277. [CrossRef]
28. Quan-Hoang, V.; Anh-Tuan, B.; Viet-Phuong, L.; Minh-Hoang, N.; Hung-Hiep, P.; Thanh-Hang, P.; Thi-Hanh, V.; Thu-Trang, V.; Manh-Toan, H. Mirror, Mirror on the Wall: Is Economics the Fairest of Them All? An Investigation into the Social Sciences and Humanities in Vietnam. *Res. Evaluat.* **2021**, *30*, 57–72. [CrossRef]
29. FAIRification Process. Available online: https://www.go-fair.org/fair-principles/fairification-process/ (accessed on 4 November 2023).
30. Buddenbohm, S.; Cretin, N.; Dijk, E.; Gaiffe, B. State of the Art Report on Open Access Publishing of Research Data in the Humanities. *HAL SHS* **2018**, 49. Available online: https://shs.hal.science/halshs-01357208 (accessed on 4 November 2023).
31. Devaraju, A.; Huber, R. F-uji-an Automated Fair Data Assessment Tool. 2020.
32. Nacionalno Vijeće za Znanost. Pravilnik o Znanstvenim i Umjetničkim Područjima, Poljima i Granama. [National Council for Science. Regulations on Scientific and Artistic Areas, Fields and Branches]. Narodne Novine 2009. p. 118. Available online: https://narodne-novine.nn.hr/clanci/sluzbeni/2009_09_118_2929.html (accessed on 4 November 2023).

33. CROSSDA. Available online: https://www.crossda.hr (accessed on 4 November 2023).
34. DABAR. Available online: https://dabar.srce.hr/ (accessed on 4 November 2023).
35. OpenAIRE | Find Research Compatible Data Sources. Available online: https://explore.openaire.eu/search/content-providers (accessed on 17 November 2023).
36. Connaway, L.S.; Radford, M.L. *Research Methods in Library and Information Science*, 7th ed.; Holtzbrinck: Santa Barbara, CA, USA, 2021; ISBN 978-1-4408-7857-2.
37. Saldaña, J. *The Coding Manual for Qualitative Researchers*, 2nd ed.; SAGE: Los Angeles, CA, USA, 2013; ISBN 978-1-4462-4736-5.
38. Tóth-Czifra, E. FAIR from the Perspective of the Humanities V2.pptx. In Proceedings of the Slides Presented at the Applying the FAIR Data Principles in Day-to-Day Library Practice Workshop at the LIBER2019 Conference, Dublin, Ireland, 26 June 2019.
39. Khodiyar, V.; Laine, H.; O'Brien, D.; Rodriguez-Esteban, R.; TÃ¼rkyilmaz-van der Velden, Y.; Baynes, G.; Brack, M.; Cambon-Thomsen, A.; Carr, D.; Carrus, E.; et al. *Research Data: The Future of FAIR White Paper*; Springer: Berlin/Heidelberg, Germany, 2021. [CrossRef]
40. Wilkinson, M.D.; Sansone, S.A.; Schultes, E.; Doorn, P.; Bonino da Silva Santos, L.O.; Dumontier, M. A design framework and exemplar metrics for FAIRness. *Sci. Data* **2018**, *5*, 180118. [CrossRef]

Disclaimer/Publisher's Note: The statements, opinions and data contained in all publications are solely those of the individual author(s) and contributor(s) and not of MDPI and/or the editor(s). MDPI and/or the editor(s) disclaim responsibility for any injury to people or property resulting from any ideas, methods, instructions or products referred to in the content.

publications

MDPI

Article

Application of ChatGPT in Information Literacy Instructional Design

Jelena Madunić * and Matija Sovulj

University Library, University of Split, 21000 Split, Croatia; msovulj@svkst.hr
* Correspondence: jmadunic@svkst.hr

Abstract: Recent developments in generative artificial intelligence tools have prompted immediate reactions in the academic library community. While most studies focus on the potential impact on academic integrity, this work explored constructive applications of ChatGPT in the design of instructional materials for courses in academic information literacy. The starting point was the use of openly licenced information resources or content infrastructure as facilitators in the creation of educational materials. In the first phase, course teaching material was developed using a prompt engineering strategy, predefined standards, and a prompt script. As a second step, we experimented with designing a custom chatbot model connected to a pre-defined corpus of source documents. The results demonstrated that the final teaching material required careful revision and optimisation before use in an actual instructional programme. The experimental design of the custom chatbot was able to query specific user-defined documents. Taken together, these findings suggest that the strategic and well-planned use of ChatGPT technology in content creation can have substantial benefits in terms of time and cost efficiency. In the context of information literacy, the results provide a practical and innovative solution to integrate the new technology tool into instructional practices.

Keywords: ChatGPT; information literacy; instructional design; open educational resources (OERs)

1. Introduction

Recent developments and the growing accessibility of generative artificial intelligence (AI) tools have had a significant impact on the higher education sector, opening remarkable opportunities for the use of new technology, while also forcing the community to re-examine traditional approaches to issues such as academic integrity and transparent science [1,2]. Generative Pre-Trained Transformer (ChatGPT 3.5) is a statistical model for generating new data based on variable relationships in a dataset. It is a specific application of a large language model (LLM), which represents a neural network trained on a large dataset. Its natural language processing capabilities enable it to generate well-structured text, written in fluent language, and based on input prompts.

Essentially, ChatGPT is a chatbot capable of remarkable simulation of human conversation and work, utilising the vast amount of data on which it has been trained. The underlying algorithms enable it to provide coherent responses to questions by filling in data from predetermined datasets. This means that ChatGPT, as a form of generative AI, creates content by combining a variety of information to provide responses to user requests.

In the context of higher education, technology initially raised concerns primarily regarding traditional assessment methods, such as written assignments and standardised tests [3]. At the formal level, recommendations have been developed for higher education institutions with basic guidelines on the use of ChatGPT in higher education and its application in teaching and learning, administration, and community involvement. Proposed solutions, in addition to providing clear guidance for students and instructors and reviewing and updating policies relating to academic integrity, also include updating higher education courses to include AI literacy and core AI competencies and skills. When choosing to use AI technology in higher education institutions, an important factor to consider is open-source access [4]. In terms of potential opportunities for educators, higher education faculties are encouraged to adapt their instructional strategies, using ChatGPT in flipped learning and student-centred approaches. Innovative assessment tasks should focus on students' creative and critical thinking abilities, rather than devising AI-proof solutions [3]. Students should be provided with clear guidance and expectations for using chatbots responsibly, including proper attribution and ethical considerations [5].

Considering the role of academic libraries in this rapidly changing information landscape, discussions have focused on understanding the future possibilities of AI text generators and the possible impact on library services. The limitations concerning training data, bias, and false information are emphasised as concepts crucial for information professionals [6]. The natural language processing abilities of ChatGPT could be used to improve search and discovery, reference and information services, cataloguing, metadata generation, and content creation [7]. Suggested applications of ChatGPT in academic libraries include the creation of virtual assistants, complementing reference services (such as a simulated reference librarian), improving user experience, the selective dissemination of information, optimising collection development, and copy cataloguing. ChatGPT technology offers possibilities for integration into library discovery tools and simplifying repetitive aspects of the research process. Academic librarians can use the content generation abilities of the tool in lesson planning and the creation of open educational resources (OER) [8,9].

A whole range of AI-powered commercial applications targeted at the higher education market appeared during the first half of 2023, ranging from literature review apps, research support tools, article summarisers, and content analysers to personalised reading assistants. The management of AI expectations is crucial for academic libraries in light of the overwhelming interest in these tools and products. Consequences faced by library professionals include reshaping their roles and becoming involved in quality assessment, algorithm literacy, the co-development of AI tools, and new search methods [10]. The persistent problem of the reliability of sources retrieved by ChatGPT can be solved by developing frameworks such as CORE-GPT, which integrates LLMs with a large-scale corpus of open-access full-text scientific articles from Core to provide a reliable and fact-based platform to answer questions [11].

In this context, it is important to note that mature AI products are costly and require large-scale training data. In addition, developers working in this field are highly trained professionals. Academic libraries, as traditionally underfunded institutions, face the problems of budget, data access, and human resources.

In summary, ChatGPT represents cutting-edge technology in natural language processing and artificial intelligence. By exploring its application in instructional design, this research expands the understanding of how emerging technologies can be integrated into educational contexts. Additionally, aligning with the principles of open educational resources, the research suggests innovative approaches to creating openly licenced resources for information literacy education.

The purpose of this paper is to investigate possible applications of ChatGPT in a small-scale environment and a specific field: instructional design for information literacy courses in academic libraries. The starting point for our research is to use openly licenced informational resources, i.e., 'content infrastructure', as facilitators in creating educational resources. It has already been widely recognised that LLMs, which use deep learning techniques to generate text based on prompts, contribute greatly to the speed of creating information resources that comprise the content infrastructure [12].

Information literacy is a critical skill in the digital age, and academic libraries play a vital role in promoting it. This research addresses the challenge of effectively teaching information literacy by leveraging ChatGPT to create interactive and adaptive learning experiences tailored to individual student needs. Through practical implementation, this research can provide insights into the effectiveness of using ChatGPT in instructional design for information literacy courses. Additionally, research contributes to the establishment of best practices and guidelines for integrating AI technologies into educational settings.

Our study focused on developing a strategy to produce an information literacy syllabus and additional resources using ChatGPT. Using free-of-charge platforms, our objective was to investigate the possibilities of creating content that would represent OER under the common definition [13]. In this study, we investigated the following questions:

1. How can the output be used in an actual classroom environment?
2. How can the chat model be adapted for a limited set of source documents?

The research questions were addressed in two phases. In the first phase of the study, the ChatGPT model was directed to produce a final text output according to predefined standards and a prompt script. In the second phase, we experimented with introducing a limited corpus of resource documents and designing a small model that could respond to queries.

The prompt script used to train the model, the output generated by this script, and the custom model instructions are all available as Supplementary Materials accompanying this article.

2. Materials and Methods

2.1. Setting the Methodological Context

Academic libraries serve as central hubs for information dissemination, resource access, and scholarly support within educational institutions. Information literacy plays a central role in this context. Due to technological advancements, the traditional definition of information literacy has been supplemented by a new concept of AI literacy. AI literacy entails a basic understanding of how artificial intelligence and machine learning work: their underlying logic and their limitations [14]. By studying ChatGPT's role in instructional practices, this research aims to bridge theory and practice, paving the way for the informed adoption of AI tools.

For the purpose of this study, ChatGPT was chosen over other generative AI tools for several reasons. Firstly, OpenAI's solution was unveiled in November 2022 and had reached a staggering number of users in the space of a few months. It should be noted that the preliminary phase of this research began in March 2023. Although the generative AI market has exploded since then, the statistics show that ChatGPT was still the most widely used text generation AI tool in the world in 2023, with an approximate 20% share of users [15]. Secondly, the decision to use ChatGPT was based on the availability of support infrastructure and community knowledge. The growing community of users on the GitHub developer platform offered invaluable advice in the process of experimental setup.

In the first part of the investigation, we adapted the method used by Eager and Brunton [16]. The method is focused on prompt engineering, i.e., writing effective text-based inputs to guide AI models in generating teaching and learning content. External reviewers, selected based on professional profiles and experience in higher education, are involved in evaluating the generated content. The method of collecting textual responses from reviewers was selected for the purpose of obtaining qualitative insights.

In the second part of the research, our approach was mainly based on testing available tools for the customisation of the chat model. The preparation stage involved the extensive research of available solutions for designing chatbots trained with user-defined content. The fundamental requirement was to find a low-code or no-code method of designing and developing custom applications. The low-code approach enables users to design and create applications using intuitive graphical tools, thus reducing the traditional coding requirements. Users with basic coding skills can use low-code tools to develop and integrate custom applications. In comparison, no-code approaches eliminate the need for programming knowledge, allowing nontechnical users to develop applications without writing any code. The proposed method allows a broader range of users to participate in building similar solutions.

In the experimental design of the custom chatbot model, we used a limited dataset with a focus on a specific topic. The main advantages of using a limited dataset are as follows:

- Computational resources: smaller datasets require less computational power for training, which can be advantageous for resource-limited environments;
- Storage and processing: limited datasets reduce storage and processing requirements.

2.2. Developing a Strategy to Produce an Information Literacy Syllabus Using ChatGPT

The model training strategy was developed for a specific task and with a specific goal in mind. The key concepts considered were the intended audience, purpose, and tone of the content generated by the model. The four steps of the strategy used in this study were as follows:

1. Assign the model the role of a subject-matter expert (SME);
2. Provide the model with context;
3. Instruct the model to use specific standards and input data;
4. Instruct the model to use a specific output format.

The task selected for this study was designing information literacy instruction material for a postgraduate course: 'Academic/Scholarly Writing', delivered at the University of Split Faculty of Economics, Business and Tourism, as part of the international postgraduate study programme in Economics and Management. The role, context, standards, and output format were developed following a detailed analysis of the course implementation plan.

Role assignment: The model was assigned a role by specifying a particular identity or perspective to ensure that the text generated by the model was relevant and appropriate for the intended audience and purpose. The prompt used for this purpose was 'Act as an instructional designer'.

Context: Specifying the intended task provided additional context for the model. The prompt used for this purpose was as follows: 'You are tasked with supporting an academic to design a syllabus for a 1st year PhD course in Academic/Scholarly Writing'.

Standards and input data: The parameters and conditions were introduced using input data from the course implementation plan (number of lecture and seminar hours, percentage of e-learning, course objectives, learning outcomes, course content, and assessment methods) and information literacy standards for higher education [17].

Output format: The model was instructed to organise the content in a specific format (e.g., modules, short summary, table, etc.).

2.3. Model Training

Training the model was conducted using a prompt script (see the Supplementary Materials, Document S1). The prompt script contained a linear series of structured prompts or queries of inputs. A systematic approach to communicating with the model is termed 'prompt engineering', and includes fine-tuning the questions in order to produce more relevant results and coherent output. The CLEAR framework for incorporating prompt engineering into information literacy instructions suggests the following method to improve AI-generated responses [18]:

- Concise: brevity and clarity in prompts;
- Logical: structured and coherent prompts;
- Explicit: clear output specifications;
- Adaptive: flexibility and customisation in prompts;
- Reflective: continuous evaluation and improvement of prompts.

The basic prompts for writing steps include defining specific outcomes and the format and type of content. After testing the initial prompt, the model output was reflected and evaluated. If the results failed to meet the expectations, the prompt was adjusted and the process was repeated. A well-written prompt includes the following components: verbal action, action outcome, task parameters, narrowed topic, alignment with goals, and any constraints or limitations, if applicable [16]. The prompt script used to train the model contained prompt examples aligned with learning goals, assessment criteria, critical thinking, problem-solving skills, and student engagement and interaction.

2.4. Conducting the Review Process

The evaluation of the final output of the ChatGPT model was carried out by two external reviewers with the following profiles: Academic Library Information Literacy Programme Coordinator and Assistant Professor of English Language. The reviewers received the raw output, without any interventions in the text. The only additions to the ChatGPT output included formatting into paragraphs and tables, for the purpose of facilitating the review process. The reviewers were informed of the purpose of the final document and the use of ChatGPT in the process of its preparation. Reviewers were asked to provide general comments, answering the following questions:

- Does it fit the purpose?
- Is it relevant to the context in which it is intended to be used?
- Is it coherent and well-organised?

2.5. Developing a Custom Chat Model

The proposed custom AI chatbot template combines the OpenAI architecture with a limited set of source documents. The selected set of documents is a list of required full textbooks and articles and additional course materials for the course 'Academic/Scholarly Writing', in the format of .pdf files. This part of the research was conducted using a GitHub account and applications and services available at no cost through the free plans offered by service providers. For the purpose of creating a custom AI chatbot, the following platforms were used:

- Flowise AI: versatile low-code/no-code platform designed to simplify the creation of applications utilizing LLMs. It offers a user-friendly drag-and-drop interface, enabling users to visualize and construct LLM apps with ease (https://flowiseai.com; accessed on 31 August 2023);
- Render: a unified cloud to build and run all apps and websites with free TLS certificates, global CDN, private networks, and auto-deploys from Git (https://render.com; accessed on 31 August 2023);
- Pinecone: a vector-based database that offers high-performance search and similarity matching (https://www.pinecone.io; accessed on 31 August 2023).

A detailed explanation of the steps is given in the Supplementary Materials, Document S2. The model design flow chart is shown in Figure 1.

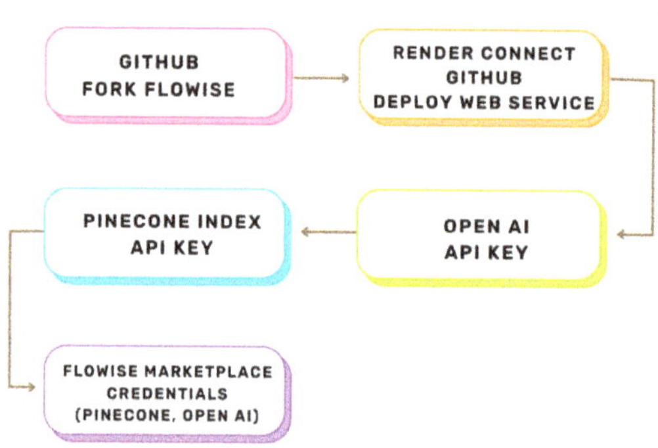

Figure 1. Model design flow chart.

3. Results

3.1. ChatGPT Output

3.1.1. Testing the Prompt Script

Conversation with the ChatGPT model using the prepared prompt script is available on the OpenAI website (https://chat.openai.com/share/6696bb02-c0a9-4693-8c7a-30f998fa5e1f, accessed on 29 January 2024). In a separate conversation, supplementary questions and script tasks were used to test how the model responds to questions related to student participation and interaction and critical thinking and problem-solving skills. (https://chat.openai.com/share/67c8ada7-5a4e-4aa7-9ebd-1d44f32988e6, accessed on 29 January 2024).

The results of the prompt script testing are presented in the format of a 15-page document (see the Supplementary Materials, Document S3) with the following subheadings:

- Introduction;
- Course Description (Course Objectives, Learning Outcomes, Course Contents, Course Schedule);
- Workshop Plan: "From Research Topic to Research Questions" (including facilitator notes and participant handouts);
- Assessment activities, criteria, and grading rubric;
- Interactive activity lesson plan (including facilitator notes and participant handouts).

The text was not changed or amended before the evaluation stage. ChatGPT answers were copied and pasted without any revisions. Limited formatting was applied to improve readability, and some sections were organised into tables.

3.1.2. Evaluation

The questions given to the reviewers reflected the basic evaluation criteria for the usability, relevance, and quality of AI-generated content. The reviews were given in the format of descriptive text and are presented in Table 1.

Table 1. Summary of reviewer's comments.

Document Section	Comment
Introduction	- The Introduction section is relevant for the context.
Course Description	- Course objectives and learning outcomes are well defined.
Learning outcomes	- In the Learning Outcomes section, formatting and style guidance, and plagiarism avoidance seem to be redundant elements at the academic level. One possible explanation could be that the tool cannot distinguish 'lower-order' and 'higher-order' skills from the Information Literacy Competency Standards for Higher Education. - Originality in scientific writing and understanding plagiarism are topics relevant at all levels of academic studies.
Course Schedule	- The structure of the Course Schedule is satisfactory - Module 1 in the Course Schedule section is unclearly formulated, as it seems unnecessary to spend as much as two weeks on the topic. - Detailed analysis of the content of other modules also indicates certain issues with clarity (e.g., addressed learning outcomes include vague phrases such as 'develop basic text analysis techniques' and 'establish coherence in scientific writing', without specifying which techniques or how to establish coherence.

Table 1. *Cont.*

Document Section	Comment
Workshop	- The workshop plan is well organised. - In terms of time management of the proposed workshop, the set time limit of 25 min for Activity 2: Advanced Literature Review and Refinement is definitely not enough for all planned activities. - One suggestion for the improvement of this section is to use one research topic selected by the workshop facilitator; students can conduct literature reviews and engage in discussion. In this way, the students could practice together, and for homework assignments each student could prepare their own research plan. - The volume of information proposed for the workshop could be separated into a combination of lectures and subsequent workshops, since it takes a significant amount of time to acquire advanced research skills. - The lecture should serve as an introduction to the set of instruments needed for formulating effective search strategies. - It should be noted that the students need to learn how to paraphrase, summarise, and condense a specific body of text without missing out on key information
Workshop notes (Advanced Resources Selection Criteria)	- The Key Concepts and Key Considerations sections contain excessive repetitions, while failing to clearly distinguish between the two areas. - The recommendation is to use only one set of clearly defined criteria for resource selection, instead of unsystematically listing various points that need to be addressed by the students. - Advanced Resources Selection Criteria should be written in a more accessible and clearer format.
Workshop notes (formulating a research question)	- Research Question criteria are clear and practical. Including examples for both well-formulated and poorly formulated research questions is a useful element and a good basis for discussion before the practical part of the workshop.
Assessment	- The Assessment section seems to be well developed. - Assessment criteria are applicable only after the mentioned skills are acquired, which is largely dependent on the students' learning pace.
Overall impression	The output document could be used only after an exhaustive editing process and certain interventions in the text, particularly in terms of adapting the complexity level to the required postgraduate level.

3.2. *Custom AI Chatbot*

3.2.1. Model Architecture

The final version of the model represents a Conversational Retrieval QA Chain, a chain for performing question-answering tasks with a retrieval component. Documents stored in a vector database are the source documents for retrieval. The chatbot generates responses from the user-defined data set, obtaining the most appropriate response. The final version of the custom chatbot model is shown in Figure 2.

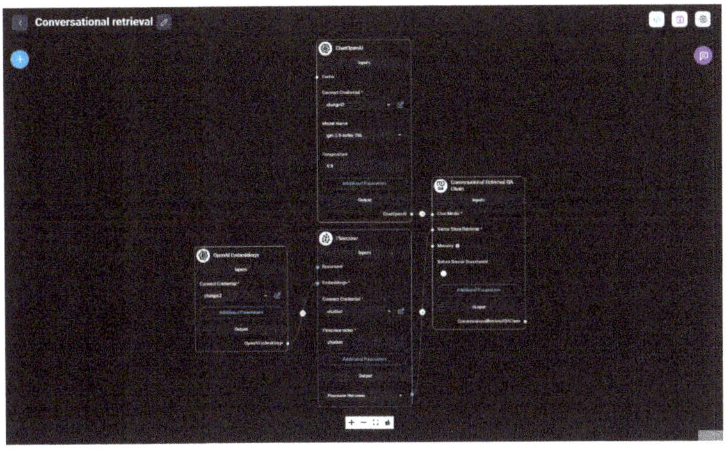

Figure 2. Final version of the custom chatbot model.

3.2.2. Model Testing

The model was tested using simple queries from the corpus text, to check the responsiveness of the model. For the purpose of this paper, we only limited the test to confirm that the chatbot is able to retrieve information from the pre-defined corpus of documents. Figure 3 shows an example of the chatbot's answer to a question formulated to ask specific information from a source text. In this example, the default temperature setting of 0.9 was used, resulting in a more creative and diverse output. Compared to the actual content of the book, it was found that the model's answer included all the points in the relevant chapter, but also added one irrelevant point, not directly related to the question.

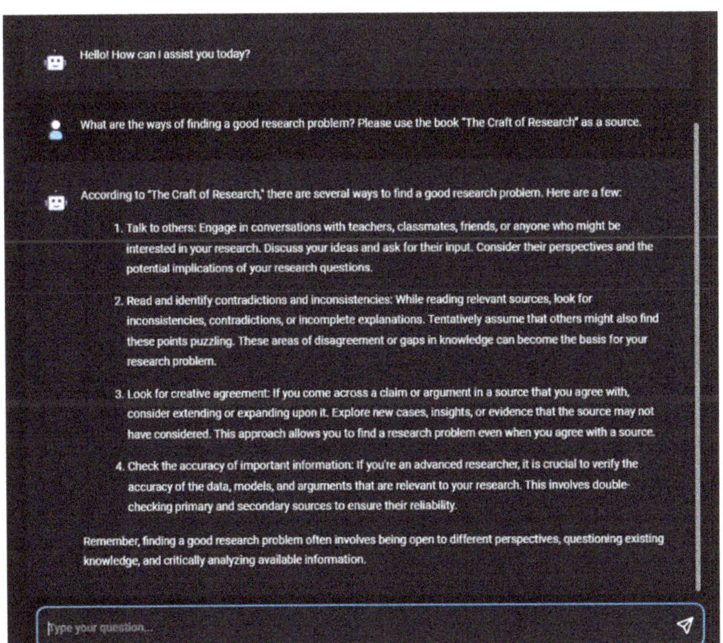

Figure 3. Custom model answering a query.

4. Discussion

4.1. ChatGPT as an Instructional Design Tool

In the first part of the study, we investigated how the output of ChatGPT could be used in instructional design. The specific subject of instruction is information literacy in academic libraries. The instructional material produced by ChatGPT was evaluated by experts in the field, as presented in Section 3. Although earlier studies have explored the possible impacts of ChatGPT in academic libraries [6,7], they have not explicitly addressed the instructional potential of the tool.

The feedback from the reviewers highlights both strengths and areas for improvement in the proposed course content. The introduction and objectives are well defined, but some learning outcomes appear redundant. Additionally, clearer criteria for resource selection and improved lecture content are recommended. Overall, the reviewers concluded that the document required editing to match the required postgraduate level.

Our study suggests that instructors may benefit from using ChatGPT as assistive tool in preparing course materials. Compared to the results of the Eager and Brunton case study [16], our results confirm that exploring features and experimenting with functionalities of ChatGPT is necessary to better understand their capabilities and limitations. In their case study, Eager and Brunton explored the transformative impact of AI-augmented teaching and learning in higher education, emphasizing the need for educators to develop prompt engineering skills to effectively utilize AI tools such as ChatGPT. The authors advocate for the strategic integration of AI and present a case study on AI-assisted assessment design to illustrate practical applications.

The results of the same case study demonstrated a significant time-saving potential of implementing AI-augmented processes in instructional design. However, this point could be argued in terms of the extensive preparation time required for drafting a prompt script that can elicit consistent and contextualised responses from ChatGPT.

In summary, the reviewers concluded that the final output generated by ChatGPT could only be used in the actual classroom environment after careful review and optimisation. Most of the positive comments of the reviewers refer to the structure of sections (course objectives, learning outcomes, workshop plan, and assessment). This was expected, since ChatGPT is trained on a large set of teaching materials and can easily generate lesson plans in an acceptable format. Instructional prompts written in a precise and unambiguous language and including fixed elements such as topic, learning goals, and type of content produced a satisfactory result. In-depth analysis of the text revealed issues concerning the vagueness of phrases generated by ChatGPT and the lack of clarity in defining certain concepts. Despite being instructed to operate as a subject-matter expert on both levels (general settings and role assignment), the model fails to retain the complexity level of the output. The described shortfalls could be resolved by training the model further and adjusting the context, instruction, or constraints.

The results can also be interpreted in the context of open educational resources. In our research, we focused on the integration of ChatGPT into teaching practices as a supportive tool for creating syllabi and lesson plans, which are listed as common open educational resources. We can compare our findings with some of the expectations voiced in the open education community regarding the use of generative AI tools in OER creation process. Lalonde [19] suggests that educators may shift towards becoming editors who validate and revise AI-generated content, ensuring its accuracy and credibility.

Wiley [12] anticipates that such tools will reduce the costs associated with drafting OERs, as they can produce reasonable first drafts much more quickly than humans. Although they can support the initial creation process, producing quality content would still require human expertise. Our results have confirmed these expectations. Reviewers' comments can easily be translated into reflective prompts, guiding the model to produce content that is more appropriate for the context or task. Repeated testing of prompts and iterating the process can give more refined results.

Methods and strategies for prompt engineering presented in this study can be used to prepare personalized lesson plans, tailored specifically to students' needs and interests. ChatGPT can be used in course design by suggesting optimal course structures, the sequencing of topics, and learning objectives. Instructors can use the presented strategies to create educational content such as quizzes, exercises, and study materials.

Overall, in the dynamic landscape of education, the integration of new technologies holds immense promise for instructional designers. Specifically, the adoption of AI tools introduces a twofold positive impact. First, it significantly enhances efficiency by automating routine tasks, allowing instructional designers to allocate more time to strategic planning and pedagogical considerations. ChatGPT can serve as a dynamic "sounding board", enabling the rapid prototyping of ideas and immediate feedback. Second, content creation with the assistance of ChatGPT has implications for open educational resources (OERs). However, rigorous evaluation is essential. Designers must assess the accuracy, relevance, and alignment of ChatGPT-generated output with learning objectives. The "four-eyes principle"—collaborative review by multiple experts—ensures the integrity of instructional materials before publication. Looking ahead, empirical research should explore the impact of AI-powered instructional design on student satisfaction and academic self-efficacy. Understanding these links would inform future design practices and ensure that AI-enhanced learning experiences align with educational goals.

4.2. Custom Chatbot Model

Adetayo [8] mentions several cases of the deployment of chatbots in a library setting, listing examples of virtual reference service chatbots from as early as 2013. These examples fall under the category of traditional chatbots, which are task-specific and rule-based, i.e., producing predefined responses and lacking the ability to handle complex queries or unclear user input. In comparison, ChatGPT offers a variety of unique benefits, including contextual understanding, natural language processing, flexibility, and adaptability.

Testing of the custom chatbot model confirmed that ChatGPT can be adapted to retrieve answers from a pre-defined set of source documents. It was found that the chatbot is able to retrieve information from the corpus. Recently developed software development kits enable the embedding of tools for accessing pre-defined custom data. The process requires minimum coding knowledge and could be used as a cost-effective solution for building custom AI chatbots. The most important limitation is the fact that we only used free plans offered by software developers to build the custom chatbot, which have restrictions on storage volume, available tokens, etc. However, the results provide the foundation for the in-house development of applications. The initial idea could be developed even further, depending on the selected text corpus fed into the model, allowing the user 'to have a conversation with the text'.

More research is needed to investigate how temperature settings and additional parameters influence the behaviour of the chatbot. There are several options available to tweak the configuration [20]. Temperature is the most common and determines the predictability level of the words generated by the model. A temperature of 0 means that the model will always choose the words with the highest probability of being appropriate. This makes it more likely to produce the same response if the request is repeated, but will be less creative and may appear less natural. Increasing the temperature allows the LLM to consider progressively less probable subsequent words. At really high temperatures, the sampling distribution from which the model is pulling for each word is so large that it tends to produce erratic and even non-sensical results. At a temperature of 2, which is the current maximum for OpenAI's models, the result becomes disordered and unusable. Generally, a temperature value should be selected on the basis of the desired trade-off between coherence and creativity for a specific application.

The top probability parameter (top_p) is associated with the top-p sampling technique, or nucleus sampling. GPT models generate the next word by assigning probabilities to all possible next words in its vocabulary. With top_p sampling, instead of considering the entire vocabulary, the next word will be sampled from a smaller set of words that collectively have a cumulative probability above the top_p value. The top_p ranges from 0 to 1 (default), and a lower top_p means that the model samples from a narrower selection of words, making the output less random and diverse. Given that top_p impacts output randomness, OpenAI recommends adjusting either top_p or temperature, but not both.

Additional parameters available for a custom-built model are the frequency penalty and the presence penalty. Both parameters address the problem of repetition in generated text and can be used to suppress or increase word frequency, thus impacting the diversity of language use.

4.3. Proper Attribution and the Responsible Use of Content Generated Using ChatGPT

The results of our study should be considered in the context of the proper attribution and responsible use of ChatGPT-generated content. Atlas [5] discusses best practices for the attribution of ChatGPT in various contexts. The standard requirement for any content used in a higher education setting is to disclose the use of LLM in the acknowledgement section or equivalent. This requirement is also in line with the OpenAI sharing and publication policy, which stipulates that the role of AI must be clearly disclosed for any content co-authored with the OpenAI API. Furthermore, the content must comply with the OpenAI content policy or terms of use.

At the end of April 2023, UNESCO published a quick-start guide [4] that addresses some of the main challenges and ethical implications of the use of generative artificial intelligence in higher education. The central theme of the document is academic integrity and the urgent need to adapt traditional assessment strategies, only marginally suggesting that teachers, researchers, and students need to be trained on how to improve the queries they pose to ChatGPT. In our study, our objective was to put a more positive spin on the dominant narrative and investigate how instructors can use the tool to improve teaching and learning practices.

In its 2023 position paper on artificial intelligence tools and their responsible use in higher education learning and teaching [21], the European University Association (EUA) highlights the need to review and reform teaching and assessment practices and adapt them in a such a manner as to ensure that AI is used effectively and appropriately. While urging the academic community to consider the academic integrity, e.g., obligation to reference the use of AI in academic and student work, and recognising the many shortcomings associated with the use of AI, EUA also acknowledges numerous potential benefits for academic work, including improved efficiency, personalised learning, and new ways of working. Our findings support this position, as they provide practical insight into how the model can be applied.

Finally, an interesting example of the implementation of recommendations comes from an independent higher education institution [22], in the form of guidance on the use of ChatGPT for teaching and learning. Since it is not accepted as a supported tool, if instructors choose to use ChatGPT for their teaching, they assume responsibility for reviewing and vetting concerns with accessibility, privacy, and security. The possibility of privacy and copyright violations is highlighted. The guidelines also include suggestions for teaching strategies, focusing on the limitations of the dataset, concerns about academic dishonesty, and economic and environmental implications. This rather conservative approach does not include any recommendations for instructors on how to explore the benefits offered by ChatGPT. However, this could be interpreted in terms of university policy and the fact that the university renegotiated a system-wide agreement with Microsoft to include Microsoft Azure OpenAI, as a solution offering higher data security and compliance with regulatory requirements.

4.4. AI in Education: Opportunities, Challenges, and Ethical Considerations

If we consider the long-term impact on student learning outcomes, possible benefits for the students may include enhanced user experiences, personalised learning, streamlined searching and study assistance.

According to a survey conducted among undergraduate students in summer 2023 in the United States [23], 85% of undergraduate students confirmed that they would feel more comfortable using artificial intelligence (AI) tools if they were developed and vetted by trusted academic sources. Furthermore, 65% also agreed that AI will improve how students learn rather than have negative consequences on learning. In this broader context of AI in education, our results validate the need to explore the potential of developing trustworthy and verified content.

While students may embrace the timesaving potential of newly available tools, this could lead to students' over-reliance on generative AI technology. It is certain that the old assessment schemes will have to be replaced, shifting focus to a student's process and approach. Instructors will be expected to use more inventive and varied assessment methods. In this context, it should be noted that tools advertised as being able to detect AI writing in student essays have been found to be very unreliable, especially if the authors are non-native English speakers [24].

The issue of academic integrity is closely associated with AI literacy. We believe that that the focus and the main concepts of information literacy remain unchanged—the reflective discovery of information, the understanding of how information is produced and valued, and the use of information in creating new knowledge and participating ethically in communities of learning [14]. How to apply these concepts in the new reality, while boundaries related to the use of generative AI tools are continuously shifting, is a challenge to be faced by library professionals. As core institutions of universities, academic libraries are important stakeholders in the innovation activities related to the digital transition of European higher education [25], focused on the common task of preparing students for the workforce of the future.

5. Conclusions

In this paper, we have presented results of two possible uses of ChatGPT in information literacy instruction in higher education. Firstly, we have outlined a method for producing written teaching material with the assistance of ChatGPT, demonstrating how the model can be used effectively. Secondly, we developed and tested a small-scale custom AI chatbot that can be used as a supplementary teaching tool.

Our research has highlighted the importance of adopting a strategic approach to interacting with LLMs such as ChatGPT, i.e., setting clear goals and defining purposes, context, and constraints of how the model interacts with the user. Prompt engineering remains an exploratory activity that requires a number of iterations. The proposed custom chatbot model provides a starting point, which can be modified for different topics or applications in instructional design.

Some limitations should be considered. Firstly, the current study was not specifically designed to test the user experience or measure student satisfaction with AI-generated instructional material. The custom chatbot model proposed in this study is designed to provide students with immediate and relevant answers to the questions related to the course materials stored in the model database. This form of learning support can motivate students to become more active in the learning process. However, the actual impact on student motivation and academic performance can only be measured by conducting in-class experiments.

Secondly, the custom chatbot model that we tested in our study is a basic configuration with a small workload. Such models can be tested using free plans; however, more serious deployment of any custom chatbot would require proprietary paid solutions. Small-scale models are appropriate for environments such as a single academic course or the testing of capabilities before considering purchasing an AI tool from a vendor. The effective evaluation of such tools requires some knowledge of how the tool was built and is necessary before any institution-wide decision is made.

The findings of this study can be helpful in understanding the collaborative potential of generative AI as a teaching assistant, tasked with planning activities, managing classroom time, and designing performance-based assessments. The method used to design a custom chatbot model can be applied in the instructional design of digital higher education courses and programmes. Considered in a more limited context, ChatGPT can allow academic libraries to bridge the financing gap caused by limited public funding, enabling the in-house development of applications adapted to the specific needs of a library.

Future studies could investigate whether the content produced in this way can meet the quality assurance standards for open educational resources (OERs). Copyright issues and the licencing of remixed content are additional areas that need to be explored further.

The integration of AI in education is approached with a healthy dose of scepticism, which can be summarised in one question: How can we trust the quality of information? The underlying concern is the transparency of data on which the models are trained. The models are vulnerable to biases in the source material or the selection process for training data, affecting the behaviour of models and causing misrepresentations or factual distortions. Additionally, learning and processing algorithms can be used to grant privilege to one group of users or reinforce stereotypes. Privacy and data security may be compromised during interaction with generative AI models, as personal data improve the quality of training models. All these concerns have been continuously voiced and addressed in the academic community since the launch of ChatGPT. As institutions traditionally focused on issues such as diversity, ethics, privacy and fair use, academic libraries occupy a crucial role in developing university frameworks on the use of generative AI tools and establishing policy guidelines. In this process, libraries can serve as meditators and collaborators, while information professionals need to educate their communities on how to navigate the new information landscape.

In conclusion, all stakeholders in the higher education process should be aware that the arrival of generative AI would bring about a paradigm shift comparable to the one we saw with the arrival of the World Wide Web. Therefore, there is a significant need to constructively integrate these tools into higher education instructional practices.

Supplementary Materials: The following supporting information can be downloaded at: https://www.mdpi.com/article/10.3390/publications12020011/s1, Document S1: Prompt Script; Document S2: Custom Model Instructions; Document S3: Prompt Script Output.

Author Contributions: Conceptualization, J.M. and M.S.; methodology, J.M.; software, M.S.; validation, M.S.; investigation, J.M. and M.S.; resources, J.M. and M.S.; writing—original draft preparation, J.M.; writing—review and editing, J.M.; visualization, M.S. All authors have read and agreed to the published version of the manuscript.

Funding: This research received no external funding.

Data Availability Statement: The original contributions presented in the study are included in the article/Supplementary Materials; further inquiries can be directed to the corresponding author/s.

Conflicts of Interest: The authors declare no conflict of interest.

References

1. Heaven, W.D. ChatGPT Is Going to Change Education, Not Destroy It. MIT Technology Review. Available online: https://www.technologyreview.com/2023/04/06/1071059/chatgpt-change-not-destroy-education-openai (accessed on 29 April 2023).
2. Tools Such as ChatGPT Threaten Transparent Science; Here Are Our Ground Rules for Their Use. Nature. Available online: https://www.nature.com/articles/d41586-023-00191-1 (accessed on 4 September 2023).
3. Rudolph, J.; Tan, S.; Tan, S. ChatGPT: Bullshit Spewer or the End of Traditional Assessments in Higher Education? *J. Appl. Teanching* **2023**, *6*, 342–363. [CrossRef]
4. Sabzalieva, E.; Valentini, A. ChatGPT and Artificial Intelligence in Higher Education: Quick Start Guide. UNESCO International Institute for Higher Education in Latin America and the Caribbean. Available online: https://www.iesalc.unesco.org/wp-

content/uploads/2023/04/ChatGPT-and-Artificial-Intelligence-in-higher-education-Quick-Start-guide_EN_FINAL.pdf (accessed on 3 September 2023).
5. Atlas, S. ChatGPT for Higher Education and Professional Development: A Guide to Conversational AI. Available online: https://digitalcommons.uri.edu/cba_facpubs/548/ (accessed on 8 September 2023).
6. Fernandez, P. "Through the Looking Glass: Envisioning New Library Technologies" AI-Text Generators as Explained by ChatGPT. *Libr. Hi Tech News* **2023**, *40*, 11–14. [CrossRef]
7. Lund, B.; Ting, W. Chatting about ChatGPT: How May AI and GPT Impact Academia and Libraries? *Libr. Hi Tech News* **2023**, *3*, 26–29. [CrossRef]
8. Adetayo, A.J. Artificial Intelligence Chatbots in Academic Libraries: The Rise of ChatGPT. *Libr. Hi Tech News* **2023**, *40*, 18–21. [CrossRef]
9. Cox, C.; Tzoc, E. ChatGPT: Implications for Academic Libraries. *Coll. Res. Libr. News* **2023**, *84*, 99–102. [CrossRef]
10. Kim, B. AI, Generative AI, and Libraries. In Proceedings of the INCONECSS Community Meeting No. 6. Artificial Intelligence: Impact on Services, Online, 12 June 2023.
11. Pride, D.; Cancellieri, M.; Knoth, P. CORE-GPT: Combining Open Access Research and Large Language Models for Credible, Trustworthy Question Answering. In *Linking Theory and Practice of Digital Libraries;* TPDL 2023. Lecture Notes in Computer Science; Alonso, O., Cousijn, H., Silvello, G., Marrero, M., Teixeira Lopes, C., Marchesin, S., Eds.; Springer: Cham, Switzerland, 2023; Volume 14241, pp. 146–159. [CrossRef]
12. Wiley, D. AI, Instructional Design, and OER. Improved Learning. Available online: https://opencontent.org/blog/archives/7129 (accessed on 29 April 2023).
13. The 2019 UNESCO Recommendation on Open Educational Resources (OER): Supporting Universal Access to Information through Quality Open Learning Materials. UNESCO Digital Library. Available online: https://unesdoc.unesco.org/ark:/48223/pf0000383205 (accessed on 25 April 2023).
14. IFLA Statement on Libraries and Artificial Intelligence. International Federation of Library Associations and Institutions (IFLA). Available online: https://www.ifla.org/wp-content/uploads/2019/05/assets/faife/ifla_statement_on_libraries_and_artificial_intelligence.pdf (accessed on 20 March 2024).
15. Statista. Leading Generative Artificial Intelligence (AI) Text Tools Market Share of Users Globally in 2023 [Graph]. In Statista. Available online: https://www.statista.com/forecasts/1423975/world-generative-ai-text-tool-market-share (accessed on 20 March 2024).
16. Eager, B.; Brunton, R. Prompting Higher Education Towards AI-Augmented Teaching and Learning Practice. *J. Univ. Teach. Learn. Pract.* **2023**, *20*. [CrossRef]
17. Framework for Information Literacy for Higher Education. Association of College & Research Libraries. Available online: http://www.ala.org/acrl/files/issues/infolit/framework.pdf (accessed on 17 August 2023).
18. Lo, L.S. The CLEAR Path: A Framework for Enhancing Information Literacy through Prompt Engineering. *J. Acad. Librariansh.* **2023**, *49*, 102720. [CrossRef]
19. Lalonde, C. ChatGPT and Open Education. Available online: https://bccampus.ca/2023/03/06/chatgpt-and-open-education (accessed on 20 March 2024).
20. OpenAI API Documentation. Available online: https://platform.openai.com/docs/api-reference/chat (accessed on 28 February 2024).
21. Artificial Intelligence Tools and Their Responsible Use in Higher Education Learning and Teaching. Available online: https://eua.eu/component/attachments/attachments.html?id=4048 (accessed on 28 February 2024).
22. Understanding AI Writing Tools and their Uses for Teaching and Learning at UC Berkeley. Available online: https://teaching.berkeley.edu/understanding-ai-writing-tools-and-their-uses-teaching-and-learning-uc-berkeley (accessed on 29 April 2023).
23. McGraw-Hill. Share of Undergraduate Students Who Have Various Opinions on the Use of Artificial Intelligence (AI) Tools in Higher Education in the United States in 2023 [Graph]. In Statista. Available online: https://www.statista.com/statistics/1445975/us-undergraduate-students-opinions-on-the-use-of-ai-in-education (accessed on 20 March 2024).
24. Liang, W.; Yuksekgonul, M.; Mao, Y.; Wu, E.; Zou, J. GPT detectors are biased against non-native English writers. *Patterns* **2023**, *4*, 100779. [CrossRef] [PubMed]
25. European Commission. 2020. Digital Education Action Plan (DEAP) Communication. Available online: https://education.ec.europa.eu/sites/default/files/document-library-docs/deap-communication-sept2020_en.pdf (accessed on 20 March 2024).

publications

MDPI

Article

Research Data Management in the Croatian Academic Community: A Research Study

Radovan Vrana

Faculty of Social Sciences and Humanities Zagreb, University of Zagreb, 10000 Zagreb, Croatia; rvrana@ffzg.unizg.hr

Abstract: This paper presents the results of an empirical research study of Croatian scientists' use and management of research data. This research study was carried out from 28 June 2023 until 31 August 2023 using an online questionnaire consisting of 28 questions. The answers of 584 respondents working in science were filtered out for further analysis. About three-quarters of the respondents used the research data of other scientists successfully. Research data were mostly acquired from colleagues from the same department or institution. Roughly half of the respondents did not ask other scientists directly for their research data. Research data are important to the respondents mostly for raising the quality of research. Repeating someone else's research by using their research data is still a problem. Less than one-third of the respondents provided full access to their research data mostly due to their fear of misuse. The benefits of research data sharing were recognized but few of the respondents received any reward for it. Archiving research data is a significant problem for the respondents as they dominantly use their own computers prone to failure for that activity and do not think about long-term preservation. Finally, the respondents lacked deeper knowledge of research data management.

Keywords: research data; research data sharing; research data reuse; research data management; Croatia

1. Introduction

The last three decades have been marked by some major developments and innovations in digital technologies, providing support to newly created paradigms of e-science and open science and to activities related to research data such as creating, collecting, storing, sharing and use of the data, making modern science increasingly digital and data-intensive [1]. Since the 1990s and the advent of e-science, research data have become a popular topic of many theoretical and practical scientific endeavors. During the same period, scientific and professional papers and books have been published describing the positive impact of research data on the development of modern science. Consequently, the value of research data has increased and, for many, they have become a new currency in science [2]. Additionally, the increased quantity of research data created a strong demand for suitable infrastructure: hardware, software, data management policies and other supporting documents and, of course, human resources for supervising the process of research data management. Suitable infrastructure, as the most crucial component, provides support to scientists, helping them focus on research itself rather than on technical and administrative aspects of research like manipulating large quantities of data.

Although science has been technically and structurally advancing through the second part of the 20th and the beginning of the 21st century, activities related to research data in digital format still lack the ease and speed with which researchers could create, collect large, complex datasets and manage them so they could be openly available. Due to the lack of adequate human (professional), technical (infrastructural) and document (guidelines and policies) support, researchers fall behind in the development and acquisition of knowledge and skills necessary to ensure data quality, integrity, shareability, discoverability and reuse over time [3]. Furthermore, researchers are not always able to spend enough time on research data management, while at the same time they neglect other activities. "Managing research data is time-consuming, costly and tedious, requiring additional resources that are not available to all researchers" [4] (p. 23). To achieve better and easier research data management with the aim to provide open access to research data resulting in broader availability and accessibility of research data and better cooperation between individual researchers, academic institutions and society must build uniform support to all researchers, which includes necessary technical infrastructure (individual, institutional and national), research data management policies and guidelines and training for researchers in research data management procedures. All these activities require a choice of good technical resources, time, good organization, professionally trained human resources (in IT and information sciences) and substantial long-term funding. The outcome of these activities will create a difference between research communities, those who are able to manage research data and those who are not.

This paper focuses on the management and use of data created by the Croatian scientists working in all scientific disciplines. Research data are "at the very heart of the knowledge life cycle and are a central ingredient to the scholarships of discovery, integration, teaching, engagement" etc. [5] (p. 345). The aim of data management is not only to facilitate the long-term preservation of research data but also to make these data available for two crucial activities: possible sharing and possible reuse by interested scientists. The latter activity adds most value to research data in general. Providing access to research data is achieved mostly by sharing research data with other people, directly upon their request or by providing access in institutional general purpose digital repositories or in specialized data repositories.

2. Materials and Methods

2.1. *Research Data Management, Data Sharing, Data Reuse*

In a growing data-intensive world, it has become difficult to assess the current volume of data created by vast number of industrial, personal and scientific endeavors, let alone predict future volumes of created data. Yet, there is a projection according to which, by 2025, global data volume will reach 175 zetabytes [6], a volume that will require meticulously created management procedures; otherwise, data will be lost, regardless of their origin or purpose. The main origin of data today is digital technology, the proliferation of which resulted in the production of big volumes of data. In the academic community, data have become an integral part of daily research processes and are more frequently counted as a standard research output [7], thus becoming a strategic commodity as well as a starting point for activities such as data sharing and data reuse (secondary analyses and new research).

Data sharing has become a symbol of open science. It promotes the transparency of research [8], provides evidence of a proper research, adds content to services such as data archiving, enables reuse (secondary analysis and comparative research), generates new research questions and results in new findings from the same data, thus creating value for money and added value [9–11]. It can inspire new and multiple perspectives [12] and enables the quality of the research through seamlessness and documentation [13,14]. Provision of data for the research quality control was a focus of the paper by Askarov, Doucouliagos, Doucouliagos and Stanley [14], in which the authors investigated publication bias and questionable research practices and they found out that data sharing and reuse may have reduced inflated statistical significance and decreased publication bias. Statistical significance was produced by authors wanting to make their paper appear more significant than it was, to be able to publish their research. Data sharing may be a tool to suppress these issues, at least partially.

Data sharing has been a holy grail of modern science. In 2023, data sharing is still not a universal activity in science, and it is burdened by barriers presented by individuals or institutions. As Khan, Thelwall and Kousha [7] point out, there have been many studies of data sharing and reuse in narrow contexts but there are no substantial science-wide research studies in this topic due to disciplinary differences. For instance, in the biotechnology sector, "individual privacy as well as intellectual property concerns often stand in the way of sharing data" [15]. Other problems include the time needed to share data effectively and fact that shared data are rarely used [7].

Successful research data sharing has technical and financial prerequisites. Technical prerequisites (personal computers, high-bandwidth Internet connections, capable storage servers) must be met so that the interested researchers can access data. Continuous funding is another prerequisite for facilitating future data reuse. The costs are related to datasets' size, complexity, different data types, metadata and documentation about the data, data quality, reuse value of data (so called "hot" and "cold" data) [16] and access control to data [17]. There are also two big categories of data that should be considered—qualitative and quantitative; both require different kinds of preparation for use [9]. Data management exists to ensure that data are "findable and accessible to both designated users and reusers, on a day-to-day basis" [16] (p. 1). However, in real life, researchers encounter different problems like diverse devices and diverse virtual places that contain digital content fragmentally, due to the fast accumulations of digital content shared [18].

The second important activity, research data reuse (a result or consequence of data sharing) includes the reproduction and verification of past research, making the results of funded research available; it supports efficiency and collaboration in research [10], interdisciplinarity and enables more frequent citation [7]. It helps in generating new questions based on the existing data and, most generally, make the advancement of science possible [19]. One of the biggest if not the biggest goal of research data reuse is to introduce reproducibility as a research quality criterion by acknowledging "the strengths and weaknesses of different ways of validating results and learn as much as possible from the methodological precepts that guide different parts of science" [20] (p. 142). Despite many efforts and initiatives in the scientific community and outside of it, reproducibility of research remains a substantial and unsolved problem in modern science [21].

Today, digital data management and related activity—data reuse—have become interconnected and essential activities in academia and elsewhere as the amount of data grows exponentially with and projection that the amount of data will only grow in near future.

2.2. Data Sharing Benefits, Motivation and Obstacles

The benefits resulting from the sharing the research data for the research community include data discovery, reuse, validation and verification of data [5]. The motives to share data include journal publishing pressure, normative pressure, perceived effort, pressure by funding agencies, perceived career benefits and scholarly altruism [22].

There are also reasons why researchers do not like to share their research data. Fecher, Friesike and Hebing [10] pointed out that research data are still not common knowledge because researchers have fears and doubts about data sharing including endangering the right to publish their research results first and the possibility of data misuse. In addition, publications that publish research data lack sufficient formal recognition for this activity, and there are also no incentives for sharing research data, so researchers remain incentivized not to share data. The lack of incentives for acknowledging and crediting researchers for sharing their own data and citing others' research data remains an unsolved problem [23]. Moreover, the authors of research data claim that other researchers cannot use their data properly because data can only exist in the specific context of their creation and, without the methodologies and ontologies adopted at the time of creation, other researchers cannot adapt data into their new research (projects) [23]. Lin Yoong, Turon, Grady, Hodder and Wolfenden [24] (p. 18) singled out the following problems to data sharing: "review access (e.g., located behind a paywall), logistical issues (e.g., lack of metadata, standardized reporting of measures, challenges with accessibility and data quality), motivational barriers (e.g., lack of author incentives), legal impediments (e.g., issues around ownership of data, intellectual property [IP]) and ethical concerns". In addition to the previously mentioned reasons (which sometimes overlap between authors), Mallasvik and Martins [12] compiled additional reasons like unavailability of funds or poor levels of knowledge regarding adequate formats and reusability, lack of recognition for those who willingly engage in research data sharing, high financial costs, uncertainties surrounding loss of control intellectual property rights and potential threats to national security.

Lewis [25] listed the rewards of good management of research data including significant potential benefits for academic research itself:

- The ability to share research data, minimizing the need to repeat work in the laboratory, field or library;
- Ensuring that research data gathered at considerable cost are not lost or inadvertently destroyed;
- The retrieval, comparison and co-analysis of data from multiple sources can lead to powerful new insights;
- The ability to verify or repeat experiments and verify findings, particularly important amid growing national and international concern about research integrity;
- New research themes—and in particular cross-disciplinary themes—can emerge from the re-analysis of existing data or comparisons with new data; increasingly, data may become the starting point for new research as well as represent an output from current research.
- If at least some of these issues were resolved, researchers would be prepared to share data if there were rewards for doing so [26].

2.3. Data Storing and Archiving

A prerequisite of achieving high reproducibility of research is reliable, long-term access to digital content [27], which is often missing or neglected. This long-terms access to research data is now commonly required by publishers, academic institutions and research project funding agencies [7,13,28,29]. However, research data are not always widely available for reuse as data sharing is not fully appreciated by researchers across all disciplines [2], restricting the reuse of data.

To be able to share research data, one must store and possibly archive them (long-term storage). Data archiving has become essential since the early days of personal computers and continues to be one of the challenges for modern science. The main goal of data archiving is to make quantitative and qualitative research data available for reuse.

Research data can come in different types: in open or controlled forms that include raw data, research data, sensitive data, government data and big data [30].

Sometimes, data are used only once and only by authors who collected data, interpreted and used them in an article, a report or a conference paper. After the publication of a journal article, conference paper or a book chapter, data may become hard to find as they were stored on scientist's personal computer, external hard disk and elsewhere where data are not widely available (online). Nowadays, in the era of Big Data, data storing and archiving has become even more important because data can be easily lost and therefore become unavailable. This is especially true for older data collected, described and stored in places other than institutional, national or other digital repositories.

Furthermore, as previously noted, "scientific publications increasingly require that the data relevant to an article be available through archives" [13] (p. 6). On the personal level, personal computing users continue to experience catastrophic personal data loss [31].

3. Research Study

3.1. Research Design

The purpose of this research study was to explore current sentiments of the Croatian scientists about three aspects of use and management of research data, which were also research questions this study aimed to answer:

Q1: Do the Croatian scientists use research data of other scientists?
Q2: Do the Croatian scientists offer access to their research data?

Q3: What are the modes of storing research data?

The main hypothesis of this research is that the Croatian scientists are only moderately ready for data sharing and data reuse, which also only partially fulfils their research mission in society.

3.2. Research Instrument

To collect data about the current sentiment of the Croatian scientists about other scientists' and their own research data, an online questionnaire (Appendix A) was designed. The questionnaire consisted of 25 closed-type questions and three open-type questions, a total of 28 questions.

The research was initiated by sending invitations to the mailing list of the Croatian scientists and by asking scientists to send the same invitation to their colleagues (snowballing). The research used a convenience sampling method. This type of sampling was used as it was not feasible to divide members of the mailing list according to their age, research experience or other criteria. The findings, especially the demographics data, helped in differentiating scientists who participated in this research.

The invitation for participation in this research was sent by e-mail to the mailing list of the Croatian scientists administered at the "Ruđer Bošković" Research Institute in Zagreb, Croatia. The mailing list included 15,000 scientists, postgraduate students, professional associates, librarians and other employees from the system of science and higher education of the Republic of Croatia, who at some point during participation in various conferences, workshops, through consent in the Croatian scientific bibliography "CROSBI" [32] or through the application form subscribed to the mailing list and received the contents sent to it. According to the Croatian Research Information System [33], which quoted the Register of scientists and artists of the Republic of Croatia created by the Ministry of science and education of the Republic of Croatia [34], 29641 scientists were listed in the register on 19 April 2024.

The research started on 28 June 2023, and the access to the questionnaire was closed on 31 August 2023.

A total of 650 respondents participated in this research study by answering questions in the online questionnaire. Since only the respondents working in science and on science-related jobs were relevant to this research study (assistant, senior assistant, assistant professor, associate professor, full professor, full professor tenure, full professor retired, professor emeritus, scientific associate, scientific advisor, Ph.D. students), a total of 584 of 650 who participated in the study were filtered out) and their answers were further analyzed. It must be noted that not all respondents answered every question in sections of questionnaire related to them, so the number of answers per question varies from question to question. That means that 584 respondents equal approx. 1.97% of all Croatian scientists listed in the register of scientists and artists of the Republic of Croatia.

4. Findings

The findings are divided into four sections (A–D) in accordance with the structure of the questionnaire.

4.1. Use and Non-Use of Other Researchers' Data

The first section (Section A) of the research aimed at identifying whether the respondents used other scientists' research data or not.

A total of 584 respondents answered the initial questions about using or not using other scientists' research data. A total of 428 respondents (73.3%) used the research data of other scientists while 156 respondents (26.7%) did not use other scientists' research data.

As an addition to this question, the scientists in this research study were asked about their years of service. The scientists had been working in science for 20 years (median). These data about years of service were compared to the number of respondents who used research data of other scientists (not all respondents provided their years of service by choice): 1–10 years of service, 82 respondents used other scientists' research data; 11–20 years of service, 185 respondents used other scientists' research data; 21–30 years of service, 114 respondents used other scientists' research data; 31–40 years of service 65 respondents used other scientists' research data and 41+ years of service, 16 respondents used other scientists' research data. The years of service for the respondents who did not use other scientists' research data were the following: 1–10 years of service, 35 respondents did not use other scientists' research data; 11–20 years of service, 59 respondents did not use other scientists' research data; 21–30 years of service, 35 respondents did not use other scientists' research data; 31–40 years of service, 23 respondents did not use other scientists' research data and 40+ years of service, three respondents did not use other scientists' research data. Again, not all respondents provided data on their years of service.

The number of scientists in this research study who claimed they used other scientists' research data is high. It is impossible to back up such results with actual numbers of the exchanged research data because researchers use other scientists' data from different resources, sometimes internally (within the same lab, department or university) and frequently there is no exact proof of these activities. This is the reason why this result should be investigated further by conducting interviews with scientists.

A total of 153 respondents (3 out of the total of 156 who did not use other scientists' data left this question unanswered) did not use other scientists' research data for the following reasons (multiple answers were possible). Table 1 shows the detailed reasons for not using other scientists' data. Predefined reasons were offered to the respondents. About three-quarters of the respondents (from those who did not use other scientists' data) did not have a need for other scientists' data, while other respondents encountered different obstacles like paywall, membership, passwords or licenses. Such obstacles have usually been met by scientists in recent decades and they have caused the inability to access published papers and books. Now they have been extended to research data.

Table 1. Not using other scientists' data (N = 153).

Not Using Other Scientists' Data	Respondents (N)	Percentage %
I did not have need for other scientists' research data	120	78.4
Access to research data was restricted by a paywall	16	10.5
Access to research data was restricted by membership in an academic institution, etc.	18	11.8
Access to research data was restricted by password	11	7.2
User interface was too complex	6	3.9
I had to agree to licenses and other terms	8	5.2
User interface used a language I did not know	1	0.7
Other reasons	12	7.8

After answering this question, the respondents were asked to go to section D of the questionnaire related to storing research data and providing access to them.

4.2. Sending Requests for Research Data to Other Scientists

The next section (section B) of the questionnaire was dedicated to sending requests for research data of other scientists.

Direct contact with other scientists for gaining access to their research data was not the first choice of the respondents (N = 182) (Table 2). Another big block of results started with scientists who sent 2–3 requests (N = 163), while the rest of the respondents sent much less requests.

The respondents were also asked to list the sources from whom or from which they received research data (Table 3), suggesting that they used multiple resources for finding research data before accessing them.

Table 2. Sending requests for data of other scientists (N = 428).

Sending Requests for Data of Other Scientists	Respondents (N)	Percentage %
Did not send a single request for research data to other scientists	182	42.5
Sent one such request	52	12.1
Sent 2–3 requests	163	38.1
Sent 6–9 requests	31	7.2
Sent 10 or more requests	34	7.9

Table 3. Information on sources of research data (multiple answers were possible) (N = 419).

Sending Requests for Data of Other Scientists	Respondents (N)	Percentage %
Scientific publications (articles in magazines, books and proceedings)	379	90.5
Colleagues with whom I work directly (in the same department, etc.)	279	66.6
Colleagues working in scientific institutions outside Croatia	270	64.4
Digital repositories outside Croatia	270	64.4
Digital repositories in Croatia	203	13.7
Colleagues working in other scientific institution in Croatia	196	27.3
Colleagues with whom I work in the same institution	182	43.4
Other sources not listed here	16	3.8

Next, the respondents were asked to estimate the number of their own requests sent to other scientists to gain access to research data (Table 4).

Table 4. Estimation of the number of their requests sent to other scientists (N = 420).

Estimation of the Number of Their Requests Sent to Other Scientists	Respondents (N)	Percentage %
Did not send requests to other scientists	165	29.1
Sent one request	49	8.6
Sent 2–5 requests	142	25.0
Sent 6–9 requests	30	5.3
Sent 10 or more requests	34	5.99

Not all the delivered requests were answered positively: 0—16 respondents; 1—30 respondents; 2—22 respondents; 3—24 respondents; 4—five respondents; 5—eight respondents; 6—three respondents; 7—one respondent; 10—six respondents; 15—one respondent. Some respondents added their own answers instead of choosing pre-defined answers: "a few"—four respondents; "less than half"—two respondents; "half"—three respondents; "almost all"—22 respondents; "all"—116 respondents

The next four questions were oriented toward estimating the importance of research data for different phases of research in general: acquiring ideas for new research (N = 580), preparation of research (N = 575), execution of research (N = 580) and verifying the quality of research (N = 579).

Figure 1 shows the importance of research data in four aspects of research: developing ideas for new research, preparation of research, implementation of research and finally, increasing quality of research. The respondents considered increasing quality of research as the most important aspect of research data over other aspects of use of research data.

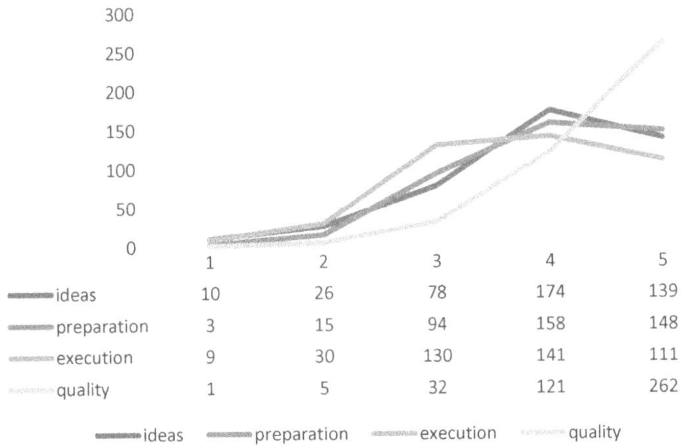

Figure 1. Importance of research data for different phases of research (1—least important; 5—most important).

In the last question in this section, the respondents were asked whether they ever tried to repeat the scientific research of another scientist based on their available research data (Table 5).

Table 5. Succes of repeating scientific research of another scientist (N = 423).

Success of Repeating Scientific Research of Another Scientist	Respondents (N)	Percentage %
No	253	59.8
Yes, I succeeded/I managed to get identical results	95	23.2
Yes, but I could not get identical results	75	17.7

The issue of reproducibility of research in science is a problem that has been well described in the scientific literature. Scientists involved in repeating one's research would most certainly like to obtain identical results to those in the original research/analysis.

This was the last question in this section that was aimed only at scientists who use other scientists' research data.

The next section (section C) was oriented toward the frequency of use of other scientists' research data as a template for new research, comparison with other research and quality control of research.

4.3. *Providing Access to Own Research Data*

The remaining part of the research study results included all the respondents, regardless of whether they used other scientists' research data or not.

The respondents were asked to estimate the number of requests they received for their own research data in the last five years (Table 6).

Table 6. Number of requests they received for their research data in the last five years (N = 584).

Number of Requests They Received for Their Research Data in the Last Five Years	Respondents (N)	Percentage %
One request	56	9.6
2–5 requests	183	31.3
6–9 requests	46	7.9
More than 10 requests	49	5.0
Did not receive any request	254	43.5

Almost half of the respondents did not receive any request from other scientists for their research data, while over half of the respondents (cumulatively) received one or more requests.

The next part of this research study was oriented toward providing access to research data for other scientists (the second part of the questionnaire).

In addition to the information found in Table 7, the respondents (N = 459) were divided according to their working experience (years of services), regardless of the mode of providing access to research data: 1–10 years of service, 82 respondents opened access to their research data; 11–20 years of service, 169 respondents opened access to their research data; 21–30 years of service, 127 respondents opened access to their research data; 31–40 years of service, 69 respondents opened access to their research data and 40+ years of service, nine respondents opened access to their research data. Next, the respondents who did not open access to their research data (N = 152) were divided according to their years of service: 1–10 years of service, 35 respondents did not open access to their research data; 11–20 years of service, 60 respondents did not open access to their research data; 21–30 years of service, 36 respondents did not open access to their research data; 31–40 years of service, 19 respondents did not open access to their research data and 40+ years of service, two respondents did not open access to their research data.

Table 7. Providing access to research data for other scientists (N = 640).

Providing Access to Research Data for Other Scientists	Respondents (N)	Percentage %
Access to all their research data without restrictions	186	29.1
Did not provide access to research data	157	24.5
Partial access to their research data without restrictions	148	23.1
Access to their research data in some other way not listed in pre-defined answers	120	18.8
Partial access to research data under certain conditions (IP address, password, etc.)	21	3.3
Access to all their research data with some restrictions (IP address, password, etc.)	11	1.7

While scientists shared their research data partially or fully, they also identified problems they encountered or feared encountering during the sharing of their own research data with other scientists (Table 8).

Table 8. Research data sharing problems (N = 430) (multiple answers were possible).

Research Data Sharing Problems	Respondents (N)	Percentage %
Fear of misuse of your research data in the form of idea theft	135	31.4
Excessive consumption of time	128	29.8
Fear of misuse of data of your research data in the form of theft of authorship	112	26.0
Lack of research data sharing infrastructure	110	25.6
Technical problems when sharing scientific research data	106	27.0
Lack of knowledge about how to share information about other scientists' data	99	23.0
Fear of misuse of your research data for commercial purposes	70	16.3
Costs of storing and sharing research data with others	44	10.2
There was no problem	27	6.3
Law restrictions and GDPR	5	1.2
Instead of research data, published works were shared	4	0.9
Improper or lack of citations	3	0.7
Research data were published in journals	3	0.7

Research data sharing depends on the good will of scientists, but it also depends on a potential system of recognition received for this activity.

Receiving recognition for sharing research data is one of the most important moments in scientists' careers, as it acknowledges scientists' efforts in certain areas. Table 9 shows that almost none of the respondents received a recognition for sharing their research data, which does not motivate scientists to start sharing their research data in the future.

Table 9. Recognition received for sharing research data (N = 488).

Recognition Received for Sharing Research Data	Respondents (N)	Percentage %
Received recognition or an award once	9	1.8
Received recognition several times	22	4.5
Never received recognition	457	93.7

The results presented in Table 10 indicate the awareness of practical aspects of opening access to research data like researchers' visibility, creating partnerships, transparency, quality and citations, which are benefits found at the top of the list (first five choices). Advancement in academic career and receiving recognition for opening/providing access to research data were least selected by the respondents. The complete lack of recognition or inadequate recognition for researchers for opening access to their research data was indicated in the previous question, and the same answer in this question was ranked very low and perceived to be less important by the respondents in this research study.

Table 10. Benefits of opening access to research data to other researchers (N = 457) (multiple answers were possible).

Benefits of Opening Access to Research Data to Other Researchers	Respondents (N)	Percentage (%)
Increasing your visibility in the scientific community	348	76.2
Creating partnerships in the preparation and implementation of scientific research	324	70.9
Increasing the transparency of scientific research	306	67.0
Increasing the quality of new scientific research	277	60.6
Increasing the citation of your scientific papers and scientific research data	249	54.5
Inspiration for starting new scientific research	237	51.9
Increasing the responsibility of scientists for conducting scientific research and presenting the results of that research	204	44.6
Confirming the accuracy of your scientific research results	201	44.0
Reducing the burden on scientists by using already existing scientific research data	134	29.3
Spotting mistakes in the scientific research of other scientists	117	25.6
Obtaining funds and/or equipment for the implementation of new research	84	19.0
Advancement to a higher scientific title based on storage activities and sharing of scientific research data	68	14.9
Receiving an award or recognition	34	7.4
Other	6	1.3
I see no benefit in providing access to my research data	5	1.1

To be able to provide access to research data, researchers must be offered some type of training/education about the process of research data management.

Based on the results in Table 11, researchers should be offered education about research data management if the scientific community in general expects them to share their research data on a wider scale.

Table 11. Training/education about the process of research data management (N = 455).

Training/Education about the Process of Research Data Management	Respondents (N)	Percentage (%)
Live lectures	24	5.3
Live workshops	24	5.3
University course	4	0.9
Live course	11	2.4
Webinars	71	15.6
Did not receive any of education about research data management	321	70.6

The next section (section D of these findings and the third part of the questionnaire) in the research study was dedicated to data archiving, a general and crucial precondition for data sharing and data reuse.

4.4. Research Data Storing and Archiving

The first question in this section was about devices or places for storing research data. Table 12 suggests that the respondents store their research data most frequently on their own computer at work, which is potentially very dangerous in the case of computer failure. Additionally, they stored research data on network drives in the cloud, which can also be dangerous if the network connection is lost, in the case of a security breach or due to another type of failure to access the data. Storing research data on offline external drives (and possibly on different locations) is a much better solution than storing data only on one's computer at work or on a shared computer. Digital repositories are not so popular, while there is a growing number of general types of repositories and data-only repositories worldwide available to scientists from different countries.

Table 12. Storing research data (N = 428) (multiple answers were possible).

Storing Research Data	Respondents (N)	Percentage (%)
On your own computer at work	255	59.6
On a network drive in the cloud	126	29.4
On an external hard drive	114	26.6
On an external SSD	48	11.2
In the institutional digital repository	46	10.8
On a shared computer at work where they store the contents of scientific research	30	7.0
I do not independently store scientific research data	8	1.9
On optical media	6	1.4
On a shared computer at work where they store the contents of scientific research	3	0.7

File format is a highly important element in research data archiving. The choice of data file format (Table 13) depends on the area of science in which different devices are used for the acquisition of data (by taking a record of a phenomenon, by recording measurements, etc.). Table 13 shows the great versatility of file formats. Some of them are standardized and appear in all areas of science, while some can be found only in particular areas of science and relate to some type of laboratory instrument paired with a computer, etc.

Time spent on data archiving is one of the biggest time eaters when considering a scientist's (monthly) workload. The results in Table 14 show that more than one-third of the respondents spend less than one hour monthly on data archiving, and that more than three-quarters of the respondents (cumulatively) spend up to 5 h monthly on data archiving. While the time spent on data archiving may differ from one research area to another and may depend on the type of research, the results show that more than three-quarters of the respondents do spend up to 5 h a month on data archiving, which is a positive result.

Table 13. File formats of research data (N = 428).

Research Data File Formats	Respondents (N)	Percentage (%)
Text files (TXT, DOC, DOCX, ODF, XML, PDF itd.)	399	93.2
Still pictures (TIFF, JPEG, PNG, SVG itd.)	268	62.6
Datasets (TSV, CSV, XLS, XLSX, XML, JSON itd.)	200	46.7
Video (MPEG4, MPEG2, QuickTime)	65	15.2
Geospatial data (ESRI, OGC, Geo PDF, GEOTIFF, etc.)	44	10.3
Sound (PCM, AIFF, MP3 itd.)	41	9.6
Other formats and applications related to specific formats like: .fasta, .abi; databases; BIN, CCS, MAT; simulator files and program code; Dwg, Excell, grib, NetCDF and other binary files; LOG, FCHK, CIF, SDF, TRJ, mgf, raw NMR specters (FID); NVvivo software; opj; various output formats of specific software; different programming languages; spss (multiple answers); SQL (dump); various database backup formats; statistical software files; Web GIS baza databases; XLS SPW	25	5.8
None of these formats	5	1.2

Table 14. Time spent on research data archiving (N = 623).

Time Spent on Research Data Archiving	Respondents (N)	Percentage (%)
Less than an hour	251	40.3
1–5 h	248	40.0
6–10 h	56	9.0
More than 10 h	32	5.1
I do not spend any time at all archiving the data of my scientific research	58	9.3

Data archiving requires knowledge about online or offline storage systems, file formats, metadata creation for data description and institutional policies for data archiving. The Croatian scientists were asked to rate their knowledge about research data archiving. A total of 644 respondents provided answers on a scale from 1 (no knowledge at all) to 5 (excellent knowledge). The results in Table 15 indicate that they acquired a certain amount of knowledge about data archiving but there is still space to reach a more advanced level of knowledge.

Table 15. Rating one's own knowledge about research data archiving (N = 644).

Research Data Archiving Level of Knowledge	Respondents (N)	Percentage (%)
1	42	6.5
2	173	26.9
3	271	42.1
4	129	20.0
5	29	4.5

5. Discussion

Empirical research studies of this type are a good base for solving different problems in research data management and could enable comparative analyses of conditions for work in different areas of science.

The results of this research study on the Croatian scientists identified several problems in use and management of research data. Roughly three-quarters of the respondents claimed they used other scientists' research data, which is a very good result. Still, they ran into different obstacles like paywalls, memberships in institutions or technical issues, which are all globally present problems that remain unsolved. Therefore, they require additional efforts on the side of different stakeholders involved in scientific endeavors.

Some obstacles, like paywalls, require cooperation with information aggregators in the commercial sector and are subject to long-term negotiations with commercial publishers. Technical issues are more easily solved but can sometimes be expensive.

Generally, some of the encountered problems are local and infrastructural and can be solved rather easily (e.g., digital research data repositories), while other problems are global and require more money, time and effort to be solved on the international level (e.g., publishing fees and research data storing as a supplement to books and articles).

Almost half of the respondents did not obtain data by sending requests to other scientists to access their data, whether they did not have a need for research data or did not receive any answer from the scientists to whom they sent requests. This latter problem could be solved by storing data in open data repositories to alleviate the problem of spending too much time on direct communication with other scientists.

The use of other scientists' research data by a larger number of scientists is practical, as a single researcher cannot discover all the problems present in some areas of research.

Also on the practical side, most of the research data that the respondents use in their analyses or new research come from their colleagues from the same department or institution, who are easily accessible and are reliable sources of research data. Research data also come from colleagues from outside the country with varying but mostly positive outcomes.

This research study showed that the Croatian scientists consider research data to be important in several cases: for obtaining ideas for new research, its preparation and execution, which is expected (if one uses research data as a starting point). The most important quality of research data for the respondents is that they are a means to increase research quality as they view research data as tools for verifying and increasing research quality. Regarding the problem of bad reproducibility of someone's research, it has been extensively addressed in the scientific literature but the solution to this problem has not been found yet. One evident reason is the need for hyperproduction of scientific output in the form of published books and articles as proof of one's scientific abilities. The hyperproduction diminishes the research quality and focuses on bureaucratic criteria for academic advancement. A growing number of research studies therefore remain irreproducible due to different problems related to low quality, which was partially confirmed by this research study. A significant number of researchers in this research study did not try to reproduce someone's research by using his/her research data, while one-quarter of the respondents claim that they managed to reproduce research and obtain the exact same results. Clearly, the results are not good.

Archiving data is another big and important topic in global science covered by this research study. The Croatian scientists who participated in this research study store research data on their own desktop computer, which could lead to a disaster in case of hardware failure. There are also other technical solutions for storing research data other than desktop computers like cloud infrastructure and external drives, each with its own problems, but they are still more reliable for long-term storing/archiving research data than desktop computers used by one or even many scientists. One possible solution is that cloud infrastructure could be better marketed to scientists.

Knowledge about data archiving has not yet reached a desirable level at which scientists will have advanced knowledge on this topic. Their knowledge is currently at an intermediate level. In Croatia, scientists have an opportunity to store research data in the national digital repository system, specially made for the Croatian academic community.

The proper storing of research data enables data sharing and data reuse. However, data sharing is not a straightforward process since there are many administrative, legal and technical obstacles and fears like misuse of research data, excessive consumption of time while sharing data to other people, idea theft, etc. These are very serious problems that are present globally in academic communities and remain unresolved. The same problems are present in the Croatian academic community and were recognized by the scientists participating in this research study. Another area that can be further researched is the benefits of opening research data to other scientists. The benefits were also clearly recognized by the respondents, but are hardly present in their daily work, and this is especially true for receiving reward for data sharing, which is a practically non-existent occurrence.

Finally, education on how to manage research data has become necessary, yet close to three-quarters of the respondents did not receive any form of education. Education in research data management will help them to overcome obstacles and spend less time on research data management.

This research study confirmed the hypothesis according to which the Croatian scientists who participated in this research study are only moderately ready for data sharing and data reuse, which also only partially fulfils their research mission in society. They will have to put more effort to achieve better results in research data management to make data sharing and data reuse more easily doable, but they should also receive recognition and rewards for doing so. This study also provided answers to all three research questions, as discussed in this part of the paper.

6. Conclusions

Research studies on research data management have now become common. While there is global interest in making research data easily obtainable, there are also local particularities that still block easy data sharing and reuse. Today, we know more about the role of research data in designing and executing new research than we knew yesterday, but we still need more marketing on research data management processes and infrastructures supporting scientists. Science is in transition toward open science, and every development that helps scientists to better and more broadly communicate the results of their research is valuable. This research study on the Croatian academic community shows that the Croatian scientists are partially ready for open science. The presumption is (which should be further researched) that those scientists who are collaborating with their colleagues outside Croatia and sharing and using the same datasets they created are more open to the idea of data sharing and data reuse and are probably actively participating in open science.

Funding: This research received no external funding.

Data Availability Statement: The original contributions presented in the study are included in the article, further inquiries can be directed to the corresponding author.

Conflicts of Interest: The authors declare no conflict of interest.

Appendix A

Questionnaire

(1) In general, until the moment of your participation in this research, have you used data (regardless of their type) of scientific research by other scientists for the purposes of your scientific work?
   - (a) Yes, I use data from other scientists and scientists from their scientific research (go to question 3)
   - (b) No, I do not use the data of other scientists from their scientific research (mark the reasons for a negative answer in the next question)

(2) If your answer to the previous question was negative, please choose the reasons for not accessing scientific research data of other scientists. AFTER THIS QUESTION GO TO QUESTION 14!
   - (a) Access to scientific research data required a password;
   - (b) The interface of scientific research data sources is too complex to use;
   - (c) The scientific research data source interface uses a language I do not know;
   - (d) To access the data, I have to agree to license and other conditions that are unacceptable to me;
   - (e) To access scientific research data, it is necessary to be a member of a certain institution, professional society, etc.;
   - (f) I had no need to use the data of other scientists' scientific research;

(g) Access to scientific research data requires payment;
(h) Other:

Use of scientific research data

(3) Among the answers offered, choose the sources of scientific research data (EXCEPT DATA FROM YOUR OWN RESEARCH) that you use in your daily scientific work (it is possible to mark several answers).

(a) The information I receive from the closest colleagues with whom I work directly (in the department, etc.);
(b) Information I receive from other colleagues in the same scientific institution where I work;
(c) Information I receive from colleagues in other scientific institutions in Croatia;
(d) Information I receive from colleagues in scientific institutions outside Croatia;
(e) Data that I find in digital repositories of scientific information in Croatia;
(f) Data that I find in digital repositories of scientific information outside of Croatia;
(g) Information that I find in scientific literature (articles in magazines, books and proceedings);
(h) Other:

(4) According to your estimation, in the last 5 years, how many requests have you sent to a scientist/scientists to give you access to the data of their scientific research?

(a) One;
(b) 2–5 requests;
(c) 6–9 requests;
(d) 10 or more requests;
(e) No, so far I have not sent a request to other scientists.

(5) If you sent one or more requests, how many of your requests were answered positively? The importance of scientific research data

(6) Mark the IMPORTANCE that the scientific research data of other scientists have on your consideration of ideas for starting your new research? They have no importance; 1 2 3 4 5 They are extremely important.

(7) Mark the IMPORTANCE that the scientific research data of other scientists have in the preparation of your scientific research? They have no importance; 1 2 3 4 5 They are extremely important.

(8) Mark the IMPORTANCE that the scientific research data of other scientists have in the implementation of your scientific research? They have no importance; 1 2 3 4 5 They are extremely important.

(9) In general, do you consider publicly available scientific research data of other scientists IMPORTANT for increasing the quality of scientific research? They have no importance; 1 2 3 4 5 They are extremely important. The purpose of using scientific research data

(10) How often do you use the scientific research data of other scientists to control the quality of their scientific research?

(a) Constantly;
(b) Most often;
(c) Sometimes;
(d) Rarely;
(e) Never.

(11) How often do you use the scientific research data of other scientists for comparison with the results of your own research?

(a) Constantly;
(b) Often;
(c) Usually;
(d) Sometimes;

(e) Rarely;
(f) Never.

(12) How often do you take the data of scientific research of other scientists as a template for formulating research questions in your scientific research?

(a) Constantly;
(b) Most often;
(c) Sometimes;
(d) Rarely;
(e) Never.

(13) Have you ever tried to repeat the scientific research of another scientist based on the available data of their scientific research?

(a) Yes, but I could not get identical results;
(b) Yes, I succeeded/I managed to get identical results;
(c) No.

Enabling access to YOUR scientific research data to OTHER scientists

(14) According to your estimation, in the last 5 years, how many requests have you received from another scientist (or more) to grant them access to the data of your scientific research?

(a) One request;
(b) 2–5 requests;
(c) 6–9 requests;
(d) 10 requests and more;
(e) No, I have not received any request.

(15) If you received one or more requests, how many of these requests did you respond to positively?

(16) Have you provided access to the data of your scientific research at THIS MOMENT?

(a) Yes, I offer open access to ALL data from my scientific research;
(b) Yes, I offer open access to ONLY ONE PART of my scientific research data;
(c) Yes, I offer access to ALL the data of my scientific research with some restriction (password, IP address, etc.);
(d) Yes, I offer access to ONLY ONE part of the data of my scientific research with some restriction (password, IP address, etc.);
(e) I offer some form of access to the data of my scientific research that is not listed here;
(f) No, I have not provided access to my research data (partially or in full) (go to question 19!).

(17) If the answer to the previous question was POSITIVE, please answer whether you have ever received any form of recognition or award for providing access to the data of your scientific research to other scientists?

(a) Yes, but only once;
(b) Yes, more than once;
(c) No, never.

(18) What problems have you encountered when sharing data from your own scientific research?

(a) Excessive consumption of time;
(b) Costs of storing and sharing scientific research data with others;
(c) Technical problems when sharing scientific research data;
(d) Lack of knowledge about how to share information with others;
(e) Lack of data sharing infrastructure;
(f) Fear of data misuse of your scientific research in the form of idea theft;
(g) Fear of data misuse of your scientific research in the form of theft of authorship;

(h) Fear of misuse of your scientific research data for commercial purposes;
(i) Other:

(19) Providing access to the data of your scientific research to other scientists can be useful for:

(a) Increasing your visibility in the scientific community;
(b) Creating partnerships in the preparation and implementation of scientific research;
(c) Obtaining funds and/or equipment for the implementation of new research;
(d) Receiving an award or recognition;
(e) Advancement to a higher scientific title based on storage activities and sharing of scientific research data;
(f) Increasing the transparency of scientific research;
(g) Increasing the responsibility of scientists for conducting scientific research and presenting the results of that research;
(h) Increasing the quality of new scientific research;
(i) Reducing the workload of scientists by using already existing scientific research data;
(j) Inspiration for starting new scientific research;
(k) Spotting mistakes in the scientific research of other scientists;
(l) Increasing the citation of your scientific papers and scientific research data;
(m) Confirming the accuracy of the results of your scientific research;
(n) I see no benefit in providing access to the data of my scientific research;
(o) Other:

(20) In the last 5 years, have you participated in any form of education dedicated to the management of scientific research data?

(a) Yes, a live course;
(b) Yes, a live workshop;
(c) Yes, a live lecture;
(d) Yes, Webinar;
(e) Yes, a university course;
(f) No.

Storage and archiving of scientific research data

(21) Where do you most often INDEPENDENTLY store the data of your scientific research?

(a) On your own computer at work;
(b) On a shared computer at work where they store the contents of scientific research;
(c) To a network drive in the cloud;
(d) In the institution's digital repository;
(e) To an external hdd;
(f) To an external SSD;
(g) On optical media;
(h) I do not independently store scientific research data.

(22) What file formats do you use to store the data of your scientific research?

(a) Text files (TXT, DOC, DOCX, ODF, XML, PDF, etc.);
(b) Images (TIFF, JPEG, PNG, SVG, etc.);
(c) Video (MPEG4, MPEG2, QuickTime;
(d) Sound (PCM, AIFF, MP3, etc.);
(e) Datasets (TSV, CSV, XLS, XLSX, XML, JSON, etc.);
(f) Spatial data (ESRI, OGC, Geo PDF, GEOTIFF, etc.);
(g) None of the above formats;
(h) Other:

(23) According to your estimation, how much time do you spend PER MONTH on archiving the data of your scientific research?
   (a) Less than an hour;
   (b) 1–5 h;
   (c) 5–10 h;
   (d) More than 10 h;
   (e) I do not spend any time at all archiving the data of my scientific research.
(24) Rate your level of knowledge about data archiving of scientific research. Completely without knowledge; 1 2 3 4 5 Excellent knowledge. Data on research participants
(25) In which field of science do you work?
   (a) Natural Sciences;
   (b) Technical sciences;
   (c) Biomedicine and healthcare;
   (d) Biotechnical sciences;
   (e) Social sciences;
   (f) Humanities;
   (g) Artistic area;
   (h) Interdisciplinary fields of science;
   (i) Interdisciplinary fields of art;
   (j) Other:
(26) Mark your gender.
   (a) Male;
   (b) Female;
   (c) I do not want to state.
(27) How much work experience do you have in jobs related to science?
(28) What is your current associate, scientific, scientific–teaching or artistic–teaching title? (Scientific–teaching professions choose only one answer!)
   (a) Scientific associate;
   (b) Senior research associate;
   (c) Scientific adviser;
   (d) Scientific advisor in permanent position;
   (e) Assistant;
   (f) Senior assistant;
   (g) Assistant professor;
   (h) Associate professor;
   (i) Full-time teacher;
   (j) Full professor in a permanent position;
   (k) Other:

References

1. Tenopir, C.; Rice, N.M.; Allard, S.; Baird, L.; Borycz, J.; Christian, L.; Grant, B.; Olendorf, R.; Sandusky, R.J. Data sharing, management, use, and reuse: Practices and perceptions of scientists worldwide. *PLoS ONE* **2020**, *15*, e0229003. [CrossRef]
2. Zenk-Möltgen, W.M.; Akdeniz, E.; Katsanidou, A.; Naßhoven, V.; Balaban, E. Factors influencing the data sharing behavior of researchers in sociology and political science. *J. Doc.* **2018**, *74*, 1053–1073. [CrossRef]
3. Whitmire, A.L.; Boock, M.; Sutton, S.C. Variability in academic research data management practices: Implications for data services development from a faculty survey. *Program* **2015**, *49*, 382–407. [CrossRef]
4. Rehnert, M.; Takors, R. FAIR research data management as community approach in bioengineering. *Eng. Life Sci.* **2023**, *23*, e2200005. [CrossRef]
5. Makani, J. Knowledge management, research data management, and university scholarship: Towards an integrated institutional research data management support-system framework. *Vine* **2015**, *45*, 344–359. [CrossRef]
6. Zinieris, M. Data: A Small Four-Letter Word Which Has Grown Exponentially to Such a Big Value. Available online: https://www2.deloitte.com/cy/en/pages/technology/articles/data-grown-big-value.html# (accessed on 12 April 2023).
7. Khan, N.; Thelwall, M.; Kousha, K. Data sharing and reuse practices: Disciplinary differences and improvements needed. *Online Inf. Rev.* 2023, *ahead-of-print*. [CrossRef]

8. Parks, N.; Fischer, T.; Blankenburg, C.; Scalfani, V.; McEwen, L.; Herres-Pawlis, S.; Neumann, S. The current landscape of author guidelines in chemistry through the lens of research data sharing. *Pure Appl. Chem.* **2023**, *95*, 439–450. [CrossRef]
9. Childs, S.; McLeod, J.; Lomas, E.; Cook, G. Opening research data: Issues and opportunities. *Rec. Manag. J.* **2014**, *24*, 142–162. [CrossRef]
10. Fecher, B.; Friesike, S.; Hebing, M.; Linek, S.; Sauermann, A. *A Reputation Economy: Results from an Empirical Survey on Academic Data Sharing*. Discussion Papers of DIW Berlin 1454, DIW Berlin, German Institute for Economic Research. Available online https://www.econstor.eu/handle/10419/107687 (accessed on 12 April 2023). [CrossRef]
11. Elman, C.; Kapiszewski, D.; Vinuela, L. Qualitative Data Archiving: Rewards and Challenges. *PS Political Sci. Politics* **2010**, *43* 23–27. [CrossRef]
12. Mallasvik, M.L.; Martins, J.T. Research data sharing behaviour of engineering researchers in Norway and the UK: Uncovering the double face of Janus. *J. Doc.* **2021**, *77*, 576–593. [CrossRef]
13. Joye, D. Qualitative or Quantitative? Data Archiving in Documentation, Research and Teaching. *Qual. Social. Res.* **2005**, *6* [CrossRef]
14. Askarov, Z.; Doucouliagos, A.; Doucouliagos, H.; Stanley, T.D. The Significance of Data-Sharing Policy. *J. Eur. Econ. Assoc.* **2023**, *21*, 1191–1226. [CrossRef]
15. Data sharing in the age of deep learning. *Nat. Biotechnol.* **2023**, *41*, 433. [CrossRef] [PubMed]
16. Pernet, C.; Svarer, C.; Blair, R.; Van Horn, J.D.; Poldrack, R.A. On the Long-term Archiving of Research Data. *Neuroinform* **2023**, *21*, 243–246. [CrossRef] [PubMed]
17. Perry, A.; Netscher, S. Measuring the time spent on data curation. *J. Doc.* **2022**, *78*, 282–304. [CrossRef]
18. Sinn, D.; Kim, S.; Syn, S.Y. Personal digital archiving: Influencing factors and challenges to practices. *Libr. Hi Tech.* **2017**, *35*, 222–239. [CrossRef]
19. Borgman, C.L. The conundrum of sharing research data. *J. Am. Soc. Form. Sci. Technol.* **2012**, *63*, 1059–1078. [CrossRef]
20. Leonelli, S. Rethinking Reproducibility as a Criterion for Research Quality. In *Symposium on Mary Morgan: Curiosity, Imagination, and Surprise (Research in the History of Economic Thought and Methodology, Vol. 36B)*; Emerald Publishing Limited: Bingley, UK, 2018; pp. 129–146. [CrossRef]
21. Limani, F.; Hajra, A.; Ferati, M.; Radevski, V. Research data repository requirements: A case study from universities in North Macedonia. *Int. J. Knowl. Content Dev. Technol.* **2023**, *13*, 75–100. [CrossRef]
22. Kim, Y.; Stanton, J.M. Institutional and Individual Factors Affecting Scientists' Data Sharing Behaviors: A Multilevel Analysis. *J. Assn Inf. Sci. Tec.* **2016**, *67*, 776–799. [CrossRef]
23. Horton, L.; Katsanidou, A. Purposing your survey: Archives as a market regulator, or how can archives connect supply and demand? *IASSIST Q.* **2012**, *35*, 18. [CrossRef]
24. Lin Yoong, S.; Turon, H.; Grady, A.; Hodder, R.; Wolfenden, L. The benefits of data sharing and ensuring open sources of systematic review data. *J. Public. Health* **2022**, *44*, e582–e587. [CrossRef] [PubMed]
25. Lewis, M.J. Libraries and the management of research data. In *Envisioning Future Academic Library Services*; McKnight, S., Ed.; Facet Publishing: London, UK, 2010; pp. 145–168. [CrossRef]
26. Kling, R.; Spector, L. Academic Rewards for Scholarly Research Communication via Electronic Publishing. CSI Working Paper. Available online: https://scholarworks.iu.edu/dspace/handle/2022/167 (accessed on 12 April 2023).
27. Faniel, I.M.; Frank, R.D.; Yakel, E. Context from the data reuser's point of view. *J. Doc.* **2019**, *75*, 1274–1297. [CrossRef]
28. Evertsz, N.; Bull, S.; Pratt, B. What constitutes equitable data sharing in global health research? A scoping review of the literature on low-income and middle-income country stakeholders' perspectives. *BMJ Glob. Health* **2023**, *8*, e010157. [CrossRef] [PubMed]
29. Wright, B.; Brunner, O.; Nebel, B. On the Importance of a Research Data Archive. In Proceedings of the AAAI Conference on Artificial Intelligence, New Orleans, LA, USA, 2–7 February 2018; p. 32. [CrossRef]
30. Zarghani, M.; Nemati-Anaraki, L.; Sedghi, S.; Noroozi Chakoli, A.; Row-hani-Farid, A. The Application of Open Science Potentials in Research Processes: A Comprehensive Literature Review. *Libri* **2023**, *73*, 167–186. [CrossRef]
31. Cocciolo, A.; Yanni, M. Personal Digital Archiving and Catastrophic Data Loss: Is it Getting Better? *Preserv. Digit. Technol. Cult.* **2022**, *51*, 133–139. [CrossRef]
32. Croatian Scientific Bibliography "CROSBI". Available online: https://www.croris.hr/crosbi/ (accessed on 19 April 2024).
33. Croatian Research Information System. Available online: https://www.croris.hr/?lang=en (accessed on 19 April 2024).
34. Register of Scientists and Artists of the Republic of Croatia. Available online: https://mzo.gov.hr/en (accessed on 19 April 2024).

publications

MDPI

Article

Towards an All-Ireland Diamond Open Access Publishing Platform: The PublishOA.ie Project—2022–2024

Jane Mahony

Trinity Long Room Arts & Humanities Research Institute, Trinity College Dublin, 2 Dublin, Ireland; mahonyjl@tcd.ie

Abstract: The Government of Ireland has set a target of achieving 100% open access to publicly funded scholarly publications by 2030. As a key element of achieving this objective, the PublishOA.ie project was established to evaluate the feasibility of establishing an all-island [Republic of Ireland and Northern Ireland] digital publishing platform for Diamond Open Access journals and monographs designed to advance best practice and meet the needs of authors, readers, publishers, and research funding organisations in Irish scholarly publishing. It should be noted in this context that there is substantial 'north–south' cooperation between public bodies in the Republic of Ireland and Northern Ireland in the United Kingdom, some of whom operate on what is commonly termed an 'all-island' basis. The project commenced in November 2022 and will run until November 2024, with the submission of a Final Report. This article originated as an interim project report presented in September 2023 at the PubMet2023 conference in Zadar, Croatia. The project is unique in its mandate to report on the feasibility of a shared platform that will encompass scholarly publishing across the two jurisdictions on the island of Ireland, which are now, post-Brexit, inside and outside the European Union (EU): the Republic of Ireland and Northern Ireland in the United Kingdom. The project is co-led by the Royal Irish Academy (RIA), Ireland's leading body of experts in the Sciences and Humanities, and the Trinity Long Room Hub Arts & Humanities Research Institute of Trinity College Dublin. There are sixteen partners and affiliates from universities and organisations from the island of Ireland. The feasibility study will be based on a review of the publishing practices in the island of Ireland, with gap analysis on standards, technology, processes, copyright practices, and funding models for Diamond OA, benchmarking against other national platforms, and specifications of the requirements, leading to the delivery of a pilot national publishing platform. A set of demonstrator journals and monographs will be published using the platform, which will be actively trialled by the partner publishers and authors. PublishOA.ie aims to deliver an evidence-based understanding of Irish scholarly publishing and of the requirements of publishers to transition in whole or in part to Diamond OA. This paper provides an interim report on progress on the project as of September 2023, ten months after its commencement.

Keywords: Ireland; open access books and journals; scholarly publishing; open research; Diamond Open Access

---

The Government of Ireland has set a target of achieving 100% open access to publicly funded scholarly publications by 2030 [1]. The *National Action Plan for Open Research 2022–2030* builds on a number of national policies and international recommendations, including the *National Principles on Open Access* (2012), the *European Commission Recommendation on access to and preservation of scientific information* (2018), the *National Framework on the Transition to an Open Research Environment* (2019), and the *UNESCO Recommendation on Open Science* (2021) [1].

Implementation of the *National Action Plan for Open Research* is led by Ireland's National Open Research Forum (NORF), established in 2017 and composed of expert representatives from policy, research funding, research performing, the library sector, research infrastructures, enterprise, and other key stakeholders in the research system across Ireland.

Implementation will be delivered under *Impact 2030: Ireland's Research and Innovation Strategy* [2] with the support of the Department of Further and Higher Education, Research, Innovation and Science.

As part of the overall action plan, the PublishOA.ie project has been tasked with conducting a feasibility study and pilot with a view to establishing a publicly owned, centralised national platform for Diamond Open Access (OA) journals and books, similar to the national platforms in Finland, Croatia, France, the Netherlands and Spain [1]. The platform will be designed to advance best practice and meet the needs of authors, readers, publishers, and funders in Irish scholarly publishing. The project is unique in its mandate to report on the feasibility of a shared platform that will encompass academic publishing across two jurisdictions, which are now, post-Brexit, inside and outside the EU: the Republic of Ireland and Northern Ireland in the United Kingdom. The project is co-led by the Royal Irish Academy (RIA) and Trinity Long Room Arts & Humanities Research Institute, working with a further sixteen institutions in the Republic of Ireland and Northern Ireland. It is funded by the National Open Research Forum (NORF). There are sixteen partners and affiliates from universities and organisations from the island of Ireland [1].

Diverse disciplinary perspectives, e.g., from the Irish Humanities Alliance, TCD Long Room Hub, Moore Institute at the University of Galway (Arts and Humanities), Irish Open Access Publishers (IOAPs) (multiple disciplines, including Social Sciences and STEM), Dublin Institute of Advanced Studies (DIASs) (Physics, Irish language), and the RIA (multiple disciplines, including STEM), will be integrated with international best practice. This will inform decisions on models and technical infrastructure tested and trialled to ensure their validity in the Irish context as well as their international validity.

Bibliodiversity and long-term sustainability are critical elements of the PublishOA.ie project. Publishing in Ireland must always regard the considerably larger and better-resourced publishing industry in the United Kingdom next-door, where Irish authors, writing in English, have historically been strongly represented [3]. The Republic of Ireland and Northern Ireland are both small countries, with current populations of approximately 5.28 million [4] and 1.9 million [5], respectively, totalling 7.18 million across the island.

Currently, there are 11 publishers of scholarly monographs in Ireland, but, by far, the majority of Irish interest monographs are published outside of Ireland, mainly in the UK, by large publishers such as Cambridge University Press (CUP), Oxford University Press, Liverpool University Press, and Manchester University Press. Similarly, several leading Irish interest journals are published outside of Ireland, including Irish Historical Studies, (CUP), the Irish Journal of Medical Science, (Springer), the Irish Journal of Economic and Social History (Sage), and Irish University Review (Edinburgh UP). The fact that so many Irish authors publish with UK university presses and commercial publishers clearly presents one of the key challenges of achieving 100% open access to publicly funded scholarly publications by 2030, since future adoption of open access publishing practices by these publishers is not yet clear [2].

In order to understand the current publishing landscape in Ireland, the first task of the PublishOA.ie project was to research, map, and publish the first digital directory of Irish publishers in the Republic of Ireland and Northern Ireland [6]. This was issued in June 2023. Together, the directory and map (Figures 1 and 2) list the activities and location of 183 publishers, publishing in both the English and Irish languages, and demonstrate the range of publishing, including fiction and non-fiction, scholarly, reference, professional, Irish language, children's and young people, and lifestyle and culture. As might be expected, there is a concentration of activities around the cities of Dublin and Belfast, but activity outside the metropolitan areas is also present.

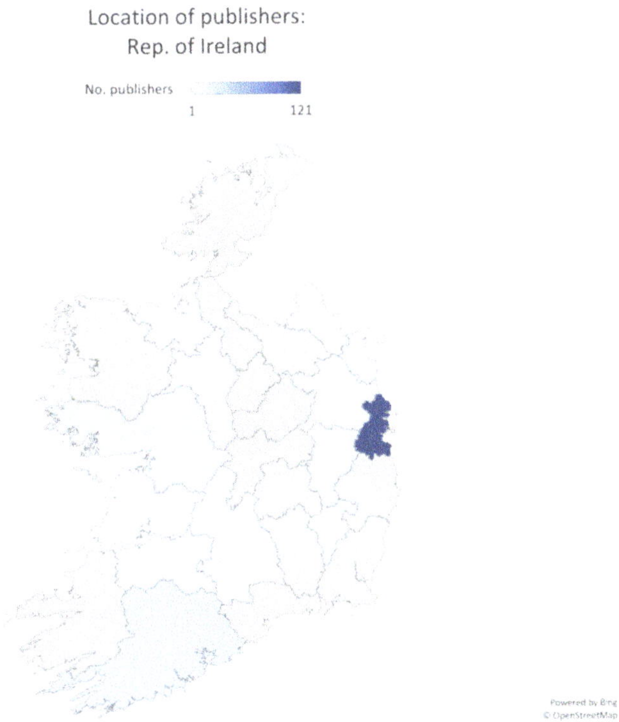

Figure 1. Map of publishing companies in the Republic of Ireland, June 2023.

PublishOA.ie is guided by the experience and expertise of members of our international advisory group. These include the Federation of Finnish Learned Societies (TSV.fi), Openjournals.nl, DOAJ, SDG Academy, and JSTOR, and other expert organisations (e.g., cOAlition S and DIAMAS). Consultation with these international organisations and institutions, all of which have demonstrable and significant experience in the field, is assisting us in analysing and discussing potential solutions to deploy, and where relevant, avail of existing developments. These discussions are proving especially valuable in the context of policy compliance (e.g., cOAlition S), technical advice (e.g., TSV and Openjournal.nl's use of Public Knowledge Project's Open Journal Systems), and potential OA content provision.

The intention is to build on and collaborate with the DIAMAS project [7], the European Union-funded consortium of 23 public service scholarly organisations from 12 European countries, whose objective is the delivery of an aligned, high-quality, and sustainable institutional OA scholarly publication ecosystem for the European Research Area. This includes setting a new shared and co-designed standard for Diamond OA publishing, a scholarly publication model in which journals and platforms are free for authors and readers (as defined by cOAlition S) [8].

PublishOA.ie is examining—with a view to adopting where assessed as relevant and appropriate—technical solutions and initiatives defined and designed by CoalitionS [9], Massachusetts Institute of Technology (MIT) Press [10], the EU's Open Science framework, defined as an approach to the scientific process that focuses on spreading knowledge as soon as it is available using digital and collaborative technology [11], and UNESCO's open access policy, defined as 'free access to scientific information and unrestricted use of electronic data for everyone. With open access, expensive prices and copyrights will no longer be obstacles to the dissemination of knowledge' [12].

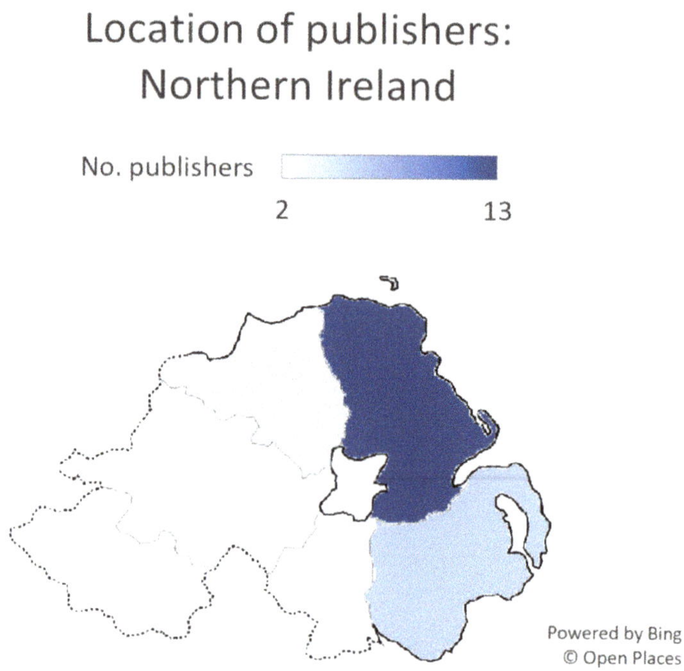

Figure 2. Map of publishing companies in Northern Ireland, June 2023.

As part of PublishOA.ie's mission to evaluate the feasibility of establishing a national publishing platform in Ireland, webinars were hosted in April, June, and July of 2023 for stakeholders, including publishers and librarians. In the first of the webinars, OpenJournals.nl and Journal.fi provided valuable technical and financial information on the operation of existing platforms in the Netherlands and Finland.

In July and August of 2023, platform providers Coko Foundation (Kotahi and Ketida), Janeway, Manifold, and the Public Knowledge Project's Open Journal Systems and Open Monograph Publishing (PKP OJS/OMP) provided demonstrations of their online publishing software and its application for editorial workflow and production. Information was shared on issues including platform maintenance and upgrading as well as data migration and journal onboarding to assist in building confidence. Other topics covered included training, IT and other support, funding sources and models, initial development budgets, annual running costs, subscription costs, as well as future planning, scaling, and sustainability.

The envisaged platform specification for Ireland will include the following elements:

- Articles will be open access on publication, accessible free of charge to anybody;
- Application of a clearly described peer review process;
- Author copyright retention;
- Application of creative commons licenses (CC BY 4.0 or similar);
- No Article Processing Charges for authors;
- Support for registration with the DOAJ/DOAB;
- Plan S compliance;
- Book publishing requirements compliance, including e-book formats, ONIX integration, author and reader engagement tools, social sharing, and tools to increase the visibility, accessibility, and impact of authors' work;
- Compliance with the 'Principles of Open Scholarly Infrastructure';

- Impact metrics and archiving—Directory of Open Access Books. Available online: https://doaj.org; https://www.doabooks.org/; https://openscholarlyinfrastructure.org/ (accessed on 16 March 2024).

As of September 2023, a set of national OA publishing principles for authors, developed in consultation with scholars, was being drafted, and it is expected in spring 2024. A set of OA publishing principles for publishers is also expected in spring 2024. A comparative technical specification, including the publishing platforms listed above, is also in preparation, complemented by an in-house examination of the technical parameters of seven further platforms: Digital Commons, Flax, Libero Reviewer, Meru, and PubPub.

PublishOA.ie aims to deliver an evidence-based understanding of Irish scholarly publishing and of the requirements of publishers to transition in whole or in part to Diamond OA. Further objectives include increasing awareness and engagement by policy makers of the system-level risks, challenges, and opportunities for a publicly owned centralised platform for the Diamond OA publication of journals and books. It is anticipated that the all-island approach will increase connections and relations within and between publishers, authors, librarians, scholars, and other stakeholders in scholarly publishing, thereby contributing to the Shared Island Initiative of the Government of Ireland [3]. This initiative aims to harness the full potential of the Good Friday Agreement of 1998 to enhance cooperation, connection, and mutual understanding on the island and engage with all communities and traditions to build consensus around a shared future. Key elements include working with the Northern Ireland Executive and the British Government to address strategic challenges faced on the island of Ireland; further developing the all-island economy, deepening north/south cooperation, and investing in the north west and border regions; and fostering constructive and inclusive dialogue and a comprehensive programme of research to support the building of a consensus around a shared future on the island.

At the time of the delivery of this paper at the PubMet Conference at the University of Zadar in September 2023, a number of key challenges had been identified and are being addressed as the project continues. These include the following:

- Scholarly publishers have articulated differing requirements for book and journal publishing. PublishOA.ie will, therefore, likely recommend and pilot two platforms (one for books, one for journals) to meet the objectives of the project. This was not anticipated at the outset of the project.
- Publisher engagement: publishers in Ireland are time- and resource-poor, especially in terms of staffing. Book publishers issue a mix of publications, and adoption of open access publishing is only one element of their activity.
- Future proofing has been identified as an issue of concern, encompassing the sustainability of the ongoing funding of both the Digital Repository of Ireland (DRI) and individual institutional repositories, and 'reference rot' (broken links), where the article or webpage resource identified by a URL no longer exists or has moved to another site. Reference rot also refers to the case whereby the resource identified has changed over time and evolved into a resource that bears no resemblance to the content originally referenced [13].
- The all-island mandate for a shared programme will require funding from the separate Governments of the Republic of Ireland and Northern Ireland. Since the UK's departure from the EU, so-called Brexit, the UK is no longer bound by EU law and directives (since this paper was delivered, the UK rejoined the Horizon Europe research and innovation programme in December 2023) [14].
- Bibliodiversity: support for smaller publishers will likely be required; the technical challenges of Diamond OA publishing may cause small publishers to outsource or divest themselves of publications to companies dedicated to this kind of publishing.
- Academic author buy-in: PublishOA.ie has identified that there are significant gaps in both knowledge and interest in open access publishing that may be mitigated by further and ongoing education and information.

Conclusions

As stated in the *National Action Plan for Open Research*, 'Ireland supports the principle of full and immediate open access to research publications to ensure the widest possible dissemination of research. Making research publications openly and freely accessible contributed to an informed citizenship, the democratisation of knowledge, and maximises the impact of research processes and outputs' [1]. In line with Ireland's *National Framework on the Transition to an Open Research Environment*, there is a national objective that all Irish scholarly publications resulting from publicly funded research will be openly available by default [1]. The Diamond Open Access model—in which journals or publishers do not charge fees to either authors or publishers—has been identified as the favoured model.

As detailed in NORF's *National Open Research Landscape Report*, Ireland's progress in the area of open access research has been demonstrated by a steady growth in repository-mediated OA and an increase in publisher-mediated OA from 2015 onwards. Initiatives supporting the growth and uptake of open access have included a growing number of transformative agreements facilitated by IReL [1].

The PublishOA.ie project, which commenced in November 2022, will conclude in November 2024, when a Final Report will be issued. The project has been tasked with conducting a feasibility study and pilot with a view to establishing a publicly owned, centralised national platform for the Diamond OA publication of journals and books for Irish-based academic journals and publishers. The project working groups have identified a series of challenges and are currently engaged with the project's management and governance, technical feasibility study and pilot platform development, funding model analysis and reporting, archiving, and communications. While the project takes reference points from both our national and international partners and collaborators, it pays specific attention to the immanent conditions and contexts of the Irish publishing ecosystem. As noted earlier, there are significant gaps in both knowledge of and interest in open access publishing, and further education for stakeholders will, therefore, remain a key element of the continuing project. PublishOA.ie welcomes comments and suggestions from all interested parties.

Funding: The research for this article was funded by the PublishOA project of the National Open Research Forum of Ireland.

Data Availability Statement: Directory of Irish Publishers. Available online: https://PublishOA.ie.

Conflicts of Interest: The author declares no conflict of interest.

Notes

1 The partner institutions are: Technological University of the Shannon (TUS); University of Galway (UG); Publishing Ireland; Dun Laoghaire Institute of Art, Design and Technology (IADT); Technological University Dublin (TU Dublin); Munster Technological University (MTU); University of Limerick (UL); South East Technological University (SETU). The affiliate institutions are the Irish Humanities Alliance (IHA); United Nations Sustainable Development Academy at University College Dublin (UN SDSN, UCD); Directory of Open Access Journals (DOAJ), Finnish Federation of Learned Societies; Openjournals.nl; Queen's University Belfast (QUB); the Dublin Institute of Advanced Studies (DIAS); JSTOR (Journal Storage).

2 See statement on Open Access from the UK Publishers Association. Available online: https://www.publishers.org.uk/our-work/open-access/. Note the statement that '[p]ublishers are committed to delivering on the Open Access agenda, but do require the necessary time, flexibility and funding to do so'. See also UK Research and Innovation (UKRI) policy statement on Open Access. Available online: https://www.ukri.org/publications/ukri-open-access-policy/uk-research-and-innovation-open-access-policy/ (accessed on 16 March 2024).

3 Available online: https://www.gov.ie/en/campaigns/c3417-shared-island/?referrer=https://www.gov.ie/sharedisland/ (accessed on 16 March 2024).

References

1. National Open Research Forum (NORF). *National Action Plan for Open Research 2022–2030*; Ireland's National Open Research Forum: Dublin, Ireland, 2022; pp. 3–15.

2. Impact 2030: Ireland's Research and Innovation Strategy. Available online: https://www.gov.ie/en/publication/27c78-impact-2030-irelands-new-research-and-innovation-strategy/ (accessed on 13 March 2024).
3. Mahony, J. (Trinity College Dublin, Dublin, Ireland). Overview and Context of Publishing in Ireland 1551–1922. Ph.D. Thesis, 2016, *Unpublished*; p. 29.
4. Central Statistics Office Ireland. Population and Migration Estimates, April 2023. Available online: https://www.cso.ie/en/releasesandpublications/ep/p-pme/populationandmigrationestimatesapril2023/keyfindings/ (accessed on 16 March 2024).
5. UK Population Data: Northern Ireland Population 2024. Available online: https://populationdata.org.uk/northern-ireland-population/ (accessed on 13 March 2024).
6. Digital Directory of Irish Publishers. Available online: https://publishoa-ie.moodlecloud.com/mod/data/view.php?id=94 (accessed on 13 March 2024).
7. DIAMAS—Developing Institutional Open Access Publishing Models to Advance Scholarly Communication. Available online: https://diamasproject.eu/ (accessed on 13 March 2024).
8. Plan S: Diamond Open Access. Available online: https://www.coalition-s.org/diamond-open-access/ (accessed on 14 March 2024).
9. Plan S: Diamond Open Access—Technical Guidance and Requirements. Available online: https://www.coalition-s.org/technical-guidance_and_requirements/ (accessed on 14 March 2024).
10. The MIT Press Announces New Initiative to Flip Existing Subscription-Based Journals to a Diamond Open Access Model. Available online: https://mitpress.mit.edu/the-mit-press-announces-new-initiative-to-flip-existing-subscription-based-journals-to-a-diamond-open-access-publishing-model/ (accessed on 16 March 2024).
11. Research and Innovation: The EU's Open Science Policy. Available online: https://research-and-innovation.ec.europa.eu/strategy/strategy-2020-2024/our-digital-future/open-science_en (accessed on 14 March 2024).
12. UNESCO. Open Access. Available online: https://en.unesco.org/open-access/ (accessed on 16 March 2024).
13. da Silva, J.A.T.; Nazarovets, M. Archiving website-based references in academic papers: Problems caused by reference rot, potential solutions and limitations. *Learn. Publ.* **2023**, *36*, 477–487. [CrossRef]
14. European Commission. United Kingdom Joins Horizon Europe Programme. Available online: https://ec.europa.eu/commission/presscorner/detail/en/IP_23_6327 (accessed on 16 March 2024).

publications

MDPI

Article

Practices and Attitudes of the Research and Teaching Staff at the University of Split about the Online Encyclopedia Wikipedia

Mirko Duić

Department of Information Sciences, University of Zadar, 23000 Zadar, Croatia; miduic@unizd.hr

Abstract: The goal of this study was to investigate the practices and attitudes of the research and teaching staff at the University of Split (Croatia) about the online encyclopedia Wikipedia. The method of a questionnaire-based survey was used to gain insights related to this topic. During February 2024, the survey was completed by 226 respondents. The results show that almost all respondents read Wikipedia articles and believe that the level of their accuracy is quite high. Almost half of the respondents strongly agree with the statement that it would be desirable for faculty staff to write Wikipedia articles with the aim of spreading knowledge about topics from their professional fields. However, a very small number of respondents participated in writing articles for Wikipedia. Also, the respondents answered that to them, the greatest motivations to write articles on Wikipedia would be if this activity were evaluated for the advancement to a higher work position and the correction of errors in Wikipedia articles. It was also found that most respondents are not very familiar with how Wikipedia works or how to add new content to it. These and other insights from this study can be used to conceive and initiate various activities that can contribute to greater participation of scientific and teaching staff of higher education institutions in writing quality content on Wikipedia, as well as activities that can contribute to a better familiarization with the principles and procedures to write and enhance its content. Other research methods, such as interviews with scientific and teaching staff of higher education institutions, could be used to acquire further, more detailed answers related to this topic.

Keywords: Wikipedia in the Croatian language; Wikipedia in national languages; higher education institutions; research and teaching staff; science communication and popularization; University of Split

1. Introduction

The spread of scientific knowledge nowadays is made possible by various web platforms, among which Wikipedia has a prominent place. This online encyclopedia has been one of the most popular websites worldwide for years [1–4]. It is used by people of different ages, from different parts of the world, with different worldviews and interests. For many, it is the first place where they obtain information about a wide variety of topics. In addition to being a significant source of information on topics from the field of popular culture and entertainment, Wikipedia has today also become a significant platform for the diffusion of science to a broader audience [4]. Given that it is one of the most visited websites in the world, Jemielniak points out that Wikipedia can also be considered 'the most important channel for the public communication of science nowadays' [5] (p. 1774). Also, Aibar points out that Wikipedia became 'the most important source of scientific and technical information for most citizens—including students at all education levels' [6] (p. 17). The diffusion of science through Wikipedia takes many forms. Wikipedia articles contain research results that were published in scholarly articles in journals and databases that are only available for a large fee and, therefore, unaffordable and unavailable for many. But when important research results from these articles are transferred in a concise and comprehensible form to Wikipedia, they become available to everyone. Articles from Wikipedia also contain numerous research results from articles that are available for free in open-access journals, and, in this way, Wikipedia, in addition to enabling its users to familiarize themselves with research results relevant to certain topics, also promotes and amplifies open-access science [4]. Also, the growing importance of Wikipedia in the scientific field is confirmed by the continuous increase in citations of Wikipedia in journal articles [7–9]. Bould cites a number of studies in which the topic of citations to Wikipedia within scholarly publishing has been investigated and points out that Wikipedia citations can also be found in journals with high impact factors [8].

Wikipedia, in addition to spreading scientific insights and strengthening the activity of science, can also influence the development of science. For example, in Wikipedia articles, scientists can find new ideas for scientific research, or they can find content that will allow them to take a new look at the ideas they already have. At the same time, scientists will sometimes come across content from scientific papers on Wikipedia that is otherwise unavailable to them because of the high subscription prices, which will enable them to better design and conduct their own research [3]. Thompson and Hanley conducted an experiment that determined the direct influence of Wikipedia on the development of science. Namely, the experiment established that scientific articles referenced in Wikipedia received more citations than scientific articles that were not referenced in Wikipedia [3]. Also, by contributing scientific and professional content to Wikipedia, scientists can improve the content of the Wikipedia articles, making them more accurate, relevant, and comprehensive. In this way, the contents of Wikipedia become better and more reliable, and the doubts about the appropriateness of using Wikipedia, which have been present since its inception until today, are reduced. Namely, given the specificity of the way articles are written on Wikipedia—where anyone can write or edit the text and add other types of content to this encyclopedia—it is not unusual that the quality of the contents on Wikipedia is often questioned, for example, their accuracy, objectivity, and comprehensibility. There are many studies related to these issues. Their findings depend on different elements, such as which language version of Wikipedia is involved or what type of Wikipedia articles are analyzed [10]. For example, Konieczny points out that according to the results of various studies, it can be determined that the quality of Wikipedia articles is slowly improving, especially for the most popular articles that are read and edited by a lot of people [10]. In this sense, versions of Wikipedia that are written in languages spoken by a large number of people are at an advantage, especially Wikipedia in English, which is read and edited by a very large number of native and non-native English speakers. On the other hand, the versions of Wikipedia that are in languages that have a significantly smaller number of speakers than the English language can have significantly fewer readers and editors, which is a factor that can contribute to the lower quality of these Wikipedia versions in terms of the number and scope of articles and their accuracy and comprehensiveness. Various aspects of Wikipedia in languages with a small number of speakers may also be considerably less researched. This is also the case with Wikipedia in the Croatian language, for which there is very little research [11]. A search of the Hrčak repository—the largest Croatian repository of scientific and professional papers, the majority of which is open-access—reveals that there are no more than 20 works related to Wikipedia, and only a few of them have this online encyclopedia as the focus of their research [12].

In this paper, this unexplored area is illuminated to some extent, considering that the goal of the paper is to investigate the practices and attitudes of the research and teaching staff at the University of Split (Croatia) related to Wikipedia.

2. Science Communication and Wikipedia

Wikipedia is an open encyclopedia, open in the sense that access to its content is free, but also open in the sense that anyone can change and edit its content. One of the main principles of Wikipedia is that its texts should be written from a neutral perspective. They should be written so that they 'document and explain major points of view' [13]. Special attention is paid to the principle of 'verifiability', which, in English Wikipedia, is defined in the following way: '. . .verifiability means other people using the encyclopedia can check that the information comes from a reliable source.' [14]. Academic and peer-reviewed publications are recommended as 'usually the most reliable sources on topics such as history, medicine, and science' [14]. In the English Wikipedia essay 'Ten simple rules for editing Wikipedia', it is written that 'there is an increasing need for the scientific community to engage with Wikipedia to ensure that the information it contains is accurate and current' and that 'for scientists, contributing to Wikipedia is an excellent way of fulfilling public engagement responsibilities and sharing expertise' [15]. These important Wikipedia principles are a clear sign that this online encyclopedia is a suitable platform for the dissemination of knowledge that can be found in academic publications and that the rules and principles of Wikipedia have considerable similarities with rules and principles that guide the activities of scholars. Therefore, it is not surprising that Wikipedia articles often reference reputable sources, among which there are a lot of articles from high-impact journals [4,16,17]. Additionally, Wikipedia articles often reference a lot of papers from open-access journals, even more frequently than papers published in closed-access journals [4]. This indicates the importance of open-access policy and philosophy, as well as the importance of open-access journals and repositories for the diffusion and advancement of science [3]. In this context, Wikipedia could be seen as an effective intermediary between the results of scientific research and the broader public. Certainly, there is a considerable similarity between the philosophy of the open-access movement and the philosophy of the Wikipedia community, in terms of their acceptance and implementation of open policy with all its associated advantages and challenges. Some studies confirm that an important motivation for many who contribute to Wikipedia is an appreciation for sharing knowledge, appreciation for the education of others, and support for open access and similar concepts [10]. Wikipedia belongs to digital platforms that enable new ways of communicating science. It allows users to present scientific content that is available to the public in open access. Therefore, it can be considered an essential part of the Open Science movement [18]. Additionally, the Citizen Science movement has been very active in recent years, and it was also significantly influenced by the development of digital technologies. One of the different definitions of Citizen Science is that it is the science that 'entails the engagement of volunteers in science and research. Volunteers are commonly involved in data collection but can also be involved in initiating questions, designing projects, disseminating results, and interpreting data [19]. Among all these mentioned activities, Wikipedia is certainly the most suitable for disseminating the results of scientific activities. Paleco et al. believe that 'it can be argued that Wikipedia is the most diverse international citizen science project in terms of usage, participants, and languages' [20] (p. 270). They also point out that Wikipedia has an important role in formal and informal education, as well as in the global democratization of information. Annette Lesmollmann believes that Wikipedia is an important part of the science communication realm and a 'valuable knowledge source open to everyone' [21] (p. 676). She also indicates that Wikipedia is a more reliable and high-quality source of scientific information than other social media platforms. The advantages of Wikipedia, compared with other social networks, are its numerous rules and quality management, as well as the fact that it has transparent criteria for editing and publication [21].

Meseguer-Artola et al. investigated the main factors that influence the teaching uses of Wikipedia among university faculty at the Universitat Oberta de Catalunya [22]. Eight hundred professors from this university, which uses a full online learning approach, completed the survey in 2012. After data analysis, it was found that these faculty members had a strong positive perception of Wikipedia's quality. Also, Aibar et al. investigated the perceptions and attitudes of 913 faculty members at two Catalan universities towards Wikipedia [6]. By using a survey as a research method, they established that almost half of the respondents saw Wikipedia as a useful teaching resource and that a striking majority of respondents gave positive answers in relation to the quality and reliability of Wikipedia articles. More than half of the respondents regularly used Wikipedia for personal and academic matters (62.6% and 55.3%). Another interesting finding was that among faculty members from these Catalan universities, 13.5% were registered users of Wikipedia, which is a considerably higher percentage in comparison with the 0.4% of registered Wikipedia users in the general population of Catalonia [6]. This finding indicates that faculty members recognize the educational value of Wikipedia and that many also contribute to it by registering as members so that they can have more convenient conditions for editing its articles. This is in strong contrast with previous negative attitudes and practices of faculty members in relation to Wikipedia. Another study that indicates a somewhat different attitude in academic circles towards Wikipedia is the study about attitudes and experiences of faculty members and students at Josip Juraj Strossmayer University in Osijek (Croatia). In that study, which is one of the very rare studies of Wikipedia by scholars from Croatia, it was established that students had a more positive opinion about Wikipedia than faculty members and that 6.6% of faculty members used Wikipedia frequently for their teaching activities, while 39.6% of them used it occasionally [11]. Also, only 2.2% of faculty members used Wikipedia frequently related to their scientific activities, and 22% of them used it occasionally. The majority of faculty members had a high level of agreement with the statement 'Accuracy and objectivity of data in articles on Wikipedia is questionable because anyone can edit and change them.' [11]. Wikipedia in the Croatian language was created in 2003 [23]. On 24 May 2024, it had 220,619 articles, 13 admins, 512 active users, and 313,467 users [24]. Wikipedia admins or administrators are Wikipedia editors who have the technical ability to perform certain actions on Wikipedia including the ability to block user accounts and IP addresses from editing, protect pages from editing, edit fully protected pages, delete and rename pages, etc. [25,26]. Active users are registered Wikipedia users who have performed an action, such as adding text to Wikipedia articles, in the last 30 days [27]. Wikipedia users are people who have registered a username on Wikipedia. The majority of users do not contribute regularly to Wikipedia [28]. We can compare the stated statistical data for Wikipedia in the Croatian language with the same type of statistical data for several Wikipedias in languages used in Eastern Europe. The following statistical data were found on Wikipedia on 24 May 2024 [24]. Wikipedia in the Slovenian language was created in 2002 [29]. It has 185,282 articles, 22 admins, 315 active users, and 232,653 users. Wikipedia in the Bosnian language was created in 2002 [30]. It has 93,486 articles, 9 admins, 126 active users, and 161,395 users. Wikipedia in the Serbian language was created in 2003 [31]. It has 689,506 articles, 15 admins, 1417 active users, and 370,844 users. Also, in 2002, Wikipedia in the Serbo-Croatian language was created [32]. It has 459,534 articles, 9 admins, 190 active users, and 213,765 users. The Hungarian-language Wikipedia was created in 2003 [33]. It has 542,252 articles, 25 admins, 1536 active users, and 562,590 users. Wikipedia in the Czech language was created in 2002 [34]. It has 546,839 articles, 32 admins, 2033 active users, and 661,559 users. Finally, the Polish-language Wikipedia was created in 2001, that is, in the same year during which the first Wikipedia was created on the web [35,36]. Wikipedia in the Polish language has 1,616,280 articles, 98 admins, 4454 active users, and 1,309,086 users. Various language versions of Wikipedia have different numbers of speakers of that language. The indicator for the activity level of speakers of a particular language in editing Wikipedia is the number of Wikipedia articles per 1000 speakers of a particular language. If we rank the previously mentioned language editions of Wikipedia according to this indicator, we can see that the most active editors of Wikipedia are Slovenian language speakers because there are 88.82 articles per 1000 speakers of Slovenian language. The Slovenian-language Wikipedia is followed by Wikipedia in the Serbian language with 76.95 articles per 1000 speakers, Wikipedia in the Hungarian language (43 articles per 1000 speakers), Wiki. in the Polish lang. (41.78), Wiki. in the Czech lang. (40.87), Wiki. in the Bosnian lang. (42.01), Wiki. in the Croatian lang. (38.33), and Wiki. in the Serbo-Croatian lang. (26.94) [37]. From these data, we can see that Wikipedia in the Croatian language, compared with almost all other listed Wikipedia editions, has the lowest number of articles per 1000 speakers. However, it should be noted that this value is similar to Wikipedia in the following languages: Hungarian, Polish, Czech, and Bosnian. Wikipedias in the Slovenian and Serbian languages have approximately twice as many articles per 1000 speakers as compared with the other listed Eastern European language Wikipedias. 'Depth' is another important indicator of individual language editions of Wikipedia. This indicator tells us about how frequently Wikipedia articles are updated [38]. If we rank the previously mentioned Eastern European language editions of Wikipedia according to the 'depth' indicator, we can see that articles on Wikipedia in the Serbo-Croatian language were most frequently updated—on 24 May 2024, the recorded value of the 'depth' indicator was 749. This Wikipedia was followed by Wikipedia in the Serbian language with a value of 167, Wikipedia in the Bosnian language (86), Wiki. in the Hungarian lang. (60), Wiki. in the Czech lang. (50), Wiki. in the Polish lang. (33), Wiki. in the Slovenian lang. (31), and Wiki. in the Croatian lang. (18). From these data, we can see that articles on Wikipedia in the Croatian language are the least frequently updated because the depth value of this Wikipedia is 18. One important element that should be noted is that the Croatian Wikipedia in the period from 2011 to 2020 'was taken over by a small group of administrators who introduced far-right bias and outright disinformation. Dissenting editorial voices were reverted, banned, and blocked' [39] (p. 612). In this situation, many of Wikipedia's principles related to neutrality, verifiability, and reliability were violated, which reduced the confidence of the readers of this Wikipedia in the accuracy of its contents. However, by 2020, through efforts of the volunteer editor community, many biased administrators had been removed or banned from their positions, which has enabled the creation of a less biased contributing environment for other editors and less biased articles for readers [39]. Nemanja Rajcic explored the differences among Wikipedia editions in the following languages: Serbian, Croatian, Bosnian, Slovenian, and Serbo-Croatian [40]. By analyzing articles about famous persons from Serbia, Croatia, Bosnia and Herzegovina, and Slovenia, he determined that 'the collaborative principle, which is one of the five pillars of Wikipedia, is rarely enforced and weakly utilized in the context of Wikipedia's from the Balkan region' [40] (p. 78). For example, many articles were written by only one editor and did not have much editing activity by editors. There are only a couple of articles with more than 10 edits. Also, the verifiability of information in articles about famous persons from other countries is not high. There is not much referencing or external linking to these articles. For example, Wikipedia in the Croatian language has many more references in articles about famous persons from Croatia than in articles about famous persons from neighboring countries. A similar situation related to the inadequate verifiability of articles about famous persons from other countries is also present in other language editions of Wikipedia explored in the research [40]. Manca Noč and Maja Zumer examined the quality of 122 featured articles from Slovene Wikipedia from 2009, 2010, and 2011. Featured articles are the best articles on Wikipedia, according to Wikipedia editors. They found that most of these 122 articles, about 75%, were adapted from the English Wikipedia [41]. Also, these adapted featured articles were problematic with regard to verifiability because they 'cite far too many sources that are definitely not available in the Slovene language and are less available in Slovenia' [41] (pp. 69–70). To alleviate this situation in the future, the authors suggested a change to Wikipedia's 'Manual of style for featured articles', where the recommendation is added that each candidate for a featured article should have 25% or more Slovene sources and articles about local topics should have 50% or more Slovene sources [41].

Wikipedia can also be used as a valuable digital pedagogy tool. It can be used by students and other users as a platform for active learning and the acquisition of knowledge and skills through various activities in the evaluation and improvement of its contents. A lot of the literature confirms and describes the value of Wikipedia as a learning tool. For example, Soler-Adillon, Pavlovic, and Freixa indicate that previous research has identified two reasons for introducing Wikipedia in the classroom. Firstly, the use of Wikipedia in the classroom can enhance students' literacy skills. Secondly, the content that students add to and enhance on Wikipedia instantly becomes visible to Wikipedia users around the world [42]. This is an additional motivation for students to engage in activities on Wikipedia as efficiently as possible. One of the issues of the scientific magazine '*Studies in Higher Education'* from 2020 was entirely dedicated to the following topic 'Wikipedia in higher education: practice what you teach'. This special issue of the magazine presents a series of studies demonstrating that higher education students who use Wikipedia are 'able to better understand the mechanisms of collaborative research and writing; practice participatory writing skills; understand the gender dynamics of Wikipedia and address these problems in practical ways' [43] (p. 947). Martín-García, Almaraz-Menéndez, and López-Esteban write that 'Wikipedia has gone from being one of the great enemies of education to becoming a great ally, especially thanks to the degree of rigor and organization it has achieved' [44] (p. 45). At the same time, they draw attention to the fact that today, Wikipedia is much more present at universities, providing teachers with numerous opportunities for educational innovation. They also describe a project started in 2013 at the University of Salamanca in which 100 professors and 584 students created 1752 Wikipedia articles. The important motivation for students participating in this project was that by publishing articles on Wikipedia, they could present their academic activities to a global audience. At the same time, a large university community was created whose members became familiar with the procedures and rules of Wikipedia editing, as well as with teaching and learning methodologies that can be used in future, similar projects [44]. Many other Wikipedia improvement projects by students have been carried out as part of university courses around the world. Information on over 500 of such projects and advice for professors and students who plan to participate in similar projects are available on the websites of Wikipedia and the organization Wiki Education [45–47]. There, information is available on more than 500 of such projects that were implemented since 2002, which, to date, have been carried out in more than 30 countries around the world and have involved several hundred professors and over 4500 students who, through these projects, have expanded and improved the contents of more than 6000 Wikipedia articles [48]. On the websites of organizations, such as Wiki Education, teachers and students involved in such projects or interested in starting them are provided with various instructions and ideas for their implementation [49–53]. Carmichael and Klock describe various Wikimedia assignments that students had to make during the course 'Natural Disturbances and Society' held at Louisiana State University (USA). It should be noted that more than 600 students from Louisiana State University had various Wikimedia assignments in 32 courses since 2014 [54]. Editing Wikipedia articles can help students and other contributors develop various skills, such as 'assessing accuracy of content; identifying needs of a target audience; using online technology and netiquette; applying and developing information literacy in the sciences; understanding scientific concepts' [54] (p. 282). Apart from these, there are other benefits of Wikipedia editing. For example, in 2018, students from a university in the Midwest USA participated in a Wikipedia edit-a-thon in order to write content about Haitian art, 19th-century women artists, and art educators. Their professors indicated that during this process, the students 'learned that authentic scholarship is collaborative, and that Wikipedia—and peer teaching and editing—are as significant sources of knowledge as a teacher or text' [55] (p. 23).

3. Participation of Academics in Writing Wikipedia Articles

Certainly, there are members of faculty staff at higher education institutions who edit Wikipedia articles. However, it is unclear what percentage of faculty staff in different countries have participated in editing Wikipedia articles. As we already mentioned, Aibar et al. investigated the perceptions and attitudes of 913 faculty members at two Catalan universities towards Wikipedia. They found that 13.5% of respondents were registered users of Wikipedia. It can be assumed that many of them edited Wikipedia articles. Namely, the main reason for someone to register as a member of Wikipedia is to have more convenient conditions for editing its articles [6]. However, in countries such as Croatia, there are no studies that explore this issue. Therefore, the percentage of Croatian academics who edit Wikipedia is unknown. Konieczny wrote that relatively few academics participate in Wikipedia editing. There are many reasons for that including a lack of career or financial incentives; unfamiliarity with Wikipedia procedures, rules, and norms; a controversial model of knowledge creation, where anyone can edit Wikipedia; negative experiences during the Wikipedia editing (i.e., declined submissions by anonymous Wikipedia reviewers); editors' contributions are frequently anonymous, without a need for the editor to have credentials related to the edited topic; and a negative attitude toward knowledge produced outside academia [10]. For example, sometimes people will try to edit some contents of Wikipedia with the claim that they are experts with academic status. However, the problem with this approach is that at Wikipedia, it is difficult to verify one's status, be it academic or otherwise. In addition, Wikipedia norms and rules are more important than the status of the editor. Therefore, anyone who wants to edit some part of Wikipedia needs to know these rules and norms very well and adhere to them [10]. Eijkman conducted a study about the attitudes of academics to Wikipedia. Ninety-nine academics from universities in Australia, Canada, the U.K., and South Africa completed the full survey. It was found that 'Wikipedia continues to be a divisive issue among academics, particularly within the soft sciences' [56] (p. 173). An important factor that can demotivate academics from participating in Wikipedia editing is that contributing to Wikipedia will not boost an academic's career. Konieczny suggested that not recognizing the advantages that Wikipedia editing can bring to academics and their institutions, advantages such as their better visibility and impact in public and academic circles, is a major failure on academia's administrative side: '. . .contributing to Wikipedia is one of the most efficient ways for scholars to have their research noticed by the general public. (. . .) The public reads Wikipedia, Wikipedia encourages its writers to cite reliable, scholarly research, and experts want to be impactful—as do the institutions that employ them. But few scholars, and even fewer university administrators, seem to follow this line of thinking to its logical conclusion.' [10] (p. 163). Various factors could motivate academics to become Wikipedia editors. We already mentioned that an important motivation for many who contribute to Wikipedia is an appreciation for sharing knowledge, an appreciation for the education of others, and support for open access and similar concepts [10]. Sharing knowledge and appreciation for the education of others are the foundational characteristics of all research and teaching institutions. Also, open-access principles, policies, and practices are today accepted by many of these institutions and their employees. Therefore, it could be concluded that many academics will be motivated to edit Wikipedia because they share these values and consider Wikipedia as a platform that can be very helpful for the advancement of knowledge sharing, education, and the Open Access movement. In addition, it is worth noting that important Wikipedia policies and principles are very similar to those in the academic field. For example, the importance attached to the verifiability policy on Wikipedia and the need to add references to quality, reliable sources of information based on which Wikipedia articles are edited [14]. Another reason for participation in Wikipedia editing is that this activity will not only improve this online encyclopedia, but the person will also improve their own skills and fund of knowledge, skills such as assessing the accuracy of content, using online technology and netiquette, integrating information from various courses and sources, and collaborating effectively with peers and editors [54].

Finally, to conclude the literature review part of this paper, there is one more aspect that is worth mentioning, which is the responsibility of academics for public interests. In an age when we are surrounded by fake news, in an age when the intentional, massive sharing of wrong information by various organizations leads to deception and manipulation of the public with the aim of achieving various interests, academics are the ones who can contribute to the accurate, impartial, and multidimensional presentation of various phenomena. Their traditional ways of working—holding lectures and publishing books and peer-reviewed papers—are still very important for spreading knowledge and skills to students and the general public. However, they now have at their disposal platforms such as Wikipedia, through which they can significantly increase the reach of their academic activities to the public. In this sense, greater participation and sharing of knowledge by academics on popular web platforms such as Wikipedia can certainly contribute to the creation of a healthier, more informed public sphere.

Each language version of Wikipedia has many articles that are comprehensive and of high quality, but there are also many articles that are poorly written in various aspects or do not contain enough content. This is indicated by various studies that investigated the quality of Wikipedia articles. One of these studies is related to the research on the quality of citations in articles about the national history of 50 countries. The research results led to the conclusion that the quality is much lower than in peer-reviewed articles from scientific journals in the field of history. The authors of that study remind us of Roy Rosenzweig's words: '. . .if Wikipedia is becoming the family encyclopedia for the twenty-first century, historians probably have a professional obligation to make it as good as possible' [57] (p. 720). Regarding the topic of the relationship between Wikipedia and academics, whether historians, academics from some other field of science, or even librarians, it is worth mentioning the opinion of Luyt and Tan that 'instead of disparaging Wikipedia, we should be probing its weaknesses to find ways to improve it. And if historians have a special responsibility to improve history writing on Wikipedia, there is also room for librarians as well, and not just in the field of history, but other subjects too.' [57] (p. 719). These thoughts and recommendations certainly encourage a positive answer to the question of whether academics should be more actively involved in the editing of Wikipedia articles in order to improve the contents of this popular online encyclopedia.

4. Materials and Methods

The goal of this study was to investigate the practices and attitudes of the research and teaching staff at the University of Split about the online encyclopedia Wikipedia, including its use in teaching and research, as well as the possibilities of supplementing it with content by the research and teaching staff. To acquire insights, data were gathered through a survey by questionnaire administered to the teaching and research staff at the following faculties of the University of Split:

Faculty of Humanities and Social Sciences; Faculty of Electrical Engineering, Mechanical Engineering, and Naval Architecture; Faculty of Law; Faculty of Civil Engineering, Architecture, and Geodesy; Faculty of Science; Faculty of Maritime Studies; University Department of Health Studies; Faculty of Economics, Business and Tourism; Faculty of Chemistry and Technology; Faculty of Kinesiology; and University Department of Marine Studies [58–69].

The questionnaire was made available on the web on 15 February 2024. E-mails with a request to participate in the survey were sent to 953 faculty employees with teaching and research responsibilities. These e-mails were sent twice, several days apart, to encourage the faculty employees who did not complete the survey after receiving the first e-mail to complete the survey. The questionnaire was filled out in full by 226 faculty members in the period from 15 February to 23 February 2024. A response rate of about 23.72% was achieved. According to the data found on the University of Split website, there are 1292 faculty employees with teaching and research responsibilities [70]. This means that 17.49% of the total number of faculty employees with teaching and research responsibilities filled out the survey.

The survey questionnaire had 31 open and closed questions. Some of the questions contained additional questions; therefore, the total number of questions was 57. Among these 57 questions, there were 32 questions in which respondents were asked to choose a grade that most precisely indicated their level of support for a specific statement. Participants had to choose one grade from the following range: one, two, three, four, and five. The grade 'one' indicated that the respondent completely disagreed with the specific statement, while the grade 'five' indicated that the respondent completely agreed with the specific statement.

The questions were based on the literature review, as well as on the personal insights and experiences of the author of this paper, who works at a Croatian university as a lecturer and researcher. The survey questions were related to the following: (a) demographic data of respondents; (b) practices and attitudes of respondents related to the use of web sources of literature; (c) respondents' practices and attitudes about Wikipedia in general; and (d) practices and attitudes of respondents related to the use and writing of Wikipedia articles. The survey was anonymous, which aimed to encourage respondents to be more open in their answers.

The University of Split was founded in 1974 [71]. Today, about 20,000 students study at the University of Split in 11 faculties, one art academy, and four university departments. Also, the University of Split has over 180 study programs in various fields of science and the field of art [72]. Among the universities in Croatia, the University of Split ranks second in terms of number of students, right after the University of Zagreb, which has around 65,000 students [73].

5. Results

5.1. Demographic Data

Out of 226 respondents, most of them are from the field of technical sciences (77 or 34.07%), followed by the field of social sciences (44 or 19.47%), humanities (41 or 18.4%), natural sciences (32 or 14.16%), biomedicine and healthcare (16 or 7.08%), and biotechnological sciences (8 or 3.54%). The least number of respondents is from the interdisciplinary field (7 or 3.1%).

Most respondents are employed as assistant professors (59 or 26.11%), followed by associate professors (39 or 17.26%), assistants (34 or 15.04%), teaching positions (29 or 12.83%), full professors in permanent titles (26 or 11.5%), and full professors (22 or 9.73%). The lowest number of respondents are employed as senior assistants, i.e., postdoctoral fellows (13 or 5.75%). Most respondents are aged 40 to 49 (78 or 34.51%), followed by respondents aged 30 to 39 (59 or 26.11%), respondents aged 50 to 59 (55 or 24.34%), and respondents aged 60 years and older (23 or 10.18%). The lowest number of respondents is between the ages of 20 and 29 (11 or 4.87%). Among the respondents, there is a noticeably higher number of women (141 or 62.39%) compared with the number of men (85 or 37.61%).

5.2. Web Sources of Literature

The majority of respondents very often read and download scientific works via the Internet (Figure 1). Overall, 32.74% of respondents download scientific works every day, and 38.94% download works several times a week. Only 1.77% of respondents never use the Internet to read or download scientific papers. These data tell us that among the respondents, the Internet is widely used for reading and downloading scientific papers.

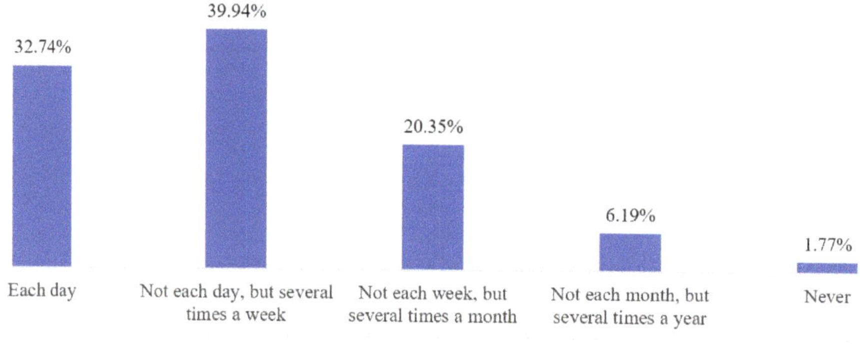

Figure 1. Frequency of using the Internet to read and download scientific papers.

On the Internet, respondents mostly use foreign web portals to access scientific and professional papers. We can see this from the grades they gave regarding claims about the use of different types of web portals (Table 1). A large share, amounting to 61.06%

of respondents, gave a grade of 5 to the statement that they use foreign web portals to access scientific and professional papers. A grade of 5 indicates the highest level of agreement with the statement, and a grade of 1 indicates the lowest level of agreement with the statement. Also, 22.57% of respondents gave this statement a grade of 4, which also indicates a strong agreement with this statement. If the percentages of respondents who graded their agreement with statement 1 as grades 4 and 5 are added up, the total percentage of those respondents is as high as 83.63%—therefore, it can be concluded that a vast majority of respondents completely or almost completely agree with statement 1, indicating that foreign web portals are very important for respondents to access scientific and professional papers.

Table 1. The frequency of using different web portals for accessing scientific and professional papers.

To what extent do you access scientific and professional papers through the following types of web portals?					
1. Croatian web portals (e.g., Hrčak portal, Croatian library portals...)					
1—Completely disagree	2	3	4	5—Completely agree	Without answer
12.83%	19.47%	15.93%	14.16%	36.73%	0.88%
2. Foreign web portals (e.g., Scopus, Web of Science, Google Scholar...)					
1—Completely disagree	2	3	4	5—Completely agree	Without answer
2.21%	3.98%	9.29%	22.57%	61.06%	0.88%

In second place in terms of frequency of use, are Croatian web portals—36.73% of respondents gave a grade of 5 to statement 2 about their use of Croatian web portals to access scientific and professional papers. Also, 14.16% of respondents gave this statement a grade of 4. It can be concluded that the majority of respondents completely or almost completely agree with statement 2 that they use Croatian web portals to access scientific and professional papers. This means that Croatian web portals are very important for respondents to access scientific and professional papers; but still, on average, they are less frequently used by respondents than foreign web portals.

As for the individual web portals through which the respondents access scientific papers, the most popular are Google Scholar and Scopus (Table 2). Approximately 63% of the respondents gave grades of 4 and 5 to the statements that they use these portals. Hrčak—the portal of Croatian scientific and professional journals—is also a very popular source for respondents, for which 50% of respondents gave grades of 4 and 5 to the statement that they use this portal [74]. This means that the Croatian portal Hrčak is not far behind in usage compared with the globally popular Google Scholar portal. A smaller share of respondents uses the portals 'DOAJ—Directory of Open Access Journals', and 'Portal of electronic resources' at the National and University Library in Zagreb (Croatia).

Respondents also had the option to name some other web portals that they often use to access scientific papers, and 18.58% of respondents used this option. Most respondents stated that they use Research Gate (seven respondents), followed by Web of Science (six), Google (four), Pubmed (three), IEEE Xplore (two), Archive.org (two), Google Books (two), and ScienceDirect (two).

As we can see in Table 3, almost all respondents strongly support the statement that all scientific works should be freely available on the Internet to all interested parties without the need to pay subscriptions for databases—74.34% of respondents completely agree with this statement (grade 5), while 12.39% of respondents almost completely agree with this statement (grade 4). Additionally, almost all respondents strongly support the statement that they are acquainted with the existence of the 'Open Access' movement. These data indicate that the vast majority of respondents are acquainted with the existence of the 'Open Access' movement and that the vast majority of respondents support one of its fundamental postulates that all scientific works should be freely available on the Internet without the need to pay for access.

Table 2. The frequency of using specific web portals to access scientific papers.

To what extent do you access scientific papers through the following web portals?					
1. Google Scholar					
1—Completely disagree	2	3	4	5—Completely agree	Without answer
4.42%	7.52%	21.68%	25.66%	37.61%	3.10%
2. Scopus					
1—Completely disagree	2	3	4	5—Completely agree	Without answer
7.08%	7.08%	20.35%	30.97%	31.86%	2.65%
3. Hrčak—portal of Croatian scientific and professional journals					
1—Completely disagree	2	3	4	5—Completely agree	Without answer
12.39%	11.50%	23.89%	15.04%	34.96%	2.21%
4. 'Portal of electronic resources' within the National and University Library in Zagreb (Croatia)					
1—Completely disagree	2	3	4	5—Completely agree	Without answer
21.24%	19.47%	24.78%	15.04%	16.81%	2.65%
5. DOAJ—Directory of Open Access Journals					
1—Completely disagree	2	3	4	5—Completely agree	Without answer
21.24%	15.93%	25.66%	18.14%	14.16%	4.87%

Table 3. Statements related to open access.

1. All scientific works should be freely available on the Internet to all interested parties without the need to pay subscriptions for databases					
1—Completely disagree	2	3	4	5—Completely agree	Without answer
1.77%	2.21%	7.08%	12.39%	74.34%	2.21%
2. Most of the scientific and professional works of which I am (co)author are freely available on the Internet					
1—Completely disagree	2	3	4	5—Completely agree	Without answer
3.54%	11.95%	17.26%	21.68%	42.48%	3.10%
3. I am acquinted with the existence of the 'Open Access' movement, which aims to achieve free access to scientific and professional works					
1—Completely disagree	2	3	4	5—Completely agree	Without answer
3.54%	1.77%	5.75%	7.52%	79.65%	1.77%

Also, 42.48% of respondents completely agree with the statement that most of the scientific and professional works of which they are (co)authors are freely available on the Internet, while 21.68% of respondents almost completely agree with this statement (grade 4).

5.3. Respondents' Practices and Attitudes about Wikipedia

The majority of the respondents do not use Wikipedia every day, nor several times a week, but about a third of the respondents use it several times a month, and about a third of the respondents use it only a few times a year (Figure 2). However, only 6.19% of respondents never use Wikipedia.

One of the research findings is that the largest number of respondents uses the English version of Wikipedia—85.84% or 194 respondents—while the Croatian version of Wikipedia is used by a much smaller percentage of respondents—65.93% or 149 respondents. These data also tell us that the large majority of respondents understand the English language. These data also indicate that the English-language Wikipedia has certain qualities that attract a larger share of respondents compared with the Croatian-language Wikipedia.

Versions of Wikipedia in other languages are used by significantly fewer respondents as follows: Italian-language Wikipedia—10 respondents, German-language Wikipedia—10 respondents, Spanish-language Wikipedia—5 respondents, French-language Wikipedia—5 respondents, Serbian-language Wikipedia—2 respondents, Portuguese-language Wikipedia—1 respondent, and Slovenian-language Wikipedia—1 respondent.

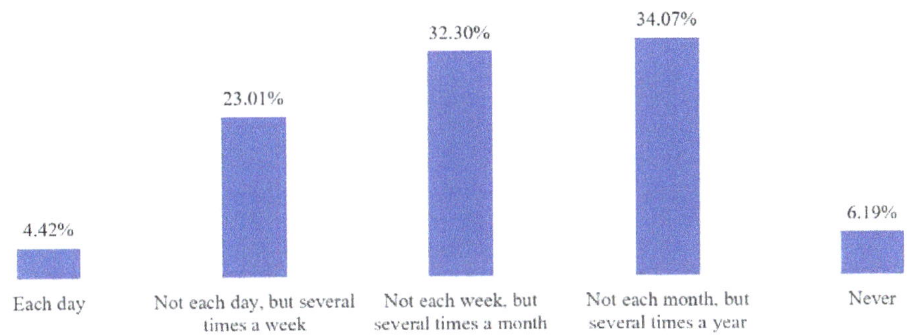

Figure 2. Frequency of reading Wikipedia articles.

As we can see in Table 4, more than half of the respondents strongly or completely agree with statement 1 that while they are reading articles on Wikipedia, sometimes they study the references based on which the articles were written. Only 13.72% of respondents completely or strongly disagree with statement 1 (grades 1 and 2). In addition, more than half of the respondents strongly or completely agree with statement 2 that while reading articles on Wikipedia, sometimes, following the references, they also read some texts based on which the articles were written. Only 17.7% of respondents completely or strongly disagree with statement 2 (grades 1 and 2).

Table 4. Exploration of Wikipedia references.

1. While reading the articles on Wikipedia, sometimes I study references on the basis of which the articles were written					
1—Completely disagree	2	3	4	5—Completely agree	Without answer
5.75%	7.96%	13.72%	22.57%	38.05%	11.95%
2. While reading the articles on Wikipedia, sometimes, following the references, I also read some texts on the basis of which the articles were written					
1—Completely disagree	2	3	4	5—Completely agree	Without answer
7.08%	10.62%	13.72%	23.89%	30.97%	13.72%

Respondents who read Wikipedia had the opportunity to state the main reasons why they do so. This question was answered by 80.53% of the respondents, and the most common reasons they cited for reading are that Wikipedia serves to inform them, that it provides quick and easy access to information, and that it helps them find basic information about the topic they are interested in. In today's world where we are bombarded with information and topics from various sides, many of which we have not had the opportunity or time to encounter before, these research findings indicate that Wikipedia is used by many respondents as the accessible starting information point for basic, orientational information gathering. The following respondents' statements confirm that Wikipedia is used because of its speed, simplicity, and general insight into many topics:

- A good general source of information provided that this information is not accepted as absolute facts.
- Considering its easy accessibility, coverage of a wide area, and almost always being among the first results of web search engines, I consider it good for getting to know a certain topic.

- I use it when I want to find an explanation of an insufficiently clear term or when I want to get to know the facts about what the person I'm interested in has been dealing with professionally.
- It is the shortest way to obtain basic information about an unknown term. According to personal experience, the information is 90% accurate.

Also, respondents often stated that their reason for reading Wikipedia is that links to articles on Wikipedia often appear in search results when using web search engines.

One of the frequently cited reasons for reading Wikipedia is that references in Wikipedia articles help respondents find additional sources of information related to topics of interest. The following statement from one respondent speaks about the use of Wikipedia because of the possibility of finding further research on the topic by following the references in Wikipedia articles:

- Well-written texts on Wikipedia (you can find everything from very bad to very good on this portal) always end by citing the sources from where what is written was taken, and then I go to those sources and use them exclusively.

Also, respondents use Wikipedia both in their work and private life. The following respondents' statements refer to the use of Wikipedia for work purposes:

- Sometimes I check some information, and it serves as a landmark for a historical and cultural course.
- As a rule, I read texts on Wikipedia when students' written term papers refer me to it, because students often use Wikipedia as a source in their term papers, even though they are advised not to do so as a rule.
- I use Wikipedia to find simpler concepts and references for explaining more complex physical systems to students.
- As a main source of information, I use published scientific articles, but if I need to find a term quickly and in Croatian, I enter it in the search engine and the first link is usually Wikipedia. I mostly use it for certain biochemical terms, medical conditions, or diseases that I would like to know more about.
- Scientific—help in preparing lectures, checking the data of final and graduate theses, and writing your own papers.

The following respondents' statements refer to the use of Wikipedia for private purposes:

- I can quickly obtain information that is often of sufficient quality; I mainly use it for information that is not from my profession.
- Gives great insight into certain areas where I am not an expert.
- I do not read it for the purposes of scientific and teaching work, except in the case of obtaining faster information about the year of birth and death of a certain person. I use it most often for information about things that interest me in my free time, for example, for information about music albums and the like.

The following respondents' statements refer to the use of Wikipedia for private and work purposes:

- Mainly for expanding general knowledge, but relatively often also due to workplace needs.
- I read it because I believe that the information I come across is correct, because I check it from several sources. Also, Wikipedia usually lists the source in small letters below the main text. My use is not directly related only to work, but also hobbies (computers, game consoles, the car industry, music, history, art, etc.).

Less often, respondents cited the following reasons for using Wikipedia:

- Credible source of information; verification of data and opinions; defining unknown terms; informing about less important topics; the comprehensiveness and variety of topics it contains; finding information that is then passed on to children in the family or at work; useful, comprehensive, and detailed information; and learning.

Respondents who do not read Wikipedia had the opportunity to state the main reasons why they do not read it. Only 27.88% of respondents answered this question, and the explanation for the relatively small percentage of respondents who answered is that, as we could see in the answers to the previous questions, most of the respondents read Wikipedia. Among those who do not read Wikipedia and who answered about the reasons for not reading it, most of them stated that the main reason for not reading it is that they consider it unreliable or inaccurate and therefore use other more reliable sources. The following respondents' statements refer to the non-use of Wikipedia because of its unreliability or inaccuracy:

- I do not use it because I am not sure of the accuracy of the data, and I have the possibility of using verified literature.
- Depending on the field under consideration, Wikipedia is an unreliable source, so it is better to avoid it.
- I read it very selectively because I know it does not always offer valid information.
- I do not use Wikipedia texts related to scientific and teaching work, given that I make sure that the information is verified (despite the fact that many articles on Wikipedia, especially in English, are well-founded and extensive). Even for the purpose of entertainment, I do not rely on articles on Croatian Wikipedia that deal with national history.

Less often, respondents gave the following reasons for not reading Wikipedia:

- Contains superficial, trivial, biased information and unverified content; not relevant and updated; anyone can write articles; does not contain enough information; and the texts are not peer-reviewed and contain wrong references.

We also asked respondents if they use Wikipedia to prepare their lessons and writing their scientific articles. As we can see in Table 5, the vast majority of respondents 'never' or 'rarely' use Wikipedia to prepare their lessons—82.3%. In contrast to that, a very small percentage of respondents 'always' and 'often' use Wikipedia to prepare their lessons—2.21%. In correspondence to these findings, it was also found that almost all respondents 'never' or 'rarely' use Wikipedia to write scientific papers—91.59%.

Table 5. Using Wikipedia in teaching and research.

1. How often do you use Wikipedia to prepare your lessons?				
Never	Rarely	Periodically	Often	Always
38.50%	43.81%	15.49%	2.21%	0%
2. How often do you use Wikipedia to write scientific papers?				
Never	Rarely	Periodically	Often	Always
68.58%	23.01%	7.52%	0.88%	0%

It is clear from these data that the vast majority of respondents do not use Wikipedia to prepare their lessons or write their scientific articles. It can be observed that the non-use of Wikipedia is somewhat more pronounced for writing scientific articles compared with the non-use of Wikipedia for preparing lessons.

As we can see in Table 6, almost half of the respondents strongly or completely agree with statement 1 that the level of accuracy of the information available on Wikipedia is quite high (grades 4 and 5). It can be concluded that there are considerably more respondents who think that the level of accuracy of the information available on Wikipedia is quite high than there are respondents with the opposite opinion.

From the answers related to statements 2 and 3, it can be seen that many more respondents consider Wikipedia useful for students' learning and writing undergraduate and master's theses than respondents who consider it useful for professors' learning and writing scientific and professional papers.

Table 6. Different statements related to the following topics and Wikipedia: accuracy of information; usefulness for learning and writing of students and professors; use for private purposes; and familiarity with the functioning of Wikipedia and with adding content.

1. The level of accuracy of the information available on Wikipedia is quite high					
1—Completely disagree	2	3	4	5—Completely agree	Without answer
3.54%	13.27%	37.61%	33.19%	8.41%	3.98%
2. Wikipedia can be useful for students' learning and writing undergraduate and master's theses					
1—Completely disagree	2	3	4	5—Completely agree	Without answer
9.37%	26.99%	30.09%	22.12%	9.29%	1.77%
3. Wikipedia can be useful for professors' learning and writing scientific and professional papers					
1—Completely disagree	2	3	4	5—Completely agree	Without answer
27.88%	37.61%	21.24%	9.73%	2.65%	0.88%
4. I use Wikipedia primarily for private purposes and not for work-related purposes					
1—Completely disagree	2	3	4	5—Completely agree	Without answer
8.41%	10.18%	18.58%	26.11%	32.74%	3.98%
5. I am very familiar with how Wikipedia works and how to add new content to it					
1—Completely disagree	2	3	4	5—Completely agree	Without answer
21.68%	19.91%	28.32%	12.39%	12.39%	5.31%

With regard to statement 4, the majority of respondents strongly or completely agree with the statement that they use Wikipedia primarily for private purposes but not for work purposes (grades 4 and 5). It can be concluded that the majority of respondents primarily use Wikipedia for private purposes, but also approximately a fifth of respondents disagree with this statement, i.e., it can be assumed that they primarily use Wikipedia for work purposes or use it equally for private and work purposes.

With regard to statement 5, it was found that a significant number of respondents are not very familiar with how Wikipedia works or how to add new content to it.

Table 7 contains data about writing for Wikipedia and learning from Wikipedia. We can see that 8.41% of respondents strongly or completely agree with statement 1 that they would like to write Wikipedia articles on topics from their professional fields (grades 4 and 5). The majority of respondents completely or strongly disagree with this statement (grades 1 and 2). In addition to that, 4.42% of respondents strongly or completely agree with statement 2 that they would like to write Wikipedia articles on topics that are not in their professional fields (grades 4 and 5). The majority of respondents completely or strongly disagree with this statement (grades 1 and 2).

Table 7. Writing for Wikipedia and learning from Wikipedia.

1. I would like to write Wikipedia articles on topics from my professional field					
1—Completely disagree	2	3	4	5—Completely agree	Without answer
43.36%	24.78%	18.14%	4.42%	3.98%	5.31%
2. I would like to write Wikipedia articles on topics outside my professional field					
1—Completely disagree	2	3	4	5—Completely agree	Without answer
61.06%	21.68%	8.41%	2.65%	1.77%	4.42%
3. The texts I read on Wikipedia are often very useful for acquiring new knowledge about topics from my professional field					
1—Completely disagree	2	3	4	5—Completely agree	Without answer
11.50%	29.65%	29.65%	16.37%	4.42%	8.41%
4. The texts I read on Wikipedia are often very useful for acquiring new knowledge about topics outside my professional field					
1—Completely disagree	2	3	4	5—Completely agree	Without answer
2.65%	10.62%	26.11%	35.84%	15.93%	8.85%

These data indicate that the vast majority of respondents would not want to write articles on Wikipedia, whether they are articles on topics from their professional field or articles on topics that are not in their professional fields. But it can be noticed that the respondents are even less likely to write articles on topics that are not in their professional fields.

Regarding the educational activities about the way Wikipedia works and the process of writing texts and developing articles on Wikipedia, it is worth noting that among the questions in the survey, there was a question about the respondents' participation in educational programs whose goals are to familiarize them with the possibilities, procedures, or principles of writing texts for Wikipedia. Only 5 respondents out of 226 participated in educational programs of this type. Thus, there is a large, currently unused space for familiarizing teaching and research staff with the way Wikipedia works and methods of writing texts and adding other content to this online encyclopedia.

As for statement 3 in Table 7, only 20.08% of respondents strongly or completely agree with this statement that the texts they read on Wikipedia are often very useful for acquiring new knowledge about topics from their professional fields (grades 4 and 5). In contrast to that, a significant share of respondents completely or strongly disagree with this statement (grades 1 and 2). In addition to that, with regard to statement 4, the majority of respondents strongly or completely agree with the statement that the texts they read on Wikipedia are often very useful for acquiring new knowledge about topics that are not in their professional fields (grades 4 and 5).

As we can see in Table 8, respondents had an opportunity to express their level of agreement with statements related to the following topics and Wikipedia: educational programs, promotion of knowledge and repositories, and participation of faculty staff.

Table 8. Educational programs for learning to write articles for Wikipedia.

1. I would be interested in participating in educational programs for learning about different aspects of writing articles for Wikipedia					
1—Completely disagree	2	3	4	5—Completely agree	Without answer
30.53%	18.14%	26.55%	15.93%	4.42%	4.42%
2. I would be interested in organizing and conducting educational programs about different aspects of writing articles for Wikipedia, aimed at scientists or students					
1—Completely disagree	2	3	4	5—Completely agree	Without answer
42.48%	20.35%	20.35%	8.41%	3.54%	4.87%

Overall, 20.35% of respondents strongly or completely agree with statement 1 that they would be interested in participating in educational programs for learning about different aspects of writing articles for Wikipedia (grades 4 and 5). In addition to that 11.95% of respondents strongly or completely agree with statement 2 that they would be interested in organizing and conducting educational programs about different aspects of writing articles for Wikipedia aimed at scientists or students (grades 4 and 5).

Out of the total 226 respondents, 14 or 6.19% of them have participated in writing articles for Wikipedia. Some of these respondents answered the question about what types of articles they wrote and what were their reasons for writing those articles. Five respondents wrote texts related to a topic in their field of science (theoretical physics, mathematics. . .). These respondents mentioned the activities of supplementing Wikipedia articles and writing introductory texts and key concepts from the scientific field they deal with, as well as writing Wikipedia articles for the purpose of researching how Wikipedia works. In addition to these five respondents, one respondent wrote a text about a mathematical method for the purpose of promoting the work of his/her colleagues. Two respondents wrote articles on Wikipedia related to the study program they attended—one respondent wrote an article for Wikipedia in the German language as an assignment during his/her studies, and the other respondent wrote an article on Wikipedia using parts of his/her thesis. Also, two respondents stated that they corrected errors on Wikipedia, and one respondent stated that he/she wrote texts about key terms related to his/her field of interest in his/her free time (linguistics, history, local history, and geography. . .).

Four respondents stated that they wrote articles on Wikipedia, but it was not clear from their answers whether they wrote articles about the topics related to the field they deal with at work or some other topics related to interests outside their work. One of the respondents gave the following answer:

- I decided to write or supplement Wikipedia content because, in Croatian, there was either no entry for a certain term or the existing one was outdated or incorrect in part, and I thought it was important for the wider social community so much so that I introduced or corrected it.

One respondent wrote about 'sports facts' on Wikipedia, and the other wrote the 'description of Prosecco' (a type of wine from Dalmatin Croatia). Finally, one respondent wrote a large number of articles in various fields.

Some of the respondents who wrote articles on Wikipedia answered the question about what were their biggest content or technical challenges or problems when writing these articles and how they solved them. Seven respondents answered that they had no challenges or problems when writing articles. This is one of their answers:

- There were no challenges, but I did not continue writing because Croatian Wikipedia was not developing at the expected speed and I lost interest.

Three respondents had certain challenges or problems while writing Wikipedia articles including the following:

- The biggest challenge was to find relevant sources for the topic (a small sports club) because the information available online was limited. I solved that problem by contacting people from the club who gave me the necessary literature.
- There are a lot of problems, from the editorial war of several authors to the large number of unverified data found there, as well as the deliberate distortion of data.
- The creation of graphic representations and use (i.e., the impossibility of using existing ones) due to copyright.

Also, some of the respondents who wrote articles on Wikipedia answered the question of whether they used scientific and professional works to support them in writing these articles. Nine respondents answered affirmatively to this question. This is one of their answers:

- Every real article on Wikipedia should be adequately referenced; unfortunately, in most cases, this is not the case. My works were always adequately accompanied by references.

Only one respondent did not answer this question affirmatively:

- Because of the topic, there was no need to use scientific or professional works, but if the topic had been different, I would definitely have used the sources mentioned.

As previously stated, out of the 226 respondents, most of them have not written articles on Wikipedia—212 respondents or 93.81%. Overall, 141 respondents answered the question asking them to state the main reasons why they did not decide to get involved in that activity. The most frequent reason given by the respondents for not participating in the activity of writing articles on Wikipedia was that they did not have time. After that, a lot of respondents also stated the following reasons:

- I am not interested; I did not think about it; and I had no reason to write Wikipedia articles.

Some respondents also stated the following reasons:

- I do not know how to do it; I did not have the opportunity; Wikipedia is not relevant; it would be too demanding; it is not my priority; no valorization for advancement in the profession; I write in other sources of information; the text would be unclear; I do not feel like it; there are more competent people for that; I doubt the validity of the whole concept; I am focused on writing scientific and professional papers; it is not my job; I have other jobs; I do not write anything on the Internet either; I do not consider the Wikipedia reliable enough; and superficial approach to the topic.

The reasons for not writing articles for Wikipedia are also explained by the following respondents' statements:

- I think that with my background in mostly writing scientific papers, writing texts on Wikipedia would be very demanding and would be too burdensome with referencing, and the text would probably be unclear to the average reader who does not deal with my topics.
- I think there are more competent people, sub-specialist oriented in the areas that are being written about.
- I never thought at all that I could write for Wikipedia, and in the academic community, Wikipedia is generally perceived as an undesirable source of information.
- I believe that it is work and that it should be approached in detail and responsibly, which I did not have time for, nor did I ever include in my plans.
- I do not know how to publish a text on Wikipedia, and I am not too interested in writing such content.
- I have not had such an idea yet because it seems to me that the site is already full of most of the information
- I often write scientific and professional papers, so, in this way, I satisfy such a need, passion, and interest.
- I still do not consider Wikipedia to be reliable enough to submit or correct texts.

In one of the survey questions, respondents were asked to indicate their levels of agreement with statements about the reasons that motivate them to write articles for Wikipedia. Among the six reasons presented in Table 9, most respondents completely or strongly agree with the following two statements—they agree that they would have the motivation to write articles for Wikipedia if it would be valued for the advancement to a higher work position, and they agree with the statement that they would have the motivation to write articles for Wikipedia if they could correct errors in its articles. After that, most respondents completely or strongly agree with statement 1 that they would be motivated if their writing on Wikipedia would contribute to the dissemination of knowledge in the community and to the popularization of science and the profession in which they work. The next most frequent motive for writing articles is when their writing on Wikipedia would contribute to the presentation of topics on Wikipedia that are not sufficiently represented.

Also, respondents had the opportunity to state some additional reasons that could motivate them to write articles for Wikipedia or to write something additional about that topic. Fifteen respondents responded to this option. Of these, five respondents stated that they would be motivated by some benefit they would gain from writing articles, for example, a financial benefit or a professional benefit, in the sense that this activity is valued during the process of advancement to higher positions. In this regard, we cite the answer of one respondent:

- Given the opportunity cost, i.e., limited time to meet the conditions for promotion, the best motive would be to value this activity for promotion. I am familiar with the way of creating text on Wikipedia, and, considering the influence of Wikipedia, it would be very important for academic institutions with their academic standards to get involved in content creation as much as possible. However, if it is not valued, then academic institutions cannot spend their limited resources on such an activity.

Table 9. Motivation to write articles for Wikipedia.

To what extent could some of these reasons motivate you to write articles for Wikipedia?					
1. Disseminating knowledge in the community and popularizing science and the profession in which I work					
1—Completely disagree	2	3	4	5—Completely agree	Without answer
11.06%	6.64%	23.01%	22.57%	18.58%	18.14%
2. Upgrading my own knowledge					
1—Completely disagree	2	3	4	5—Completely agree	Without answer
13.27%	13.27%	24.34%	15.93%	13.27%	19.91%
3. Correcting errors on Wikipedia					
1—Completely disagree	2	3	4	5—Completely agree	Without answer
11.50%	7.08%	18.14%	25.22%	22.12%	15.93%
4. Presentation of topics on Wikipedia that are not sufficiently represented					
1—Completely disagree	2	3	4	5—Completely agree	Without answer
10.62%	9.73%	24.34%	21.24%	15.93%	18.14%
5. I am motivated to contribute to Wikipedia by the possibility of participating in a useful and interesting activity					
1—Completely disagree	2	3	4	5—Completely agree	Without answer
14.16%	17.26%	23.01%	15.04%	7.96%	22.57%
6. I would have the motivation to write articles for Wikipedia if it would be valued for the advancement to a higher work-position					
1—Completely disagree	2	3	4	5—Completely agree	Without answer
12.83%	7.52%	11.95%	14.16%	33.19%	20.35%
7. There is no reason that can motivate me to write articles for Wikipedia					
1—Completely disagree	2	3	4	5—Completely agree	Without answer
30.97%	15.04%	15.04%	2.65%	10.62%	25.66%

Two respondents answered that their motivation for writing articles on Wikipedia would be if they had more free time at their disposal. One respondent saw the expansion of his/her knowledge and contribution to the general culture as a motivation for writing. One respondent stated that he/she would participate in writing articles on Wikipedia if it was performed as part of a project and if several other colleagues participated in it. Another respondent stated that he/she has not yet thought about writing articles on Wikipedia, while five respondents answered that they would not write articles on Wikipedia for various reasons. For example, one respondent had the following opinion about writing articles on Wikipedia:

- After getting to know Wikipedia and how to work on it, there is no way I can contribute anymore.

Among this group, two respondents preferred to write texts elsewhere, not on Wikipedia:

- I prefer to publish original scientific texts and books that occupy and fulfill me.
- If it is about the popularization of science, I write biographical lexicographical units, for example, in the Croatian Biographical Lexicon.

Table 10 contains data about the role of Wikipedia in the promotion of scientific and professional knowledge and repositories, as well as the participation of university researchers and teaching staff in writing articles on Wikipedia. With regard to statement 1, 32.74% of respondents almost completely or completely agree with the statement that Wikipedia is a very suitable platform for the promotion of scientific and professional knowledge (grades 4 and 5). In addition to that, 29.65% of respondents almost completely or completely agree with statement 2 that Wikipedia is a very suitable platform for the promotion of scientific and professional repositories, such as the Hrčak portal with articles from Croatian scientific and professional journals (grades 4 and 5).

Table 10. Different statements related to Wikipedia and the following topics: promotion of knowledge and repositories and participation of faculty staff.

1. Wikipedia is a very suitable platform for the promotion of scientific and professional knowledge					
1—Completely disagree	2	3	4	5—Completely agree	Without answer
10.18%	16.37%	36.73%	23.01%	9.73%	3.98%
2. Wikipedia is a very suitable platform for the promotion of scientific and professional repositories, such as the Hrčak portal with articles from Croatian scientific and professional journals					
1—Completely disagree	2	3	4	5—Completely agree	Without answer
12.83%	18.58%	33.19%	20.35%	9.29%	5.75%
3. It would be desirable for university researchers and teaching staff to write articles on Wikipedia with the aim of spreading knowledge about topics from their professional field					
1—Completely disagree	2	3	4	5—Completely agree	Without answer
11.06%	9.29%	30.97%	25.22%	19.91%	3.54%

Based on the respondents' answers related to statements 1 and 2, we can see that there is a significant share of respondents who almost completely or completely agree with these two statements (grades 4 and 5), but also, there is a significant share of respondents who completely or almost completely disagree with these statements (grades 1 and 2).

With regard to statement 3, it is an interesting finding that 45.13% of respondents almost completely or completely agree with the statement that it would be desirable for university researchers and teaching staff to write articles on Wikipedia with the aim of spreading knowledge about topics from their professional fields (grades 4 and 5).

Respondents also had the option to write comments related to the topics covered in the survey or to highlight something that was not covered by the questions in the survey. Thirteen respondents responded to this option. These are several respondents' comments:

- I believe that the survey should have included—in my opinion—the main problem of Wikipedia, which is also the main source of its unreliability, which is the freedom to self-assess the author's competence because people simply immodestly self-assess themselves, that is, they consider themselves competent enough to open a profile and write; this applies especially to Croatian Wikipedia.
- I think that such a simple and freely available open (both in terms of access to readers and in terms of access to authors) encyclopedia is a very good idea and that everyone should have the *opportunity* to write, but I also think that not everyone should get the opportunity to realize that opportunity, and some kind of screening that guarantees the author's competence must exist. Self-correction of the system from other authors apparently does not work.
- I must clarify that Wiki is unfortunately not considered a reliable source, that is why I said that I do not use that source when writing, but I also think that if the academic community were to get involved in the formatting of the texts, it could be a great way to obtain reliable information easy and efficient.
- I am currently at a stage in my life where I do not have time to write on Wikipedia (two small children). But in about 10 years, it would be interesting to me.
- Political and social topics are often quite distorted. The references are, to put it mildly, funny, and the truth of the content is often questionable.

- The English version has some quality, while the Croatian version is at the level of the yellow press (often, the references are articles from the yellow press).
- Wikipedia is a project I grew up with since my student days. At first, it seemed a bit hippie. And now it is one of the main sources of information for smart and AI internet searchers, such as ChatGPT, Bing AI, Bard, etc. I do not like that because Wikipedia has a concept that I never liked: the truth is what the majority say! That is how writing Wikipedia articles works, especially if they turn into a discussion. The majority wins. This means, for example, from the aspect of history, that the history of small nations can always be overcome and written by historians of larger nations because there are more of them. One should search for the objective truth, and not agree on the truth. For me personally, Wikipedia is a potentially very dangerous project!

6. Discussion

In this study, numerous insights were gained about the practices and attitudes of the research and teaching staff at the University of Split, Croatia, regarding the online encyclopedia Wikipedia. This section presents and discusses the implications of the results.

It was found that almost all respondents read articles on Wikipedia. The most common reasons they cited for reading Wikipedia are that it serves to inform them, that it provides quick and easy access to information, and that it helps them find basic information about the topic they are interested in.

Respondents often stated that their reason for reading Wikipedia is that links to articles on Wikipedia often appear in search results when using web search engines. This aspect is closely related to the previously mentioned positive aspect of Wikipedia, namely, that by using this online encyclopedia, information can be found quickly and easily. If the user searches for a topic through a web search engine, such as the Google search engine, and if the user is offered links to Wikipedia articles among the first-listed search results related to that topic, then the user can quickly and easily find relevant content, even when not specifically searching for articles on Wikipedia. The high ranking of links leading to Wikipedia in the search results of web search engines can be influenced by a number of factors, among which are the number of users, the amount of content on Wikipedia, and the representation and visibility of the topic that the user is searching for on Wikipedia. Many language versions of Wikipedia have a lot of users, a lot of content, and the representation of a large number of topics that may be interesting for users to research, so it is not surprising that Wikipedia articles are frequently highly positioned in web search engine results.

It was also confirmed that respondents use Wikipedia both in their work and private life. This finding indicates that Wikipedia can be a useful source of information in different spheres of life. Many general classic, printed encyclopedias certainly have this dual function, but Wikipedia may have a certain advantage over them, in that it is quickly and easily accessible via the Internet, as well as the advantage that, because of the way it was created and its availability on the web, it can present many diverse topics that cover a wide range of work and private interests. Another frequently cited reason for reading Wikipedia is that references in Wikipedia articles help respondents find additional sources of information related to topics of interest. This finding confirms the previously mentioned considerations about the importance of using quality sources based on which Wikipedia is written, as well as placing as many references as possible within Wikipedia text [3,14,16–18,41,54]. In addition, it was found that more than half of the respondents strongly or completely agree with the statement that while they are reading the articles on Wikipedia, sometimes they study references based on which the articles were written. These findings confirm that it is important to use quality sources based on which Wikipedia is written, as well as to place as many references as possible within Wikipedia text. This is also emphasized by the Wikipedia editing rules, in which special attention is paid to the principle of 'verifiability' so that 'other people using the encyclopedia can check that the information comes from a reliable source' [14]. Not only do the quality sources based on which Wikipedia was written enhance the quality of content on this online encyclopedia, but they also enable users to find and study these sources more easily through Wikipedia articles. However, findings from the study about differences between Wikipedia editions in the Serbian, Croatian, Bosnian, Slovenian, and Serbo-Croatian languages indicate that in these editions of Wikipedia, the verifiability of information in certain types of articles is not high because there is not much referencing of sources used to write these articles [40]. The quantity and quality of references in articles of Wikipedia in the Croatian language is an important issue that should be explored in more detail in future studies. Adding more references to Wikipedia articles and finding quality sources to develop Wikipedia articles could be a valuable contribution of Croatian faculty members to Wikipedia. Their working positions have made them skilled in these activities and aware of their values.

One of the important results of this study is that almost half of the respondents strongly or completely agree with the statement that the level of accuracy of the information available on Wikipedia is quite high. This is an interesting finding, which indicates that Wikipedia has gained the trust of a significant number of respondents for its accuracy. The results of some previous studies conducted outside Croatia are similar to the results of this study with regard to the positive attitudes of faculty members towards the accuracy of Wikipedia. For example, the faculty members at the Universitat Oberta de Catalunya in Spain also have a strong positive perception of Wikipedia's quality [44]. In another study about the attitudes of faculty members of two Catalan universities towards Wikipedia, it was found that a striking majority of respondents gave positive answers in relation to the quality and reliability of Wikipedia articles [6]. It would be valuable to explore the attitudes of Croatian faculty about Wikipedia accuracy by conducting further studies with faculty members of other Croatian higher education institutions. In that way, we could determine whether the results of this study are representative of other Croatian higher education institutions, not only the University of Split. It is worth mentioning that a partly similar study was conducted in Croatia among students and teachers at J. J. Strossmayer University in Osijek. It was found that students at that university had a more positive opinion of Wikipedia than teachers. It was established that the majority of faculty members at Osijek have a high level of agreement with the statement that the accuracy and objectivity of data in articles on Wikipedia are questionable because anyone can edit and change them [11]. However, it needs to be said that the study was conducted in 2016 and, therefore, it is possible that the attitudes of a considerable number of faculty members about this issue could have changed.

In this study about practices and attitudes of the research and teaching staff of the University of Split, it was also established that respondents strongly or completely support the statement that all scientific works should be freely available on the Internet to all interested parties without the need to pay subscriptions for databases. Also, the majority of respondents strongly or completely agree with the statement that most of the scientific and professional works of which they are (co)authors are freely available on the Internet. These findings were seen in the context of many other studies, some of which established that people who support collaborative and open knowledge-creation models have more positive attitudes towards Wikipedia and others that confirmed that an important motivation for many who contribute to Wikipedia is an appreciation for sharing knowledge, appreciation for the education of others, and support for open access and similar concepts [10]. Therefore, it is not surprising that another finding of our study was that almost half of the respondents strongly or completely agree with the statement that it would be desirable for university researchers and teaching staff to write articles on Wikipedia with the aim of spreading knowledge about topics from their professional fields. It could be said that Wikipedia is seen by many respondents as an effective intermediary between the results of scientific research and the broader public—the people who do not read scientific journals in their everyday lives but who frequently browse articles on Wikipedia looking for answers to various questions. Faculty members who share this view could initiate, organize, and conduct Citizen Science projects in which they could cooperate with volunteers from the general public in the creation and dissemination of new knowledge through Wikipedia and other open, crowdsourcing platforms.

From the survey answers, it could also be seen that a lot more respondents consider Wikipedia useful for students' learning and writing undergraduate and master's theses than respondents who consider it useful for professors' learning and writing scientific and professional papers. A possible explanation for this difference is that more respondents believe that professors' learning and writing scientific and professional papers are activities that, to a greater extent, require the use of more reliable and high-quality sources of information than Wikipedia, compared with the activities of students' learning and writing of undergraduate and master's theses. A lot of the literature, in accordance with these findings, confirms and describes the value of Wikipedia as a learning tool for students. For example, Soler-Adillon, Pavlovic, and Freixa indicated that previous research confirmed that the use of Wikipedia in the classroom can enhance students' literacy skills and that adding and enhancing Wikipedia's content could be a motivating activity for students [42]. Also, Martín-García, Almaraz-Menéndez, and López-Esteban wrote that today, Wikipedia is much more present at universities and that it provides teachers with numerous opportunities for educational innovation [44].

Next, our study showed that significantly more respondents consider Wikipedia very useful for acquiring new knowledge about topics that are not in their professional fields, compared with respondents who consider it very useful for acquiring new knowledge about topics from their professional fields. From this, it can be concluded that it is possible that Wikipedia contains more instructive information about topics that are not in respondents' professional fields or that perhaps Wikipedia also contains instructive information about topics that are in their professional fields but only basic information about which respondents are already familiar. Both of these cases indicate information gaps on Wikipedia that can be filled by having experts write articles that are currently incomplete or non-existent. The teaching and research staff at higher education institutions are experts on various topics, and they could make valuable contributions to the content of Wikipedia. In that way, they could contribute to the dissemination of knowledge in the community and to the popularization of science and the profession in which they work. Also, they could contribute to the presentation of topics on Wikipedia that are not sufficiently represented. Finally, by writing Wikipedia articles, they could upgrade their own knowledge. Although the activity of writing articles on Wikipedia is simple in technical terms, it is much more complex with regard to its intellectual challenges, and, therefore, it can be valuable for the advancement of editors' knowledge. Finally, it is also an activity that could advance editors' skills of clear and meaningful knowledge communication.

It was also found that 8.41% of respondents have high motivation to write Wikipedia articles on topics from their professional fields, and 4.42% of respondents have high motivation to write Wikipedia articles on topics that are not in their professional fields. Although at first glance it may seem that these are not large percentages of respondents, they are nevertheless significant. Namely, previous research about Wikipedia editors indicates that a very small number of Wikipedia editors create a very large amount of content on Wikipedia [75]. Therefore, if the majority of faculty members at the University of Split who have a great motivation for writing articles on Wikipedia were to participate in this activity, it could significantly contribute to the increase in the quantity and quality of the content of this encyclopedia. These highly motivated members could also be initiators and leaders of educational initiatives that could encourage students and members of the wider community to get involved in editing Wikipedia. Also, activities and contributions of highly motivated faculty members could serve as examples and incentives for other faculty members to consider becoming involved in contributing to Wikipedia development.

Most respondents completely or strongly agree with the following two statements—they agree that they would have the motivation to write articles for Wikipedia if it would be valued for the advancement to a higher work position, and they agree with the statement that they would have the motivation to write articles for Wikipedia if they could correct errors in its articles. Based on these responses, it can be concluded that many respondents, with adequate motivation, could start to write articles on Wikipedia or that they at least could further consider the decision whether to get involved in writing articles on Wikipedia. It should be emphasized that many respondents indicated that they would be particularly motivated to write articles on Wikipedia if this activity would be valued for their advancement to a higher work position. Currently, in Croatia, there is no incentive of this type. The decision to acknowledge the activity of writing articles on Wikipedia as an activity that can support the advancement to a higher work position of university employees could be considered by governing bodies of a specific university, the alliance of universities, the ministry in charge of the field of science and teaching at higher education institutions, or/and some other relevant institutions. This is not an easy decision to make because there are many aspects related to this topic and there are arguments for and against that kind of approach. But one thing is quite certain—if decisions regarding this were to be confirmed, then, at least judging by the responses of the respondents from this survey, many more employees of higher education institutions would be willing to write articles on Wikipedia. Also, if writing articles on Wikipedia is officially recognized in the future by educational authorities, then it will be necessary to have a reliable method for proving of their authorship. Although Wikipedia is an information system on which anyone can write articles anonymously, it is also possible to write articles under one's own name and surname, if the user creates a user account. Given that each Wikipedia article contains a 'view history' link that allows viewing past revisions of that article, anybody can see which specific users have edited a specific article and when these edits were made. In this way, it is possible to prove the authorship of Wikipedia articles.

As it was already said, an equally strong motive for respondents' editing of Wikipedia is to correct errors in its articles. This motivation can be used to encourage the writing of articles on Wikipedia by employees of higher education institutions, by organizing various activities such as workshops or edit-a-thons in which one of the main goals is to search for and correct errors on Wikipedia in the thematic field in which the participants are experts [76]. This can also be performed in the form of a competition to correct errors, which can be an additional incentive to participate in this type of activity. When attracting participants to edit-a-thons or other similar activities, the fact that many respondents have high levels of motivation for writing articles on Wikipedia related to the following aspects of their contribution can also have an impact: contribution to the dissemination of knowledge in the community and to the popularization of science and the profession in which they work and presentation of the topics on Wikipedia that are not sufficiently represented on it. Therefore, these motivations should also be considered when designing the content of activities to encourage and implement the writing of articles on Wikipedia, as well as when describing and promoting these activities. Among the rules for editing Wikipedia, it is written that 'there is an increasing need for the scientific community to engage with Wikipedia to ensure that the information it contains is accurate and current' and that 'for scientists, contributing to Wikipedia is an excellent way of fulfilling public engagement responsibilities and sharing expertise' [15]. This is especially important for editions of Wikipedia that do not have as many editors, articles, and references in articles, as some other more popular and developed editions of Wikipedia. As we saw in one of the previous sections of this article, Croatian-language Wikipedia does not have a very high number of articles per 1000 speakers of Croatian language.

In comparison with Wikipedia editions in the Hungarian, Polish, Czech, and Bosnian languages, and especially in comparison with Wikipedia editions in the Slovenian and Serbian languages, Croatian-language Wikipedia has the lowest number of articles per 1000 speakers [37]. Also, among these Wikipedia editions, articles on Croatian-language Wikipedia are the least frequently updated [38]. Both of these factors could be an additional motivation for some members of the Croatian higher education community to begin to write and enhance articles on Croatian-language Wikipedia.

In this study, it was also found that a significant part of respondents are not very familiar with how Wikipedia works or how to add new content to it. Knowledge about this could help them to better understand various aspects of Wikipedia, to be in a better position to evaluate various phenomena on Wikipedia, to contribute to its development and quality, and to be able to use Wikipedia to share their professional and other knowledge with the wider community. From the respondents' answers, we can see that some respondents would be very willing to participate in educational programs to learn about different aspects of writing articles for Wikipedia, as well as to organize and conduct these types of educational programs. It is not necessary to involve a large number of faculty staff in this type of educational program. In contrast, even a small number of participants who are sufficiently motivated and willing to participate in educational activities of this type can strongly contribute to the development of Wikipedia's content and the creation and encouragement of the creation of new communities of its editors. It should be mentioned that Wikipedia has a sandbox page, where users can experiment with editing. Anything they write will not remain indefinitely on that page, but it will be automatically deleted in regular periods. This is one of the ways to practice various aspects of writing Wikipedia articles. However, the activity of writing Wikipedia articles contains many important aspects that cannot be learned by only using the sandbox page. For example, Wikipedia editors should learn about the guidelines, principles, procedures, and rules for adding various types of content to Wikipedia. They should have a good understanding of the criteria and procedures for including some parts of the content in Wikipedia articles and they should have to learn about Wikipedia's style of writing, the methods and principles of making references in articles, adding images and audiovisual material to Wikipedia articles, logical and successful integration of newly added content with existing content, and so on. Therefore, comprehensive and inspirational educational programs for learning about different aspects of writing and enhancing the quality of Wikipedia articles are required.

7. Conclusions

Wikipedia is one of the most popular websites on the web. Among its authors, there are certainly a lot of employees of higher education institutions who, using their expert knowledge, improve and expand the articles of this online encyclopedia. In this research, the practices and attitudes of the research and teaching staff at the University of Split about the online encyclopedia Wikipedia were investigated.

The results showed that almost all respondents read Wikipedia articles. Also, the results showed that there are respondents who would like to write Wikipedia articles on topics from their professional fields and articles on topics that are not in their professional fields. As already mentioned in a previous part of this paper, a large amount of content on Wikipedia is created by a very small number of editors. Therefore, a small number of faculty staff involved in Wikipedia editing could achieve a great impact regarding the development and improvement of Wikipedia's content. They could make a significant and valuable change to Wikipedia's content with their own editing, and also by encouraging, promoting, and organizing participation in Wikipedia editing by their students and other members of the faculty staff. Additionally, some of the respondents who answered that they would not want to write articles on Wikipedia themselves might change their opinion if they participate in educational programs related to Wikipedia. There was also a finding that a relatively small number of respondents have participated in writing articles for Wikipedia. At the same time, it should be taken into account that compared with employees from other professions in Croatia or compared with the faculty staff of other higher education institutions in Croatia, it is possible that the faculty staff from the University of Split participate significantly more in editing Wikipedia articles. Unfortunately, there are no studies that would allow these comparisons. Respondents stated that in terms of writing articles on Wikipedia, they would be motivated the most if this activity would be valued for the advancement to a higher work position. Currently, in Croatia, there is no incitement of this type. The decision to acknowledge and reward this activity could be considered and accepted by governing bodies of a specific university or other relevant institutions related to higher education. There are arguments for and against this kind of approach. Judging by the responses of the respondents, if such a decision were to be adopted, it could have a significant impact on increasing the interest of research and teaching staff in higher education institutions to get involved in writing and improving the quality of Wikipedia content. A large number of respondents also stated other strong motivations for getting involved in writing articles on Wikipedia including, first of all, correcting observed mistakes in articles, and then contributing to the spread of knowledge in the community and the popularization of science and their professions. Also, some of them stated that their motive for writing or improving articles on Wikipedia may be to present topics that are not sufficiently represented in this online encyclopedia.

All these motivations for writing articles on Wikipedia should therefore be considered when designing activities to encourage and initiate the writing of articles on Wikipedia, as well as when describing and promoting these activities. The high levels of various types of respondents' motivations are not surprising given that the mission and goals of higher education institutions coincide well with the mission and goals of Wikipedia—members of both communities value the dissemination of knowledge and the popularization of science, the accuracy of information, and the representation of different perspectives and topics. Therefore, it is not surprising to find that almost half of the respondents strongly agree with the statement that it would be desirable for university scientists and teaching staff to write articles on Wikipedia with the aim of spreading knowledge about topics in their professional fields.

The majority of respondents are currently not very familiar with how Wikipedia works or how to add new content to it. Less than 3% of respondents participated in educational programs whose goal was to familiarize them with the possibilities, procedures, or principles of writing texts for Wikipedia.

In such a situation, the following question arises: in which ways could one try to encourage a change in attitude among a larger number of employees of higher education institutions about their own participation in writing articles on Wikipedia? The insights gained through this study can help to illuminate different inter-related aspects of this situation, can be a starting point for more grounded thinking about it, and can support the consideration and initiation of various activities that could help change the attitudes of the faculty staff about their own participation in writing articles on Wikipedia. Also, the insights gained through this study could help to launch activities such as the following: educational workshops about Wikipedia and the creation of its content; educational workshops on the benefits that the incorporation of Wikipedia's content from scientific and professional journals can have on the journals and repositories where these contents are located; edit-a-thons in which a specific thematic group of Wikipedia articles is expanded and qualitatively improved; and initiatives for recognition and formal evaluation of quality contributions to Wikipedia by faculty staff with teaching and research responsibilities.

Finally, it needs to be said that this study has some limitations that should be considered. The first limitation is the survey method used to gather data. When survey respondents answer certain questions, some of them may answer in such a way that presents some of their attitudes or practices in a different way than they really are. Sometimes the individual practices or certain attitudes of respondents could be determined in more detail and more reliably if other research methods are used, such as observing the practices of respondents while using Wikipedia. Another limitation of this research is that the research sample consisted only of respondents from the University of Split. In order to obtain a more representative picture of the practices and attitudes of the research and teaching staff in Croatia about Wikipedia, it is necessary to conduct research with respondents from other Croatian higher education institutions.

Therefore, in future research on Wikipedia, the practices and attitudes of the research and teaching staff of higher education institutions in Croatia, as well as outside Croatia, can be investigated if one wants to determine and compare the situation related to this topic in several countries. In addition, other research methods can be used in future research in order to determine practices and attitudes about Wikipedia in more detail and more comprehensively. For example, the interview method can be used. When selecting respondents for interviews, one can focus on specific groups of research and teaching employees, for example, on those employees who have already edited Wikipedia or on those who have a high motivation to edit Wikipedia. Also, the quality of articles on Wikipedia in the Croatian language can be analyzed and evaluated, given that there is almost no research of this type.

Funding: This research received no external funding.

Data Availability Statement: The original contributions presented in this study are included in this article. Further inquiries can be directed to the corresponding author.

Acknowledgments: I would like to thank all the respondents who completed the survey.

Conflicts of Interest: The author declares no conflicts of interest.

References

1. SimilarWeb. Top Websites Ranking—Most Visited Websites in The World. Available online: https://www.similarweb.com/top-websites (accessed on 19 March 2024).
2. SimilarWeb. Top Websites Ranking in Croatia in February 2024. Available online: https://www.similarweb.com/top-websites/croatia (accessed on 19 March 2024).
3. Thompson, N.; Hanley, D. Science is shaped by Wikipedia: Evidence from a randomized control trial. In *Wikipedia in Academia*; Gallo, V., Petrucco, C., Eds.; Padova University Press: Padova, Italy, 2020; pp. 105–126.
4. Teplitskiy, M.; Lu, G.; Duede, E. Amplifying the impact of open access: Wikipedia and the diffusion of science. *J. Assoc. Inf. Sci. Technol.* **2017**, *68*, 2116–2127. [CrossRef]
5. Jemielniak, D.; Aibar, E. Bridging the gap between Wikipedia and academia. *J. Assoc. Inf. Sci. Technol.* **2016**, *67*, 1773–1776. [CrossRef]
6. Aibar, E.; Lladós-Masllorens, J.; Meseguer-Artola, A.; Minguillón, J.; Lerga, M. Wikipedia at university: What faculty think and do about it. In *Wikipedia in Academia*; Gallo, V., Petrucco, C., Eds.; Padova University Press: Padova, Italy, 2020; pp. 17–22.
7. Ball, C. Defying easy categorization: Wikipedia as primary, secondary and tertiary resource. *Insights* **2023**, *36*, 7. [CrossRef]
8. Bould, M.D.; Hladkowicz, E.S.; Pigford, A.E.; Ufholz, L.; Postonogova, T.; Shin, E.; Boet, S. References that anyone can edit: Review of Wikipedia citations in peer reviewed health science literature. *BMJ* **2014**, *348*. [CrossRef] [PubMed]
9. Tomaszewski, R.; MacDonald, K.I. A study of citations to Wikipedia in scholarly publications. *Sci. Technol. Libr.* **2016**, *35*, 246–261. [CrossRef]
10. Konieczny, P. Teacher from Adversaries to Allies? The Uneasy Relationship between Experts and the Wikipedia Community. *J. Des. Econ. Innov.* **2021**, *7*, 151–170.
11. Faletar Tanacković, S.; Đurđević, A.; Badurina, B. Wikipedija u akademskom okruženju: Stavovi i iskustva studenata i nastavnika. *Libellarium* **2015**, *8*, 161–199.
12. Hrčak. Portal of Croatian Scientific and Professional Journals. Search Results for the Search Term: Wikipedia. Available online: https://hrcak.srce.hr/en/pretraga?q=WIKIPEDIA (accessed on 19 March 2024).
13. Wikipedia. Five Pillars. Available online: https://en.wikipedia.org/wiki/Wikipedia:Five_pillars (accessed on 19 March 2024).
14. Wikipedia. Verifiability. Available online: https://en.wikipedia.org/wiki/Wikipedia:Verifiability (accessed on 19 March 2024).
15. Wikipedia. Ten Simple Rules. Available online: https://en.wikipedia.org/wiki/Wikipedia:Ten_simple_rules_for_editing_Wikipedia (accessed on 19 March 2024).
16. Evans, P.; Krauthammer, M. Exploring the use of social media to measure journal article impact. In *Proceedings of the American Medical Informatics Association Annual Symposium*; American Medical Informatics Association: Boston, MA, USA, 2011; pp. 374–381.
17. Nielsen, F.A. Scientific citations in Wikipedia. *First Monday* **1997**, *12*. Available online: http://firstmonday.org/ojs/index.php/fm/article/view/1997 (accessed on 19 March 2024). [CrossRef]
18. Curtis, V. *Online Citizen Science and the Widening of Academia*; Palgrave Macmillan: Cham, Switzerland, 2018.
19. Mordechai, H.; Dörler, D.; Heigl, F.; Lemmens, R.; Manzoni, M.; Hecker, S.; Vohland, K. What is citizen science? The challenges of definition. In *The Science of Citizen Science*; Vohland, K., Land-Zandstra, A., Ceccaroni, L., Lemmens, R., Perelló, J., Ponti, M., Samson, R., Wagenknecht, K., Eds.; Springer Nature: Berlin/Heidelberg, Germany, 2021; pp. 13–33.
20. Paleco, C.; Peter, S.G.; Seoane, N.S.; Kaufmann, K.; Argyri, P. Inclusiveness and Diversity in Citizen Science. In *The Science of Citizen Science*; Vohland, K., Land-Zandstra, A., Ceccaroni, L., Lemmens, R., Perelló, J., Ponti, M., Samson, R., Wagenknecht, K., Eds.; Springer Nature: Berlin/Heidelberg, Germany, 2021; pp. 261–281.
21. Leßmöllmanno, A. Current trends and future visions of (research on) science communication. In *Science Communication*; Leßmöllmanno, A., Dascal, M., Gloning, T., Eds.; Walter de Gruytere: Berlin, Germany, 2019; pp. 657–688.

22. Meseguer Artola, A.; Aibar, E.; Ammetller, G.; Lladós, J.; Minguillón, J.; Lerga, M. Factors that influence the teaching use of Wikipedia in higher education. *J. Assoc. Inf. Sci. Technol.* **2016**, *67*, 1224–1232. [CrossRef]
23. Wikipedia. Wikipedija na Hrvatskome Jeziku. Available online: https://hr.wikipedia.org/wiki/Wikipedija_na_hrvatskome_jeziku (accessed on 29 May 2024).
24. Wikipedia. List of Wikipedias. Available online: https://meta.wikimedia.org/wiki/List_of_Wikipedias (accessed on 29 May 2024).
25. Wikipedia. Wikipedia: Administrators. Available online: https://en.wikipedia.org/wiki/Wikipedia:Administrators (accessed on 29 May 2024).
26. Wikipedia. Wikipedia Administrators. Available online: https://en.wikipedia.org/wiki/Wikipedia_administrators (accessed on 29 May 2024).
27. Wikipedia. Wikipedia: Statistics. Available online: https://en.wikipedia.org/wiki/Wikipedia:Statistics (accessed on 29 May 2024).
28. Wikipedia. Wikipedia: Wikipedians. Available online: https://en.wikipedia.org/wiki/Wikipedia:Wikipedians (accessed on 29 May 2024).
29. Wikipedia. Slovene Wikipedia. Available online: https://en.wikipedia.org/wiki/Slovene_Wikipedia (accessed on 29 May 2024).
30. Wikipedia. Bosnian Wikipedia. Available online: https://en.wikipedia.org/wiki/Bosnian_Wikipedia (accessed on 29 May 2024).
31. Wikipedia. Serbian Wikipedia. Available online: https://en.wikipedia.org/wiki/Serbian_Wikipedia (accessed on 29 May 2024).
32. Wikipedia. Serbo-Croatian Wikipedia. Available online: https://en.wikipedia.org/wiki/Serbo-Croatian_Wikipedia (accessed on 29 May 2024).
33. Wikipedia. Hungarian Wikipedia. Available online: https://en.wikipedia.org/wiki/Hungarian_Wikipedia (accessed on 29 May 2024).
34. Wikipedia. Czech Wikipedia. Available online: https://en.wikipedia.org/wiki/Czech_Wikipedia (accessed on 29 May 2024).
35. Wikipedia. Polish Wikipedia. Available online: https://en.wikipedia.org/wiki/Polish_Wikipedia (accessed on 29 May 2024).
36. Wikipedia. Available online: https://en.wikipedia.org/wiki/Wikipedia (accessed on 29 May 2024).
37. Wikipedia. List of Wikipedias by Speakers Per Article. Available online: https://meta.wikimedia.org/wiki/List_of_Wikipedias_by_speakers_per_article (accessed on 29 May 2024).
38. Wikipedia. Wikipedia Article Depth. Available online: https://meta.wikimedia.org/wiki/Wikipedia_article_depth (accessed on 29 May 2024).
39. Kharazian, Z.; Starbird, K.; Hill, B.M. Governance Capture in a Self-Governing Community: A Qualitative Comparison of the Croatian, Serbian, Bosnian, and Serbo-Croatian Wikipedias. In *Proceedings of the ACM on Human-Computer Interaction 8, Issue CSCW1*; Nichols, J., Ed.; Association for Computing Machinery: New York, NY, USA, 2024; pp. 1–26.
40. Rajcic, N. Comparison of Wikipedia Articles in Different Languages. Master's Thesis, Vienna University of Technology—Informatics, Vienna, Austria, 2017.
41. Noč, M.; Zumer, M. The completeness of articles and citation in the Slovene Wikipedia. *Program* **2016**, *48*, 53–175. [CrossRef]
42. Soler-Adillon, J.; Pavlovic, D.; Freixa, P. Wikipedia in higher education: Changes in perceived value through content contribution. *Comunicar* **2018**, *26*, 39–48. [CrossRef]
43. Johinke, R.; Di Lauro, F. Wikipedia in higher education: Practice what you teach. *Stud. High. Educ.* **2020**, *45*, 947–949. [CrossRef]
44. Martín-García, T.; Almaraz-Menéndez, F.; López-Esteban, C. Wikipedia at the University: Engaging students and teachers in open knowledge and collaborative work. In *7th International Conference on Higher Education Advances (HEAd'21)*; Domènech, I., Soria, J., Merello Giménez, P., De La Poza Plaza, E., Eds.; Universitat Politècnica de València: València, Spain, 2021; pp. 235–242.
45. Wikipedia. Education Program. Available online: http://en.wikipedia.org/wiki/Wikipedia:Education_program (accessed on 19 March 2024).
46. Wikiedu. About Us. Available online: https://wikiedu.org/about-us (accessed on 19 March 2024).
47. Wikipedia Foundation. Available online: https://wikimediafoundation.org (accessed on 19 March 2024).
48. Lerga, M.; Aibar, E. Best Practice Guide to Use Wikipedia in University Education. 2015. Available online: https://openaccess.uoc.edu/bitstream/10609/41662/6/Best_Practice_Guide_Wikipedia_2015.pdf (accessed on 19 March 2024).
49. Wikipedia. Education Program/Educators. Available online: https://en.wikipedia.org/wiki/Wikipedia:Education_program/Educators (accessed on 19 March 2024).
50. Wikiedu. Instructor Orientation Modules. Available online: https://dashboard.wikiedu.org/training/instructors (accessed on 19 March 2024).
51. Wikipedia. Education Program: Students. Available online: https://en.wikipedia.org/wiki/Wikipedia:Education_program/Students (accessed on 19 March 2024).
52. Wikiedu. Student Training Modules. Available online: https://dashboard.wikiedu.org/training/students (accessed on 19 March 2024).
53. Wikimedia Foundation. Instructor Basics—How to Use Wikipedia as a Teaching Tool. Available online: https://upload.wikimedia.org/wikipedia/commons/9/92/Instructor_Basics_How_to_Use_Wikipedia_as_a_Teaching_Tool.pdf (accessed on 19 March 2024).

54. Carmichael, B.J.; Klock, M.M. Incorporating Wikipedia in the Classroom to Improve Science Learning and Communication. In *Scientific Communication—Practices, Theories, and Pedagogies*; Yu, H., Northcut, K., Eds.; Routledge: New York, NY, USA, 2018; pp. 278–300.
55. Pratesi, A.; Miller, W.; Sutton, E. Democratizing knowledge—Using Wikipedia for Inclusive Teaching and Research in Four Undergraduate Classes. *Radic. Teach.* **2019**, *114*, 22–33. [CrossRef]
56. Eijkman, H. Academics and Wikipedia: Reframing Web 2.0+ as a Disruptor of Traditional Academic Power-Knowledge Arrangements. *Campus-Wide Inf. Syst.* **2010**, *27*, 173–185. [CrossRef]
57. Luyt, B.; Tan, D. Improving Wikipedia's credibility: References and citations in a sample of history articles. *J. Am. Soc. Inf. Sci. Tech.* **2010**, *61*, 715–722. [CrossRef]
58. University of Split. Available online: https://www.unist.hr/en (accessed on 19 March 2024).
59. Faculty of Humanities and Social Sciences (University of Split). Available online: https://www.ffst.unist.hr/en (accessed on 19 March 2024).
60. Faculty of Electrical Engineering, Mechanical Engineering and Naval Architecture (University of Split). Available online: https://eng.fesb.unist.hr/ (accessed on 19 March 2024).
61. Faculty of Law (University of Split). Available online: https://www.pravst.unist.hr/en/ (accessed on 19 March 2024).
62. Faculty of Civil Engineering, Architecture and Geodesy (University of Split). Available online: https://gradst.unist.hr/eng (accessed on 19 March 2024).
63. Faculty of Science (University of Split). Available online: https://www.pmfst.unist.hr/?lang=en (accessed on 19 March 2024).
64. Faculty of Maritime Studies (University of Split). Available online: https://www.pfst.unist.hr/en (accessed on 19 March 2024).
65. University Department of Health Studies (University of Split). Available online: https://ozs.unist.hr/en/ (accessed on 19 March 2024).
66. Faculty of Economics, Business and Tourism (University of Split). Available online: https://www.efst.unist.hr/en (accessed on 19 March 2024).
67. Faculty of Chemistry and Technology (University of Split). Available online: https://www.ktf.unist.hr/index.php/en/ (accessed on 19 March 2024).
68. Faculty of Kinesiology (University of Split). Available online: https://web.kifst.unist.hr/en/ (accessed on 19 March 2024).
69. University Department of Marine Studies (University of Split). Available online: https://more.unist.hr/en/ (accessed on 19 March 2024).
70. University of Split/Sastavnice. Available online: https://www.unist.hr/sastavnice-56/56 (accessed on 17 March 2024).
71. Sveučilište u Splitu. Razvoj Sveučilišta. Available online: https://arhiva.unist.hr/sveuciliste/o-sveucilistu/razvoj-sveucilista (accessed on 29 May 2024).
72. Sveučilište u Splitu. Sveučilište Danas. Available online: https://arhiva.unist.hr/sveuciliste/o-sveucilistu/sveuciliste-danas (accessed on 29 May 2024).
73. Agencija za Znanost i Visoko Obrazovanje. Broj Studenata Prema Ustanovi Izvođača Sveučilišta u Zagrebu, Splitu, Osijeku i Rijeci (2022/23). Available online: https://www.azvo.hr/broj-studenata-prema-ustanovi-izvodaca-sveucilista-u-zagrebu-splitu-osijeku-i-rijeci-2022-23/ (accessed on 29 May 2024).
74. Hrčak. Portal of Croatian Scientific and Professional Journals. Available online: https://hrcak.srce.hr/en (accessed on 19 March 2024).
75. Haklay, M. Participatory citizen science. In *Citizen Science: Innovation in Open Science, Society and Policy*; Hecker, S., Haklay, M., Bowser, A., Makuch, Z., Vogel, J., Bonn, A., Eds.; UCL Press: London, UK, 2018; pp. 52–62.
76. Wikipedia. How to Run an Edit-a-Thon. Available online: https://en.wikipedia.org/wiki/Wikipedia:How_to_run_an_edit-a-thon (accessed on 19 March 2024).

publications

MDPI

Article

Is This the End of Anthropology as We Know It? Some Implication of FAIR Principles on Tales in Ethnological and Anthropological Qualitative Research

Olga Orlić

Institute of Ethnology and Folklore Research, 10000 Zagreb, Croatia; olga@ief.hr

Abstract: Open science, accessibility and knowledge sharing, especially of articles and monographs stemming from publicly funded research, seem to be moving in quite a positive direction toward scientific development and have received almost unanimous approval from the scientific community. However, when it comes to data sharing, the existing practice reveals a different picture, and not exclusively a discipline-dependent one. FAIR principles are developed and promoted as guiding tools for creating contextualized standards. The fact that data obtained by a qualitative methodology deserve special attention and treatment regarding the accessibility principle is recognized. Although FAIR principles provide ways to anonymize the data and interlocutors, individuals coming from smaller communities or even communities of practice can sometimes be easily recognized by members of the same community if data are openly accessed. Sometimes the interlocutors might agree with these terms, but sometimes they do not. According to the disciplinary code of ethics, a researcher is obliged to thoroughly describe the ways of the raw data management and usage, and in the case of mandatory raw data sharing (e.g., for receiving funding), it can inevitably impact the narratives collected. The prerogative to make all data open inevitably leads to autocensorship among interlocutors, i.e., resulting in a kind of FAIRy tale being collected. The article discusses the results obtained from the survey carried out among Croatian ethnologists and cultural anthropologists about the currently practiced data sharing, their attitudes about data sharing and their perceived behavior in hypothetical situations connected with data sharing. The results show mixed opinions about data sharing and a desire to follow the disciplinary code of ethics first, i.e., to follow the interlocutors' wishes in the case of data management and usage.

Keywords: open science; data sharing; FAIR principles; CARE principles; ethnology; cultural anthropology; humanities and social sciences; qualitative methodology; confidentiality

1. Introduction

Open science is praised as a great step toward reducing some of the inequalities existing between scientific communities all over the world and paving the avenues for science in the future [1]. This is especially true, among other things, for the open access journal agenda that has been democratizing access to scientific results, diminishing existing hierarchies and power relations. Having the financial resources to access pay-walled journals and papers is a significant form of capital [2] that can make a difference in generating scientific achievements, receiving access to funding and enabling someone to pursue a successful academic career. The pros and cons of open access are still being evaluated and negotiated [3], and the distinction between true and fake open access should become clearer [4,5], but a major part of the scientific community agrees that open access represents a positive change.

However, the open science agenda has one more goal: to make data accessibility or data sharing praised as a vehicle that not only speeds up science and its achievements but also strengthens trust in the scientific process [1,6,7].

Data sharing is praised as a beneficial practice, but Tenopir et al. have noted differences between what scientists practice and preach [8]. In other words, there "is a willingness to share data, but it is difficult to achieve or is done only on request" [8].

Tenopir et al. point out studies revealing how the type of data impacts the willingness to data sharing (e.g., "Whereas 90% of scientists working in atmospheric science were willing to share their data, only 58% of the questioned social sciences scientists were ready to do this" [8]). This indicates the specific nature of data as well as the specific nature of the research process.

Pampel and Dallmeier-Tiessen emphasize some reasons for this "unwillingness". Enhanced documentation of data is a time-consuming task competing with many other activities and/or priorities and many disciplines lack standards by which data can be described, and researchers do not have proper incentives to publish data, despite several already-developed ideas. The ideas about so-called data papers or enriched publications (research data published as an enrichment of an article) are good, but one has to keep in mind that in a competitive academic environment, scientists are still ranked and promoted upon the publishing of scientific papers, monographs and edited volumes [9].

Nevertheless, the scientific debate about open data has resulted in the creation of the FAIR principles (FAIR stands for Findable, Accessible, Interoperable and Reusable). The FAIR principles were introduced by the open science agenda in 2016 [10], after a workshop held in Leiden, The Netherlands, in 2014. They were formulated with the aim of enabling digital resources in order to become more FAIR for machines as well as for humans [10]. Although they were most commonly considered unproblematic and had a positive impact on various levels (e.g., speeding up the research, enabling evaluation processes, and raising trust in science), some voices shared different experiences and pointed to the barriers [11,12].

The most prestigious and competitive research funding program in Europe, HORIZON, as well as other competitive funding agencies, adopted the open science agenda as an appropriate way of performing science. Soon, this made open data according to FAIR principles a desirable practice with different implementation choices, making it difficult to achieve convergence. Some researchers consider that FAIR certifications or requirements for funding could prove a strong driving force toward convergence in creating Data Management Plans (DMPs) [13]. However, the joint DMP is unachievable and undesirable. It should be "tailored to the context in which research is conducted" [14].

Open science and its goals are promoted in the Croatian context through various platforms and initiatives, websites, blogs and conferences [15], with the annual PUBMET conference in Zadar being a very important event. The National Initiative for Open Science in Europe (NIOS) has published a document in Croatian language, explaining the mentioned principles (https://training.ni4os.eu/pluginfile.php/3637/mod_resource/content/0/HR-NI4OS%20-%20FAIR.pdf (accessed on 3 February 2024)) [16].

The Croatian Science Foundation (CSF), the most important Croatian funding institution, strives to follow the trends set by the European Commission. As of 15 March 2022, the Research Data Management Plan (RDMP) became e a mandatory part of the application documents for all projects funded by the Croatian Science Foundation [17]. Although it puts more demands on researchers, the main goal is to improve a research methodology and science in general, as stated in the following sentence: "Sharing research data increases visibility, citation of publications and collaboration between scientists". The online documentation contains examples, even specific ones, for social sciences and humanities, where the researcher can find the options available.

Given the fact that Social Science and Humanities (SSH) still has a quite marginal position within interdisciplinary funding (such as EU funding) [18] and that SSH include economics, business, management and law, it is not a surprise that arts and humanities receive only 5% of EU funding (humanities being within the SSH umbrella).

This means that the perspective of cultural anthropology and ethnology in some aspects of data sharing can be considered as a kind of "minority report". This means that their perspective can be inaudible in comparison to disciplines that do not question the accessibility aspect of the FAIR principles and simultaneously receive significantly higher funding. Therefore, a rather "weak" position of SSH and especially of humanities in the global funding market cannot be a reason not to take into consideration their disciplinary "minority reports" on data sharing.

The accessibility and reusability of data are being questioned in qualitative research, due to the sensitivity of data, GDPR and licenses [19]. Likewise, the security aspect of the intelligence data has been identified as an important challenge to the FAIR principles in terms of accessibility requirements [20]. Speaking about FAIR principles, one has to bear in mind that:

"FAIR is not a new standard; is not a top-down requirement; is not an all-or-nothing binary state (FAIR or not FAIR). The FAIR principles were conceived and designed as a resource for optimal choices to be made during many aspects of data and tool generation as well as (re)use and long-term stewardship" [21].

Furthermore, Mons et al. explained what FAIR principles are intended to serve:

"FAIR refers to a set of principles, focused on ensuring that research objects are reusable, and actually will be reused, and so become as valuable as is possible. They deliberately do not specify technical requirements, but are a set of guiding principles that provide for a continuum of increasing reusability, via many different implementations. They describe characteristics and aspirations for systems and services to support the creation of valuable research outputs that could then be rigorously evaluated and extensively reused, with appropriate credit, to the benefit of both, creator and user" [21].

Some authors have also elaborated on levels of accessibility, ranging from non-existent to fully accessible, stressing that "The letter A' in FAIR stands for 'Accessible under well-defined conditions" [19] while others mentioned personal privacy, national security and competitiveness as reasons for data to be shielded as well" [20]. Mons et al. [22] have elaborated the varying degrees of FAIRness (Figure 1.) in order to explain, even in visual form, how data sharing can have different degree for different kinds of data and contexts.

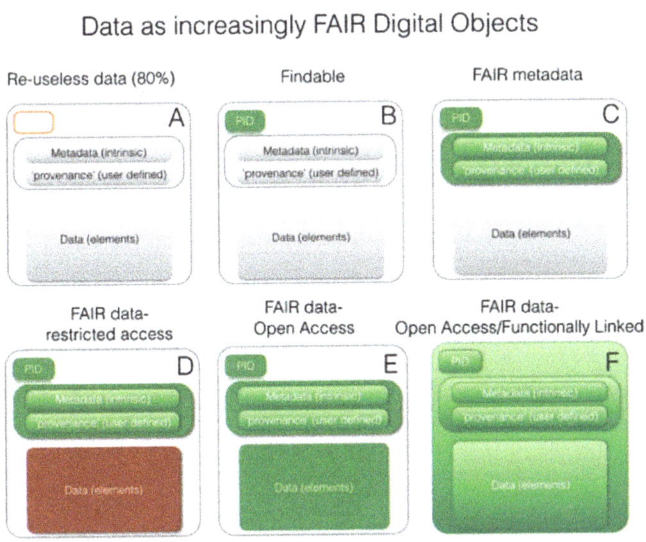

Figure 1. Varying degrees of FAIRness, taken from Mons et al. [22].

Researchers dealing with people are always under particular ethical scrutiny, and rightly so. Since the implementation of the GDPR into the European legislation, data sharing can also be considered a kind of violation, especially if the individuals did not agree or sign the informed consent to allow data sharing. Some of the data collected by qualitative research can be quite sensitive and confidential and should be treated with caution, especially when it comes to further possible exploitation for the advancement of science. And exploitation is quite common with indigenous data. Therefore, only three years after the FAIR principles were introduced, the CARE principles for indigenous data management were also introduced after an important scientific and public debate [23]. There are even examples of indigenous community archives, such as the one promoted by the Mukurtu platform, that tends to "put cultural protocols around access to knowledge", as Kim Christen described in an interview[24]. The idea that "indigenous community members curate the content through their own narratives" (ibid.), as well as co-writing processes, is quite exciting as an idea for adhering to building principles in relation to access" [24].

They refer to people and the purpose of data: "Collective Benefit, Authority to Control, Responsibility and Ethics and their respective sub-principles" and specifically target the data of communities that were "Historically plagued by data inequities and data exploitation, Indigenous Peoples" [25]. They seek to ensure that data collected from indigenous peoples lead to "tangible benefits for Indigenous collectives through inclusive development and innovation, improved governance and citizen engagement, and result in equitable outcomes" [23].

The CARE principles refer to "data, information and knowledge in any format that impact Indigenous Peoples, nations and communities at collective and individual levels; data about their resources and their environment, data about them as Individuals and data about them as collectives" [23]. This article argues for extending these principles to all communities' data, from which professional benefits are collected from.

The CARE principles should not be, therefore, associated exclusively with indigenous peoples. Some studies have made this clear. For example, the study of data repositories conducted by Dunning et al. [26] analyzed 37 data repositories. Certain data sets (described in social sciences as personal) did not comply with FAIR principles, despite the fact they could. This led the authors to the conclusion that "disciplinary norms have developed specific ways of making data accessible that do not always tally with the FAIR principles". The authors concluded that "Compliance should not be seen as a stick, but rather a desirable goal, with the recognition that some of the guidelines are open to interpretation and to debate. Indeed, the term compliance, at least for some of the facets, is misguided. Rather facets provide targets that will help with getting a recognition and a reward for the publication of data. Given that the EU now includes FAIR guidance as a part of its H2020 program, it is important that funders and peer reviewers take heed of this, so the principles do not get misused as sanctions" [26].

Apart from the impossibility of achieving full compliance with the FAIR principles in the repository, some researchers pointed out the "selfish scientist paradox" [27] according to which the same group of researchers (usually individual scientists, as the survey was conducted in the life sciences research community) were happy to receive the shared data but reluctant to provide any [27]. Their research showed that early career researchers reluctantly shared their data prior to publication (but wanted to consider data sharing in case of publishing in high-ranking journals), and that experienced researchers saw the receipt of funding (or collaboration under certain conditions) as a strong incentive to data sharing [27].

Based on an online survey conducted among working members of the small but active Croatian community of ethnologists and cultural anthropologists, this article argues for (1) a discipline-specific RDMP that prevents the mandatory disclosure of the raw data and (2) an extension of the application of CARE principles to all population/individuals whose data are collected using qualitative methodological tools (and not to Indigenous Peoples exclusively).

The need to protect interlocutors and not harm them is the core part of disciplinary ethics. If interlocutors wish to share their stories with the rest of the world, this should be clearly stated in the informed consent form. If they express that they do not want to share their narratives, researchers are obliged to abide by this will. This should be recognized and applied by funding organizations. Not all raw data are the same, and therefore they have to be protected differently. Anthropologists and ethnologists have been applying this principle, together with the anonymization processes (if requested) for a long time. The collected data are shared (and especially un-anonymized) only if the interlocutor provides permission to do so. This means that he/she is a priori familiar with ways of data processing.

The informed consent form (together with the information about the project) is the crucial part of the documentation submitted to Ethical Boards before the research approvement and therefore this part has to be carried out very carefully. Apart from "project information", it contains the "permissions" part that regulates the accessibility aspects of the collected data. This argues that the standard for application of FAIR principles in ethnology and anthropology must be based on interlocutors' permissions clearly marked in the informed consent form. This means that the permissions are and can be different from case to case and that in cultural anthropology and ethnology, one cannot apply "one-size-fits-all".

Qualitative research, especially ethnological and anthropological, in most cases implies an encounter between the interlocutor and the researcher. The encounter can sometimes be very deep and emotional, and in some cases, it can mark the beginning of a long-lasting friendship. The trope of the "field" is linked to people anthropologists meet "there" and to their relationships with "them". Interlocutors are not just providers of data, as the shift in anthropological thinking shows [28]. This space of confidentiality, empathy and emotion created during such encounters is perceived by each participant as a unique one. The bumpy road and unpredictable ways in which you manage to find and engage an interlocutor and gather data are also an important part of becoming an anthropologist, which is perceived as a disciplinary initiation process. Therefore, it is also difficult to simply share data as if you have never been emotionally involved in the process.

2. Methodology

In January 2024, the questionnaire was created by using Google Forms and sent to 145 e-mail addresses of working ethnologists and cultural anthropologists. The Croatian Ethnological Society consists of less than 300 members and some of them are not professionals. There are between 150 and 180 membership fee-paying members, including several students and many non-paying retired colleagues. Students and retired ethnologists and cultural anthropologists were deliberately excluded from the survey in order to assess current practice only. This means that the number of e-mail addresses to which the questionnaire was sent approximately corresponds to professionals actively working in the field. Therefore, this small sample should be perceived as a result of purposive/purposeful [29,30] sampling, used as a research strategy, according to Patton "when one wants to learn something and come to understand something about certain select cases without needing to generalize to all such cases" [29]. The same principle is used in proper qualitative research. This study was quantitative, but the whole professional community in question is quite small, and therefore the study could not have aimed at larger numbers and in the end did not seek statistical significance [30].

The questionnaire consists of 18 + 1 questions (the last question is intended for those who want to add something), and the first three are foreseen for socio-demographic data deemed important for the research, i.e., gender, age and occupation).

Then follows a first set of questions about how respondents inform the public about their research results, how they store their raw data, and the existing practice of their own data sharing and using other researchers' data.

Aside from current practices, respondents are also asked about their opinion on who should have access to the raw data and on the practice of data sharing in general. The last question is considered more complex, so this section is followed by a single open-ended question asking respondents to explain the previous answer.

The second part of the questionnaire consists of six statements (partly adopted from Damalas et al. [27]) in which the degree of agreement with certain statements in relation to hypothetical situations is checked according to the Likert scale.

Here are these statements:

1. I would agree to share the raw data before publication.
2. I would agree to share data if it is a requirement for funding.
3. I would agree to share raw data to achieve open science' goals.
4. I support open science's goals of the raw data sharing.
5. I would agree to share raw data if it ensures publication in high-ranking scientific journals.
6. I would agree to share raw data if it means I can collaborate with reputable scientists.

The final question was yes/no question targeting attitudes about raw data sharing under certain conditions. This section is followed by an open question where respondents are asked to explain their answer to the previous yes/no question.

3. Results

Within two weeks, 33 responses were received (i.e., 22.7%). The majority of respondents were women (87.9%, 12.1% men), reflecting the fact that is a fairly female profession (this unproportionable gender ratio (compared to the general population) was already noted by Lidija Sklevicky [31] for members of CES (a ratio 70.7: 29.3%)). Despite the low response rate (22.7%) of quite a small number of potential respondents, the conclusions could easily be a point of critique but there have been several reasons to consider them valid. The first and most important one was the above-mentioned fact that the professional community of Croatian ethnologists and cultural anthropologists is very small. Also, the retired colleagues and students were deliberately excluded from the survey.

The low response rate can be explained by the fact that respondents do not perceive the topic as relevant to their particular situation.

The age of respondents was from 29 to 62, reflecting the fact that only the working population of Croatian ethologists and anthropologists was included. The majority of respondents were from academia, research institutions, and museums (including several responses from museum pedagogists) and only one response was from a cultural heritage protection service.

3.1. *Analysis of the First Set of Questions in the Questionnaire*

3.1.1. Analysis of the Closed Questions in the First Set of Questions

In the first set of questions, respondents had to provide information about the ways of informing the public about their research results. In total, 90.9% of responses stated that it was in scientific papers, book chapters or similar and 45.5% referred to exhibitions and catalogs, 18.2% included blogs and social media posts, while 15.1% named documentaries and serials, 15.1% named public (and popular) lectures and performances for audience. One respondent (3%) mendtioned TV, one (3%) radio, and one (3%) open repositories such as PhD thesis repository.

The second question was "How do you keep/store your data?". Responses to this question were: On my own computer, I do not print transcripts (27.3%); I keep the data in the computer and in the documentation of the institution I work at, I do not print transcripts (39.4%); I keep printed transcripts and audio recordings on my own computer (24.2%); I store on an institutional server (15.2%); I am storing it as secondary material of the institution (6.1%); If funding sources ask for it, I make them available (18.2%); Other (6.1%) (Appendix A, Figure A1).

The following question "Do you share data with other colleagues?" was aimed to check the current practice of data sharing within a professional environment. Responses were the following: With collaborators, completely (30.3%); With collaborators, partially (27.3%); No (21%); Other (15.2%); Yes (3%); Only transcripts, not audio files and photos (3%) (Appendix A, Figure A2).

Answers pointed to the conclusion that the majority of ethnologists and cultural anthropologists in Croatia were practicing data sharing, completely or partially, but this referred mainly to collaborators (i.e., peers). In total, 21.2% of respondents did not share data, while almost the same percentage (21%) contextualized their answers into particular situations, i.e., added their own sentences to the questionnaire: depending on the project propositions; depending on the research, the topic, the project's propositions and the interlocutors' informed consent; depending on the sensitivity of data; depending on topics discussed and on agreements with the interlocutors. One respondent (3%) claimed that usually there is no interest in sharing and that he/she usuallyshares data with colleagues.

The next question was "Do you use other researcher's data?" The majority of the answers stated that the use of other researchers' data happened during the collaboration process. Together with the rest who claimed that they shared data, it totaled 60.6%. A further 39.4% of respondents claimed that they did not share data (Appendix A, Figure A3).

The next question was "Who should have access to the data?". More than 50% (54.5%) thought that all members of a research team and interlocutors should have data access, 33.3% thought that the data access should be granted only to the researcher and the interlocutor, and 9.1% thought that only the data collecting researcher should have the data access. A further 15.2% thought that, apart from the above-mentioned (researchers, interlocutors), the sources of financing (regardless of the funding type—private or public) should have data access as well. A further 21.2% of the respondents agreed with the following sentence: "If the research project was financed with public money, then all collected data should be publicly available". Finally, 15.2% of the respondents marked Other (Appendix A, Figure A4).

Then respondents were asked "Do you think data should be shared?" and if so, several options were offered. The majority of respondents answered negatively—33.3%. Further, 24.2% of the respondents answered data should be shared, while 15.2% specified that this should be related only to transcripts, not audio tapes and photographs. However, 21% stressed the complexity of data sharing by adding explanations in the section where open-ended answers were allowed. The decision was to be made depending on a research and an agreement with the interlocutors, according to several explanations. Others stressed that data should be shared within members of the research/project. One respondent stated that data should be shared after the researcher himself uses everything he needs, and other, similarly, stressed that data should be shared only if there is no fear that someone will use data and thus prevent original work to be published. According to other respondent, the data should not be shared as a rule, but in some situations they could be shared. One respondent stressed the need to strictly observe the indicated method of protection. One answer provided summarized it all: "I do not thin that it is possible to answer these questions with an exclusive answer. I think that everything depends on the research, the topic and the participants.

This analysis showed that for 1/5 of the respondents the YES/NO questions were oversimplified, and they felt the need to elaborate the answers more deeply and explain their opinion (Appendix A, Figure A5).

3.1.2. Analysis of Open-Ended Question in the First Set of Questions

The following question was the open one, and was provided as the further elaboration of the previous question (Do you think data should be shared?). The majority of responses were grouped around the idea of data sharing with colleagues of the same team (project or research team). Some stressed the need for prior agreement within the research team:

> *"If there is an agreement between researchers at the beginning of the project, I share the data in the form of an anonymized transcript."*

Some stressed the fact that data should be anonymized, while others simply described the existing protocol of keeping/safeguarding the data in their institution:

"This practice I carry out according to rules of the institution I work at, and with which I agree as a rule: the research team has access to the raw data, with storage in documentation of the institution that is the holder of the research project, and with the participants in the research at their own request."

Some of the respondents recognized the potential benefits of data sharing but also emphasized the need to define rules of sharing.

"I believe it can be useful to share because it will make it easier for us to speed up our work, but it must be under clearly defined rules."

The other set of answers stressed the sensitivity and confidentiality of the data collected, together with the need to grant protection and anonymity to those who provided this kind of, mostly personal, data.

"Care should be taken and the interlocutor protected in case of dealing with sensitive topics".

"During the conversation, the informant can tell us, for example, some personal things that are not necessarily related to the topic of the conversation. Such things are (at the request of the informant or at the discretion of the examiner) omitted from the transcript."

"Within qualitative research, everyone is a subject to confidentiality, because interlocutors can be easily recognized, scientific research is not a gossip column!!!!"

"Anthropological research in practice has very broad topics and spectrums of possibilities. If we work with vulnerable groups on sensitive topics or with very small easily recognizable communities, then it is not easy to categorically ensure the principles of data sharing. As a rule, I believe it is necessary to share data, but only if it does not inconvenience our participants and when they themselves have clearly chosen to do so."

Also, the attitude that a research interview is an authorial act, or an act of confidentiality between the researcher and interlocutors that cannot be simply reused because of the possible superficial or even incorrect interpretation, was indicated:

"Interviews are an authorial act between two or more participants. The other researcher cannot always understand the context of the interview and it is possible that data will not be interpreted correctly. The interviewer and the interviewee necessarily develop some interaction, deeper or more superficial, and it is unique to each individual interview. The teller decided to share his information and time with a certain researcher, without going into the motivation. It is much more acceptable to me not to hand over the raw data, but to publish and structure them".

Several respondents mentioned a kind of moratorium as a possible solution for data access in case of sensitive topics, similar to archival praxis. But even then, one respondent expresses the inadequacy of using other researchers' data.

"I believe that the biggest problem of using the raw data "from a second hand" is of an ethical nature, precisely because of possibly wrong or superficial interpretation."

Two of the most elaborated answers tackled principles of data interoperability and reusability in ethnographic research. While accessibility of the numerical raw data makes it possible to evaluate the data collected or to use them in your own research, it is not possible to do the same with transcripts of interviews, because of the specific nature of the discipline and its methodology:

"The ethnographic research is rather complex and often intimate in nature, biographical and inseparable from the context of its origin. That being said, the transcript can appear in one of three versions—it can be arranged for consultation and sharing, and it can serve as an image of the audio track. Since it is a conversational relationship that does not register repeatable and totally comparable data that can be extrapolated and used out of context, my opinion is that sharing data is counterproductive and dangerous."

The second quotation refers, additionally, to the fear of not being able to "find" interlocutors for future research, if one cannot grant them anonymity.

> *"If all raw data are available to everyone, there is a fear that it could be difficult to find interlocutors for the research of "tricky" topics. I also wonder how misuse of such data could be prevented. And finally, in the context of cultural anthropology and ethnology, the raw data obtained as a consequence of a field research represent a result of the ineraction of two people (a researcher and an interlocutor), i.e., the raw data are contextual by nature. Another researcher might get different answers to the same questions in a conversation with the same interlocutor. This is the reason, why the use of the raw data by other researchers, especially in other projects and analyses, is not necessarily justified. In this case, the use and analysis of the raw data makes sense only if the research is based on the anthropologist/ethnologist himself and his approach to the field."*

Other respondents stressed the fact that, regardless of the technique used, it was impossible to anonymize interlocutors from small communities. One of them even emphasized the need to primarily rely on the disciplinary code(s) of ethics (the Code of Ethics of Croatian Ethnological Society [32] and American Anthropological Association were mentioned) and to show responsibility toward the researched community and interlocutors.

Some respondents saw the need to define raw data first, and stressed the fact that personal notes in anthropology could be considered as data as well. In this answer, the care of exposing a researcher himself/herself i.e., of the researcher's personal data was expressed.

Only one respondent admitted that Croatian ethnologists need to have a wider discussion about the issue, and only one stressed the fact that exclusive metadata sharing (a solution incorporated into one of the FAIR principles) was the acceptable one for the discipline.

This section showed that some negative attitudes toward data sharing could be caused due to unclear data definitions.

According to the answers to these questions, ethnologists and cultural anthropologists were open to transcripts sharing with colleagues. The answer about metadata, being the only acceptable solution for sharing (more broadly), seemed to pinpoint the appropriate way toward using the principles of data sharing that are acceptable to disciplinary ethics of ethnology and cultural anthropology.

3.2. Analysis of the Second Set of Questions in the Questionnaire

3.2.1. Analysis of the Closed Questions in the Second Set of Questions

In the next set of questions, the respondents were asked to express levels of agreement, ranging from strong agreement to strong disagreement, with some claims.

According to the provided data, over 50% (66.6%) of respondents were against data sharing prior to publication, while 12.2% would not mind data sharing prior to publication. Further, 21.2% of them opted for "Undecided" (Appendix A, Figure A6).

If data sharing was a prerequisite for funding, then again, according to the collected responses, 54.6% of respondents did not take into consideration data sharing, while 15.2% considered data sharing. Further, 30.3% opted for "Undecided" (Appendix A, Figure A7).

The claim related to raw data sharing as a way of achieving open science goals had the most "Undecided" respondents—42.4%. This could reflect the fact that ideas and concepts of open science related to data were not very well known within the researched community. A further 30.3% of respondents did not agree to share data in order to achieve open science goals, while 27.3% agreed to share the data having this particular goal in mind (Appendix A, Figure A8).

A further 27.3% of the respondents agreed with the claim that they supported open science goals related to raw data sharing, 36.3% did not agree with this claim, and the option of individual largest percentage chose the "Undecided" option (36.4%) (Appendix A, Figure A9).

The next two questions, adapted from Damalas et al. [27], were offered to evaluate to what extent Croatian ethnologists and cultural anthropologists were ready to compromise their ideas in order to reach certain types of praised achievement within the scientific/academic community (such as publishing in high ranked journals and collaboration with praised scientists).

A high percentage—63.4% of them—do not agree to share data if this could guarantee them the publication in high-ranking journals. On the other side, 15.2% are willing (or at least willing to admit so) to do so. The "Undecided" option was chosen by 21.2% of respondents (Appendix A, Figure A10).

Almost the same percentage of respondents declared they would agree to share the raw data if it could allow them to cooperate with respected scientists (57.4%). Further, 18.2% of the respondents reported that they would not be willing to do so, while 24.2% of those remained "Undecided" (Appendix A, Figure A11).

3.2.2. Analysis of the Open-Ended Question in the Second Set of Questions

The following question addressed the data sharing under certain conditionsattitude. According to 84.8% of respondents, the answer in case of data sharing under certain conditions was "yes" and according to 15.2% of them the answer was "no".

The open question followed this one, with the request made to the respondent to elaborate/explain their answer.

For the majority of interlocutors, data sharing related primarily to already existing practices of sharing data with the interlocutor(s) and colleagues with whom the collaboration on the particular project/topic was carried out. This was often described as data sharing with colleagues you trust (with whom you usually collaborate). Some stressed the need to clearly state this in the informed consent, as it had also been partially practiced.

> *"In addition to the previous explanation, I would like to note that I believe the partial sharing of the raw data with scientists and colleagues from a joint project is justified because it contributes to the overall research of a certain topic or area, analysis and interpretation of data with the aim of ensuring excellence. However, I consider important to clearly indicate it to the interlocutor in the process of creating the Informed Consent form. Interlocutor must be familiar not only with the re-search objectives, but also with the information to whom the data will be made available."*

The majority of answers were imbued with a care for the interlocutor primarily, and not so much for the open science goals. The emphasis was on the protection of the interlocutor, and on the "do no harm" principle, indicating that the disciplinary code of ethics has priority over the open science agenda.

> *"Protection should be ensured for both, the interlocutor and the researcher."*

> *"The raw data may contain information that whistleblowers, for example. . .(. . .). . .do not want to be known to anyone".*

However, there are researchers that are clearly against data sharing and some of them acknowledge the fact that ethnography is a special cognitive strategy and therefore the data collected cannot be treated the same way as numbers and impersonal data.

> *"As in the previous answer, I consider data sharing in ethnography to be a missed way of understanding ethnography as a cognitive strategy."*

Of course, there are also anthropologists and ethnologists who do not see any problems in data sharing:

> *"The raw data should be shared in any case. Just as we have access to the data in the archives, so we should enable others to access our data. Of course, in addition to solving ethical issues, sensitive information and extracting the transcript of the conversation from the field notes."*

Also, some stress the need to thoroughly explain the interlocutor what the raw data mean, prior to the interview:

> *"The respondent or teller must be familiar with the term "the raw data" and its further distribution within open access. This is a prerequisite for agreeing to an interview. The raw data should not be shared afterwards, if the interlocutor was not previously informed. It is common to introduce the teller to the purpose of the research, which is almost always*

limited to a certain topic, and to collect "the raw data" for tellers can be too general and vague."

Although none of the respondents mentioned that autocensoring interlocutors do and will apply during the interview, many of them have encountered such a praxis during field work. For example, sometimes the interlocutors tell one story while being recorded, and then at the end of the conversation, they add something controversial or oposite.

Sometimes interlocutors ask the researcher to stop the recording at a certain point. Some researchers working with vulnerable groups do not use dictaphones, in order for the interlocutors to feel safer and freer.

The main fear that raw data sharing could bring to qualitative research is the fact that researchers might receive the "polished" data, and might never receive information revealing topics, e.g., frictions within the community, certain secrets or uncommon or sensitive practices, or intimate information. This might in the long run make ethnologists and anthropologist FAIRy tale collectors.

However, respondents emphasized the other side of the medal, too. Some of them mentioned the need to take more care about the raw data by the researchers themselves, because they quite often store the data on personal computers and do not share it. The worst is if they do not analyze or publish it.

"From my own work experience, I know that many raw data from research in Croatia (not only ethnological and anthropological) are kept in researchers' private computers, external hard drives, printed out on shelves at home, in offices and the like. It would be necessary to increase researchers' awareness of taking more care and at the same time providing more open storage for this data, which can serve other researchers as well."

"If the researcher plans to use data for his work, it is logical that he will not share it. If he does not intend to publish the data, it is better to make it publicly available."

However, the attitude that the final decision should be left to the interlocutors was also mentioned here, as stressed by one respondent: *"They determine what can and must be public"*.

4. Discussion

The results obtained from the questionnaire reveal that Croatian ethnologists and cultural anthropologists do not consider the topic very relevant to their particular situation. This is indicated by a low response rate of 22%. Such attitude (if this is the reason) could mean that they have not yet encountered the requests to make raw data they have collected available or that they think this could relate to them. In this sense, more research is needed, especially after a certain period of time, to see if the situation has changed. However, the first set of questions aimed at the current practice of data management (including sharing) reveal that the majority of respondents share data to a certain extent and usually during collaboration with other colleagues. The last two questions from this section aimed to obtain not only the opinions about who should have access to raw data, but to see what they think about the practice itself. This required further explanations via open-ended questions. Open-ended questions revealed that data sharing is acceptable within the team, and that the protection of the interlocutors and, especially, sensitive information has priority. However, some respondents stressed the need to acknowledge different cognitive and emotional efforts involved in qualitative research. Especially important was the argument which stressed the fact that in qualitative research it is the researcher who does the interpretation, not the scale. Therefore, "second hand" interpretation is not considered to be a "validation" of results, but more of a threat to data, because the context of the research is lost.

This kind of research is considered, by some respondents, as an authorial act, deserving special status. Some respondents stressed that in this kind of research conversation [33] (with a purpose, despite the fact that it might look like a "regular" conversation to other people), the researcher sometimes reveals personal data about him/herself and that maybe he/she would not like to share it. However, this attitude shows certain hypocrisy within the discipline, since it is precisely diaries and personal notes of famous anthropologists (for example, Malinowski's [34]) that revealed the difference between the researcher's front/back stages [35] (front stage being the published manuscript positioning the researcher into the scientific community while diaries revealed the back stage i.e., the personal experiences of the researcher in the process of research). These diaries were extremely worthy for understanding disciplinary development and for betterunderstanding of diverse processes underlying the published materials.

In the second part of the questionnaire, the respondents were asked to mark their level of agreement with certain statements in order to see how they believe they would act in hypothetical situations.

While in the first question, the willingness to share data prior to publication is low as expected, in the second question, the unwillingness to share data as a prerequisite for funding was also quite high, as opposed to results in Damalas et al. [27] This might be a reflection of the situation in which the respondents came from various areas, not only from academia, combined with the situation where they were not under high pressure to seek funding. Also, this might be a socially desirable answer. The following two questions related to data sharing with the aim of supporting open science goals had quite a high response rate for the "Undecided" option. This might reflect the insufficient information about the goals of open science.

In the end, publication in high-ranking journals or collaboration with reputable scientists does not seem to be a relevant incentive for data sharing, according to respondents. These attitudes might also reflect socially desirable answers.

The following question asked respondents to express their opinion about the need to share data under certain conditions. Since this was a complex topic with a yes/no answer, it was followed by an open-ended one where respondents were able to further elaborate their opinions.

The majority were for at least partial data sharing, especially in collaboration. However, here again, the emphasis was on the care for the protection of the interlocutors (and their data) and the confidentiality of the data. The code of ethics of the discipline was to be followed, and the respondents stressed the need to obtain the permissions in the informed consent allowing various degrees of data sharing.

Some of the respondents were aware of the fact that data shouldbe shared and used, instead of being neglected in the private documentation of the researcher (in the case of unpublished results). Some even stressed that it would be beneficial, and were critical of the fact that in some cases the raw data are not stewarded with care.

The results point to an important topic for qualitative researchers, especially in the long run. Researchers skilled primarily in qualitative methodology always struggle with the interpretation of the data collected, especially in the light of interlocutors describing "order imagined" vs. "order achieved" [36,37]. Having in mind these differences between narratives recollected and the realities lived, the ethical considerations of the raw data sharing options being presented to interlocutors were not the only ones.

The obligation or possibility to share the raw data will inevitably lead to changes in the nature of narratives told in all qualitative research. The personal narratives could become autocensored or less intimate (in some cases) and in the case of small communities, the "desirable" narrative could become the one shared with the researcher. Of course, this would not be the case with all interviewees, but the tendency could be anticipated.

The anonymization processes are often mentioned as possible solutions for such a situation [6]. Landi et al. admit that "health data deriving from patients affected by rare diseases should be considered more sensitive (e.g., identifiable) and additional safeguards measures should be taken" [19]. The interlocutors from small communities or particular groups could be more easily identified as well and therefore additional measures should be taken for them.

Landi et al. display an argumentation that is in line with anthropologists' and ethnologists' opinions and their primary concerns to protect the interlocutors. They also agree that informed consent (providing a priori information to data subjects about the way their data will be processed) should be the main guideline [19].

"Additionally, considering the GDPR aims to strengthen the rights of individuals to be better informed about the processing of their data, which should be lawful and fair, and give them greater control over their own data; it is important to verify that existing metadata take into account the original consent and all existing and applicable data sharing, data use agreements and data protection policies. Moreover, it should be investigated that metadata have already been implemented with the information provided to the data subject in personal data processing according to Articles 13 and 14 of the GDPR, and that all the data subject's rights have been and will be respected" [19].

Furthermore, these authors stress the need for metadata, not data, to be shared, and this is in line with certain opinions expressed in the survey. These metadata should have clearly stated the conditions under which accessibility is possible, if at all.

Other authors, e.g., Mons et al. [21], underline that "The A' in FAIR stands for 'Accessible under well-defined conditions'" and mention personal privacy, national security and competitiveness as reasons for data to be shielded.

It is important, however, to keep in mind what Briggs [38] has pointed out, i.e., that "Once informed consent" is "obtained", researchers ordinarily gain exclusive rights over how that discourse circulates and is interpreted, along with who receives it and who benefits from it.

"Interviews thus impose standardized social scientific knowledge production and circulation practices that further subordinate and obscure the knowledge-making practices that interviewees use in making social worlds and challenging forms of symbolic and other violence" [38].

This power imbalance can be mitigated with the CARE approach toward raw data and metadata sharing. As mentioned above, CARE principles are developed for Indigenous People and their protection. They are developed having in mind the power imbalance of colonial encounters. However, even in cases where the interlocutor and researcher belong to the same community, the power imbalance exists and the majority of the respondents of the survey take this protective and caring standpoint when elaborating their opinions. They clearly express the need to protect the sensitive data and confidentiality obtained in the process of research.

A standard procedure in conducting an in-depth interview (the most common qualitative methodological tool used in cultural anthropology (today mostly anthropology by appointment [39])) is providing enough information for the interlocutor in order to sign an informed consent form. Apart from describing the research, the informed consent form has to contain the data explaining the procedure of keeping and managing the data, as well as mentioning the media in which the data will be presented (articles, exhibitions, documentaries, etc.). Anonymity is always one of the possibilities the informed consent offers, and the majority of interlocutors opt for it, but not all. Occasionally, the interlocutor insists on periodically switching off the recorder by the researcher, usually when something delicate is being recollected. Also, quite often, after the interview ends, the researcher can hear the information not intended for recording. Although there are ways to anonymize the data (as explained in Celjak et al. [6]), interlocutors from smaller communities or groups could be recognized due to the transcript parts not being removed, not to mention by voice.

While preparing the informed consent form for the Solidarity Economy in Croatia: Anthropological Perspective (SOLIDARan) project (SOLIDARan) project Informed consent form, Appendix B), the research team tried to follow disciplinary ethics requirements. The process prior to the interview related to the informed consent form went as follows: each interlocutor takes a personal copy of the informed consent form, so they can later review the documents they have signed. However, the researchers often had to explain everything orally because most of them did not want to take the time to read it prior to interview. They made decisions about their anonymity and the modes of receiving the raw data (if at all). While preparing the documentation for the Ethical Board (to approve the research), the Ethical principle of CES, as well as other relevant sources, were followed. Also, it was clearly stated who will have access to the raw data and how the data will be used. This is the way all collaborators on the project have to treat the data obtained.

All these issues raise a question: is it really the ideal goal for all the data to be only FAIR ones? The answers received with the questionnaire revealed that sharing data among Croatian ethnologists and cultural anthropologists means primarily sharing data within the team or project members and keeping it within institutional documentation. The majority of the respondents expressed accordance with the principle "do no harm" to the community researched. They also stressed the interview topic-dependent decision about data sharing, and the need to protect sensitive and personal data. Some of them constantly stressed the fact that anonymization does not fully work in small communities. Also, the majority emphasized the fact that the interlocutors should be in charge of deciding to what extent the data provided by them, should be subject to sharing, if at all. Some ethnologists and cultural anthropologists stated that raw data obtained by the qualitative methodology and ethnography are not the kind of data one can simply reuse because they can be simplified or incorrectly interpreted without knowing the rich context of the research encounter. Some of them went even so far as they envisage the production of digital waste that in the end will not be useful. However, some researchers thought that raw data should be made available in the same way as the archival data and that if the researcher will not use the data, then it is better to share them.

Related to two questions adopted from Damalas et al. [27] that would reveal the selfish scientist paradox, the Croatian answers were a bit different. Respondents mainly claimed that they would not share data if it grants them funding, publishing in high-ranking journals or collaborating with reputable scientists.

FAIR should not be a top-down requirement, but an increasing projectification of science (grants received and project funding have become an important means of scientists' validation), as well as the publish-or-perish principle, create a clear IF NOT—THEN causal logic. Therefore, not only further research is needed in order to evaluate the above-mentioned claims and praxis, but continuous discussions within the broader scientific community would facilitate the incorporation of specific values and ethical principles of ethnology and cultural anthropology more clearly into open science.

5. Conclusions

The results of the study suggest that Croatian ethnologists and cultural anthropologists consider the disciplinary code of ethics and care for interlocutors as their most important obligation. They do share data, but usually only within a limited circle of collaborators, usually while working on the same project or topic. For the majority, this was the only meaningful option. This is in line with the ethical principles of disciplines and is not in conflict with the FAIR principles related to metadata sharing exclusively. This is in line with the authors mentioned above (Figure 1) [22] who emphasize that the degree of openness (i.e., accessibility) varies depending on the context of the discipline.

Metadata should be open, but accessibility should be applied to each particular case, regulated by the informed consent in each particular case (the interlocutors have different attitudes toward the idea of their data being revealed). Some researchers stress the need for data to undergo a moratorium time, or that only metadata should be fully accessible.

Some consider ethnology and acultural anthropology to be a special cognitive strategy where there is no meaningful way of reusing someone else's raw data. The need to have a further discussion and to clearly define what raw data are (especially if they are considered the researcher's own data, such as notes and opinions and personal information revealed to the interlocutor during the interview).

Results of the questionnaire carried out within the purposeful sample of working ethnologists and cultural anthropologists in Croatia showed that the majority of the respondents would follow a kind of combined FAIR/CARE approach to data sharing (although the respondents did not use these terms!), because of reasons of complying with the disciplinary Code of Ethics primarily. They stressed the need to protect the interlocutors. Different situations and topics also dictate the approach the researchers have to take toward data sharing as a desirable goal of open science.

If FAIR principles fail to be considered as guidelines, and become a standard, in ethnology and anthropology (and disciplines using the qualitative methodology) it may lead to collecting auto censored narratives from interlocutors, (and therefore can be perceived as a kind of FAIRy Tales). In the long run, it can impoverish the data available for interpretation, even for the ones who collected the data, not to mention the ones reusing it.

Funding agencies, including our national one too, may fund the research of so-called "hard" sciences more intensively, but they nevertheless fund the humanities as well, regardless of the marginality of such endeavour. They must keep in mind that not all disciplinary raw data cannot be shared in the same way.

In the case of data collected by interviewing a simple additional question in the informed consent form related to interlocutors' willingness to open access data sharing could be a solution:

Do you want your data (anonymized/not anonymized) to be completely available in the open access (available in various online repositories)?

YES/NO

Additionally, a set of options (as elaborated in Mons et al. [22] and Celjak et al. [6]) can be offered to interlocutors to choose the option that does not make them feel exposed.

This is in line with opinions expressed by respondents who often mentioned the need to inform the interlocutor and to follow their wishes related to data processing. Some respondents followed the institutional procedure, while others criticized the fact that there is a praxis that shows neglect toward data-keeping.

The results of a survey point to the need for further advocacy for both FAIR and CARE principles as important and ethical building blocks of open science in Croatia. This includes not only further research but further educational activities as well, especially among the researchers who are not sufficiently aware of the open science requirements and their meaning. The requirements for each discipline concerning evaluation and proposing of the optimal model for implementing FAIR and CARE principles in their perspective RDMP have to be met. Apart from this, differences between disciplines have to be taken into account (and respected) by funding agencies when promoting open science and FAIR principles as their standard or prerequisite for funding.

Funding: This paper is part of the research project "Solidarity Economy in Croatia: Anthropological Perspective" (SOLIDARan), funded by the Croatian Science Foundation (IP-2019-04-3946).

Data Availability Statement: The data presented in this article are not readily available because of the lack of direct permissions for data sharing. It is not possible to get permissions due to the anonymity of the survey. However, some of the raw data are included in the article. Further inquiries can be directed to the author.

Acknowledgments: I also want to thank all the anonymous respondents to the questionnaire. Without them, this analysis would not be possible. I would like to thank to my colleagues with whom I have openly discussed the matter (Lidija Nikočević, Duga Mavrinac, Ivona Orlić, Koraljka Kuzman Šlogar, and Mojca Ramšak (but others as well)), and to the members of the Managing Board of Croatian Ethnological Society (Željka Petrović Osmak, Tihana Rubić, Marija Mesarić, Ivana Radovani Podrug, Danijela Birt Katić, Jasmina Jurković Petras, Klementina Batina and Melita Trbušić) with whom I have had vivid discussions concerning the formal request on data sharing opinion in museum(s). I also want to thank the editors of this Special Issue and to the anonymous reviewers for their tremendous patience and work.

Conflicts of Interest: The author declares no conflict of interest.

Appendix A

The results of the survey (n = 33)

The numbers in the brackets refer to the actual number of respondents to a particular question.

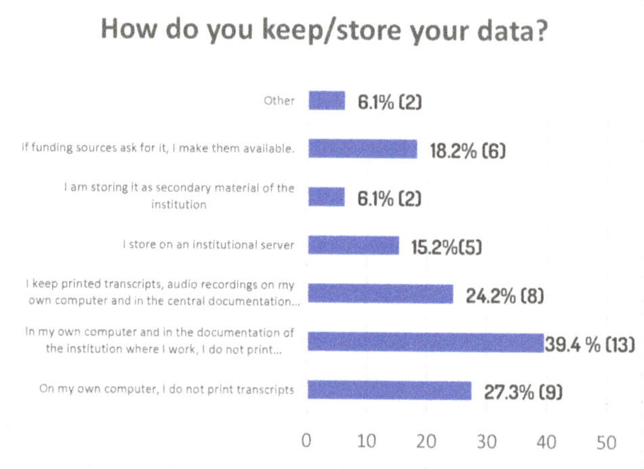

Figure A1. How do you keep/store your data?

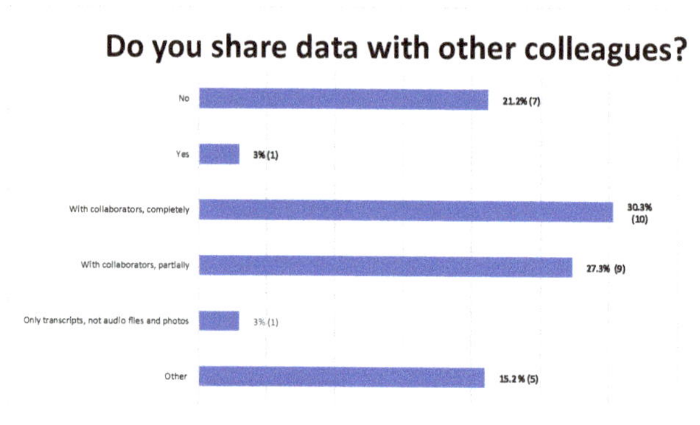

Figure A2. Do you share data with other colleagues?

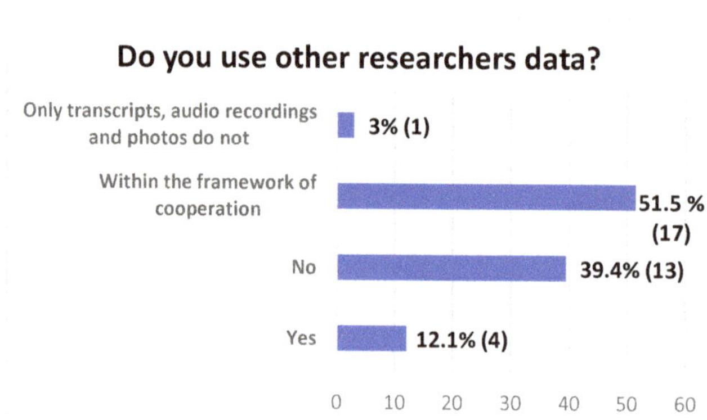

Figure A3. Do you use other researchers data?

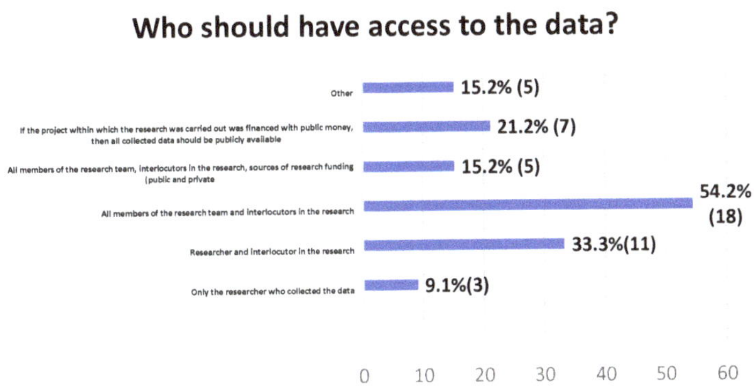

Figure A4. Who should have access to the data?

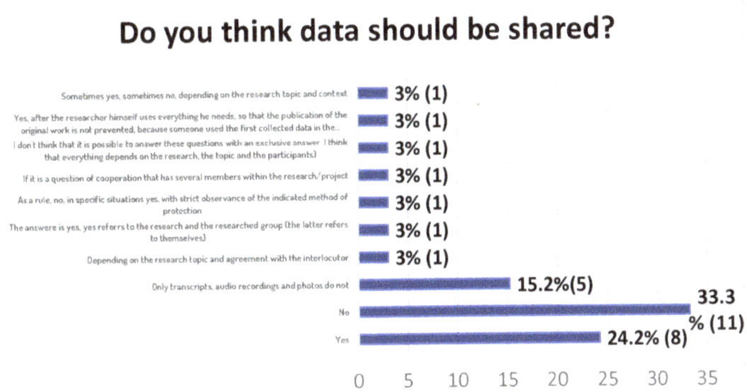

Figure A5. Do you think data should be shared?

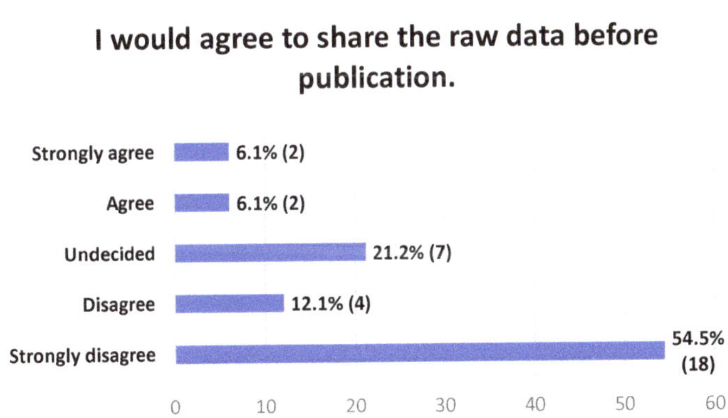

Figure A6. I would agree to share the raw data before publication.

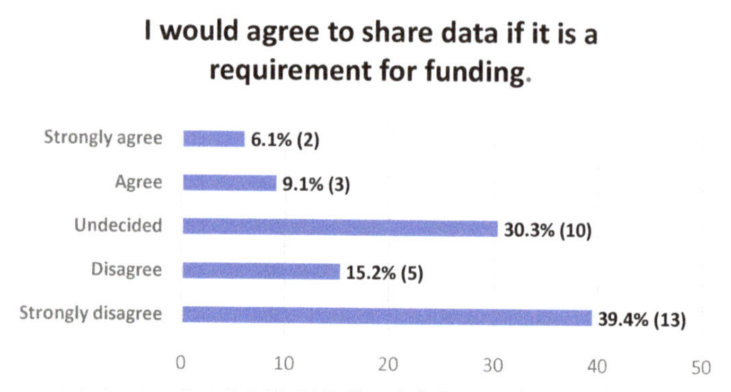

Figure A7. I would agree to share data if it is a requirement for funding.

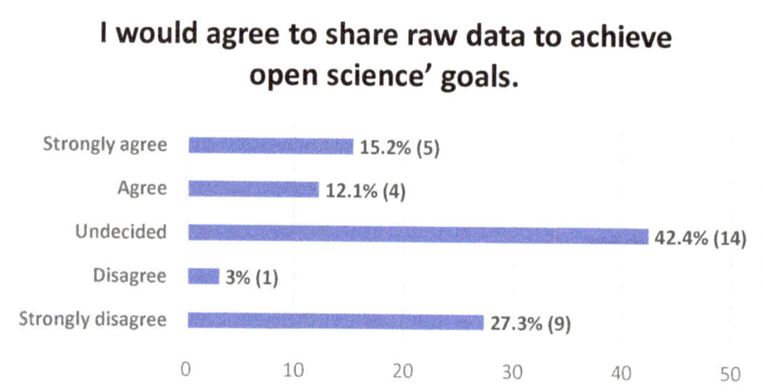

Figure A8. I would agree to share raw data to achieve open science' goals.

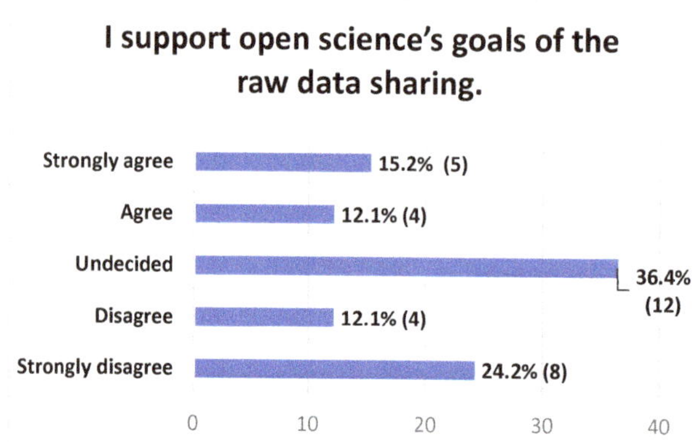

Figure A9. I support open science's goals of the raw data sharing.

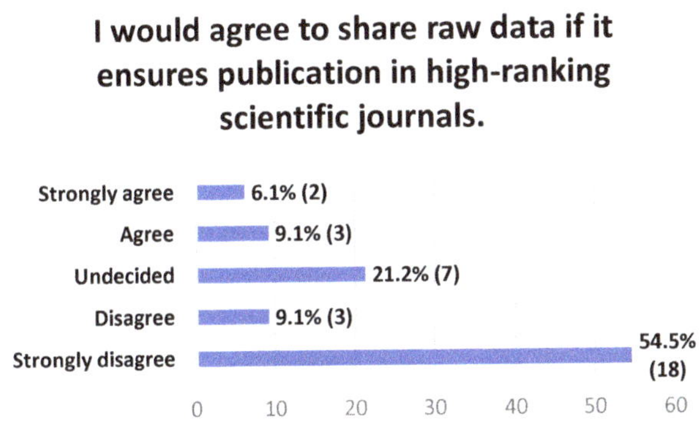

Figure A10. I would agree to share raw data if it ensures publication in high-ranking scientific journals.

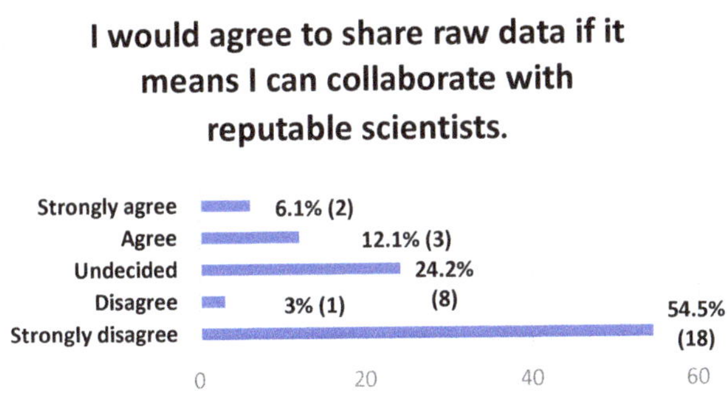

Figure A11. I would agree to share raw data if it means I can collaborate with reputable scientists.

Appendix B

Informed consent was created and used for the "Solidarity Economy in Croatia: Anthropological Perspective" (SOLIDARan) project.

Informed consent—information for interlocutor

Dear Madam or Sir,

You are invited to participate as an interlocutor in the scientific research conducted by the Institute for Anthropological Research (Zagreb) as a part of the "Solidarity Economy in Croatia: Anthropological Perspective" (SOLIDARan) project, financed by the Croatian Science Foundation.

The principal investigator of the research is dr.sc Olga Orlić, the senior research associate at the Institute for Anthropological Research (Zagreb). The research will be conducted on the territory of the Republic of Croatia (Zagreb and its surroundings, Slavonia Dalmatia, Istria and Primorje regions). The main goal of the research is to provide a contribution to theoretical reflections on a solidarity economy. In this part of the research, the elements of the solidarity economy phenomenon in the contemporary Croatian context is to be explored, primarily from the anthropological perspective. This is to gain a better insight into practices and potential problems different actors in the practices of the solidarity economy have as well as into ways of solving them, if such exist.

For this project, its applied goal is also extremely important—to create a model (guidelines) for implementation of solidarity economy practices' elements in public policies, but also to encourage such practices in a wider society. The data collected in this way can significantly contribute to the creation of such guidelines that can be useful to practitioners of the solidarity economy, if implemented in an appropriate manner.

For all additional questions about the research, please contact dr.sc Olga Orlić at: xxxx.xxxx@inantro.hr

Please read this Informed Consent for Research Participation carefully. In case you do not understand any part of the Informed Consent, please contact the examiner or the project manager for an explanation. Your participation in this interview is voluntary and you may withdraw or choose to skip any of the questions at any time. If you decide to participate in this research, you will be asked to sign the Informed Consent with an indication of the date. Beside by the project leader/principal investigator, the Informed Consent is signed by the interlocutor and the researcher who conducts the research interview before the start of the interview. The informed consent is signed in 2 copies, one of which remains in the possession of the research interviewee.

Your personal data collected through this research interview will be used exclusively for scientific purposes. The data from your interview can be used (in the form of quotes or isolated statements) during the dissemination of research results by all collaborators on the project: in scientific papers, books or during conference presentations, at presentations or on posters. If you want to remain anonymous, your name and surname will not be mentioned anywhere, and your anonymity is guaranteed. In that case, you can choose a pseudonym The audio recording of the conversation and/or the transcript of the interview can, if you wish, be delivered to you by e-mail or to your home address.

The audio recording of the research conversation will be stored in the main researcher's computer and in the Audio Materials Database of the Institute for Anthropological Research. Transcripts of the conversation (coded information about the interlocutor, the code book will be stored the project leader) will be printed and stored in the Database of Qualitative Research of the Institute for Anthropological Research under a project number. Also, the transcripts of the research interview will be available for use only to collaborators of this research, for purposes of scientific analyses.

Informed consent—permissions

I want my data to remain anonymous during the abovementioned form of use (please circle the desired answer)

YES/NO

If the answer is YES, I want the following pseudonym to be used in addition to the statements and data I provided to the researcher:

____

I would like to receive an audio recording and a transcript of the conversation after the research completion (please circle the desired answer)

YES/NO

If the answer is YES, please, indicate the e-mail address to which you would like to receive the materials, considering that we are unable to send the audio recording by post.

e-mail address:

____

Home address (in this case, only the conversation transcript's printout will be sent by mail):

____

I confirm with this signature that I am informed about the goals, advantages and risks of this research, that I agree to participate in it, and that the abovementioned approved ways of using my data and statements in the dissemination of research results are correct.

______________________, ______________(Date).

______________________ ______________________

Signature of the interlocutor, Dr.sc. Olga Orlić,
SOLIDARan principal investigator
Institute for Anthropological Research

____

Name and surname of the interlocutor (printed letters)

I, the researcher, hereby confirm that I verbally provided the necessary information about this study and gave one copy of the informed consent, signed by the interlocutor and the researcher, to the interlocutor before the research interview.

____

The name and surname of the researcher—project collaborator, the institution of the collaborator (printed letters and signature).

References

1. Miedema, F. *Open Science: The Very Idea;* Springer: Dordrecht, Netherlands, 2022.
2. Bourdieu, P. *Distinction: A Social Critique of the Judgement of Taste;* Nice, R., Translator; Harvard University Press: Cambridge, Massachusetts, 1984.
3. Frank, J.; Foster, R.; Pagliari, C. Open access publishing—Noble intention, flawed reality. *Soc. Sci. Med.* **2023**, *317*, 115592. [CrossRef] [PubMed]
4. Mehrpour, S.; Khajavi, Y. How to spot fake open access journals. *Learn. Publ.* **2014**, *27*, 269–274. [CrossRef]
5. Hebrang Grgić, I. Otvoreni pristup—Deus ex machina za izdavaštvo znanstvenih časopisa? [Open access—Deus ex machina for publishing scientific journals?]. *Libellarium* **2015**, *8*, 1–11. [CrossRef]
6. Celjak, D.; Dorotić Malič, I.; Matijević, M.; Poljak, L.; Posavec, K.; Turk, I. *Istraživački Podaci—Što s Njima? Priručnik o Upravljanju Istraživačkim Podacima [Research Data—What to Do with it? Handbook of Research Data Management];* Sveučilište u Zagrebu, Sveučilišni Računski Centar: Zagreb, Croatia, 2020.
7. Bartling, S.; Friesike, S. (Eds.) *Opening Science. The Evolving Guide on How the Internet Is Changing Research;* Springer Open: Cham, Switzerland, 2014.
8. Tenopir, C.; Allard, S.; Douglass, K.; Aydinoglu, A.U.; Wu, L.; Read, E.; Manoff, M.; Frame, M. Data Sharing by Scientists: Practices and Perceptions. *PLoS ONE* **2011**, *6*, e21101. [CrossRef] [PubMed]
9. Pampel, H.; Dallmeier-Tiessen, S. Open Research Data: From Vision to Practice. In *Opening Science. The Evolving Guide on How the Internet is Changing Research;* Bartling, S., Friesike, S., Eds.; Springer: Cham, Switzerland, 2014; pp. 213–224.
10. Wilkinson, M.; Dumontier, M.; Aalbersberg, I.; Appleton, G.; Axton, M.; Baak, A.; Blomberg, N.; Boiten, J.-W.; da Silva Santos, L.B.; Bourne, P.E.; et al. The FAIR Guiding Principles for scientific data management and stewardship. *Sci. Data* **2016**, *3*, 160018. [CrossRef]
11. Kolbe, V. Open Science versus Data Protection—Challenges and Solutions in Sign Language Acquisition Studies. *Hrvat. Rev. Za Rehabil. Istraživanja* **2022**, *58*, 109–120. [CrossRef]
12. Burrows, T. Sharing humanities data for e-research: Conceptual and technical issues. In *Sustainable Data from Digital Research;* Thieberger, N., Ed.; PARADISEC: Melbourne, Australia, 2011; pp. 177–192. Available online: http://hdl.handle.net/2123/7938 (accessed on 15 January 2024).
13. Jacobsen, A.; Azevedo, R.d.M.; Juty, N.; Batista, D.; Coles, S.; Cornet, R.; Courtot, M.; Crosas, M.; Dumontier, M.; Evelo, C.T.; et al. FAIR Principles: Interpretations and Implementation Considerations. *Data Intell.* **2020**, *2*, 10–29. [CrossRef]
14. Jones, S.; Pergl, R.; Hooft, R.; Miksa, T.; Samors, R.; Ungvari, J.; Davis, R.I.; Lee, T. Data Management Planning: How Requirements and Solutions are Beginning to Converge. *Data Intell.* **2020**, *2*, 208–219. [CrossRef]
15. Stojanovski, J. Promicanje ideja otvorene znanosti u Hrvatskoj. [Promoting the ideas of open science in Croatia]. *Soc. Teme* **2019**, *1*, 166–170.
16. FAIR. Sve što Trebate Znati o FAIR Podacima. NI4OS-Europe. Nacionalne Inicijative za Otvorenu Znanost u Europi. Available online: https://training.ni4os.eu/pluginfile.php/3637/mod_resource/content/0/HR-NI4OS%20-%20FAIR.pdf (accessed on 3 February 2024).
17. Plan Upravljanja Istraživačkim Podacima [Research Data Management Plan]. Hrvatska Zaklada za Znanost [Croatian Science Foundation]. Available online: https://hrzz.hr/plan-upravljanja-istrazivackim-podacima-za-projekte-hrvatske-zaklade-za-znanost/ (accessed on 15 January 2024).
18. Välikangas, A. The Limited Role of Social Sciences and Humanities in Interdisciplinary Funding: What are Its Effects? *Soc. Epistemol.* **2023**, *38*, 152–172. [CrossRef]
19. Landi, A.; Thompson, M.; Giannuzzi, V.; Bonifazi, F.; Labastida, I.; Bonino da Silva Santos, L.O.; Roos, M. The "A" of FAIR—As open as possible, as closed as necessary. *Data Intell* **2020**, *2*, 47–55. [CrossRef]
20. Brewster, C.; Nouwt, B.; Raaijmakers, S.; Verhoosel, J. Ontology-based access control for FAIR data. *Data Intell* **2020**, *2*, 66–77. [CrossRef]
21. Mons, B.; Schultes, E.; Liu, F.H.; Jacobsen, A. The FAIR principles: First generation implementation choices and challenges. *Data Intell* **2020**, *2*, 1–9. [CrossRef]
22. Mons, B.; Neylon, C.; Velterop, J.; Dumontier, M.; Santos, L.O.B.d.S.; Wilkinson, M.D. Cloudy, increasingly FAIR; revisiting the FAIR Data guiding principles for the European Open Science Cloud. *Inf. Serv. Use* **2017**, *37*, 49–56. [CrossRef]

23. Carroll, S.R.; Herczog, E.; Hudson, M.; Russell, K.; Stall, S. Operationalizing the CARE and FAIR Principles for Indigenous data futures. *Sci. Data* **2021**, *8*, 108. [CrossRef]
24. Kimberly, C.; Davis, L.; Griffith, Z.; Neely, J. Traditional Knowledge and Digital Archives: An Interview with Kim Christen. *Discl. A J. Soc. Theory* **2018**, *27*, 5. [CrossRef]
25. Carroll, S.R.; Garba, I.; Figueroa-Rodríguez, O.L.; Holbrook, J.; Lovett, R.; Materechera, S.; Parsons, M.; Raseroka, K.; Rodriguez-Lonebear, D.; Rowe, R.; et al. The CARE Principles for Indigenous Data Governance. *Data Sci. J.* **2020**, *19*, 1–12. [CrossRef]
26. Dunning, A.; de Smaele, M.; Boehmer, J. Are the FAIR Data Principles fair? *Int. J. Digit Curation* **2017**, *12*, 177–195. [CrossRef]
27. Damalas, D.; Kalyvioti, G.; Sabatella, E.C.; Stergiou, K.I. Open data in the life sciences: The 'Selfish Scientist Paradox'. *Ethics Sci. Environ. Polit.* **2018**, *18*, 27–36. [CrossRef]
28. Leve, L. Interlocutors: Language, Power and Relationality in Decolonial Ethnographic Practice. *Fieldwork Relig.* **2022**, *17*, 47–61. [CrossRef]
29. Patton, M.Q. *Qualitative Research and Evaluation Methods*, 3rd ed.; Sage Publications: Thousand Oaks, CA, USA, 2002.
30. Miles, M.B.; Huberman, A.M. *Qualitative Data Analysis*, 2nd ed.; Sage Publications: Thousand Oaks, CA, USA, 1994.
31. Sklevicky, L. Profesija etnolog—Analiza pokazatelja statusa profesije. In *Simboli Identiteta. Studije, Eseji, Građa*; Rihtman-Auguštin, D., Ed.; Hrvatsko etnološko društvo: Zagreb, Croatia, 1991; pp. 45–67.
32. Ethical Code of Croatian Ethnological Society. Available online: https://hrvatskoetnoloskodrustvo.hr/o-nama/eticki-kodeks/ (accessed on 3 February 2024).
33. Milas, G. *Istraživačke Metode u Psihologiji i Drugim Društvenim Znanostima*; Naklada Slap: Jastrebarsko, Croatia, 2009.
34. Malinowski, B. *A Diary in the Strict Sense of the Term*; Guterman, N., Translator; Athlone Press: London, UK, 1989.
35. Goffman, E. *The Presentation of Self in Everyday Life*; Doubleday & Company: Garden City, NY, USA, 1959.
36. Rihtman-Auguštin, D. Pretpostavke suvremenog etnološkog istraživanja. *Nar. Umjet.* **1976**, *13*, 1–25.
37. Rajković, Z. Obilježja etnografske građe i metode njezina terenskog istraživanaja. *Etnološki Pregl.* **1974**, *12*, 129–134.
38. Briggs, C. Against Methodological Essentialism, Fragmentation and Instrumentalism in Times of COVID-19. *Am. Anthropol.* **2021**, *123*, 954–956. [CrossRef] [PubMed]
39. Hannerz, U. Studying down, up, sideways, through, backward, forwards, away and at home: Reflections on the field worries of an expansive discipline. In *Locating the Field: Space, Place and Context in Anthropology*; Coleman, S., Collins, P., Eds.; Berg: Oxford, UK, 2006; pp. 23–42.

MDPI AG
Grosspeteranlage 5
4052 Basel
Switzerland
Tel.: +41 61 683 77 34

Publications Editorial Office
E-mail: publications@mdpi.com
www.mdpi.com/journal/publications